The Best Years of British Film Music

1936–1958

The Best Years
of British Film Music

1936–1958

Jan G. Swynnoe

THE BOYDELL PRESS

First published 2002
The Boydell Press, Woodbridge

ISBN 0 85115 862 5

The Boydell Press is an imprint of Boydell & Brewer Ltd
PO Box 9, Woodbridge, Suffolk IP12 3DF, UK
and of Boydell & Brewer Inc.
PO Box 41026, Rochester, NY 14604–4126, USA
website: http://www.boydell.co.uk

A catalogue record for this book is available
from the British Library

Library of Congress Cataloging-in-Publication Data
Swynnoe, Jan G.
   The best years of British film music, 1936–1958 / Jan G. Swynnoe.
      p. cm.
   Includes bibliographical references (p.) and index.
   ISBN 0–85115–862–5 (alk. paper)
   1. Motion picture music – Great Britain – History and criticism.   I. Title.
ML2075 .S93 2002
781.5′42′0941–dc21   2001043610

This publication is printed on acid-free paper

Typeset by Joshua Associates Ltd, Oxford
Printed in Great Britain by
St Edmundsbury Press Ltd, Bury St Edmunds, Suffolk

Contents

Plates

For George and Joan

Acknowledgements

The following people helped me in many different ways and at various stages in the preparation of this book:

Doreen M. Alwyn (Carwithen), Barbara Davies, Roy Douglas, the late Brian Easdale, Marian Glyn Evans, Lewis Foreman, Sandie Gray, Barry Halsey, John Huntley, John Hywel, Echo Irving, Philip Lane, Sam Mercer, Rodney Newton, Graham Parlett, Nigel Shipway, Bertha Stevens, Eric Tomlinson, Alfred Tubb, Bruce Wood.

I should like to thank them very much for the generous way they gave of their time and resources.

*   *   *

A list of source acknowledgements for the musical examples is located at the back of this volume.

Note

The dates of all British feature films and their categorization into genres such as 'war' or 'comedy' have been taken from Dennis Gifford's *The British Film Catalogue: 1895–1970* (Newton Abbott, 1973). Statistics are compiled only from feature films over 45 minutes long. The date in each case is the year of release.

Introduction

> There isn't a country anywhere in the world with half as much
> musical inspiration as there is here.[1]

When the Paramount moguls sent Alexander Korda, the Hungarian film
director and producer, from Paris to London in November 1931, it was with
the express intention of injecting new life and vigour into their subsidiary
company, which, along with the British film industry as a whole, was suffering
a serious decline. They were not to know that, by a curious combination of
circumstances arising directly from this unpromising union between two
nations of little temperamental affinity, the future of British film music was
to be vitally affected. Within a few months of his arrival, Korda was in a
position to establish his own company, London Film Productions, with a
group of associates who both put up the money and formed a board of
directors. When it came to filling the vacant positions in his new company,
including those for the music staff, Korda resorted to the method of
preferment based on nepotism, the notorious practice of *protekció*, which
was widespread in, though possibly not exclusive to, Hungary. Korda wanted
to employ the German opera coach, Kurt Schroeder, as his musical director.
Schroeder's brother-in-law had worked with Korda in Hollywood, and it was
on the basis of his recommendation that Korda made this very important
appointment. Fortunately for the course of British film music, Korda was
obliged by law to employ a British subject to work as an 'apprentice' in order
that Schroeder might obtain a work permit. By this means was the young
student of the Royal College of Music Muir Mathieson inducted into the film
industry.[2]

Mathieson, who was born in January 1911, and who studied with Arthur
Benjamin and Malcolm Sargent at the Royal College, was blessed with two
attributes in particular that were to play a key role in the development of music
for film in Britain. He was an extraordinarily strong-minded individual, and he
had an unshakeable faith in the value of the work being produced by
contemporary British composers. Mathieson deplored the fact that Britain
had such a low status as a musical nation at the time. The strength of his feelings
on the subject can be judged by this extract from an interview with Leslie
Mitchell given in 1947:

---

[1] Muir Mathieson, quoted in Towers and Mitchell (1947), 62.
[2] Kulik (1990), 75.

For years and years we have been brought up on the belief that while we may have some poets, we certainly have no musicians. That's been going on for so long that musicians themselves have grown to believe it. But it's an absolute fallacy. Do you realize that at this moment we have the biggest and most exciting output of music in the world? But as France, Italy and Germany have always sold us the idea that they are the only producers of composers and musicians since the eighteenth century, music has become their biggest export. What about our big people? Walton, Bax, Ireland, to mention only three. I want to see the British genius for music exploited throughout the world, and recognized by other countries.[3]

It was with this passionate conviction in the worth of British music, and the intention of promoting it, that Mathieson laid down his terms for accepting Korda's offer to become musical director of London Film Productions in 1934 after Kurt Schroeder had left. Passionate conviction was a quality which Korda had probably found sadly lacking in the British character. He was certainly swayed sufficiently to accede to the unprecedented demands of the twenty-three-year-old Mathieson. These were that, being fully aware of his own shortcomings as a composer, he should not be required to compose himself, but should have a say in the choice of composers. He argued that, as Korda was investing in the highest production values in all other departments, it made sense to employ only the finest composers for his films, even if that meant a fair proportion of British composers who had no experience of film scoring. It is to Korda's credit that he had sufficient trust in Mathieson to take such a risk. Without Mathieson's strength of character, British composers might not have been granted the opportunity to work in a medium which offered them such new scope for creativity.

There was resentment among members of Korda's team at Denham studios that so many foreigners were in key positions. Mathieson was one of only three Britons to head a department. Miklós Rózsa, the Hungarian composer who was to become enormously successful in Hollywood, but who cut his teeth at Denham and worked closely with Mathieson, says of him in his autobiography:

> He was kind and helpful to me when I was first learning the job, although he didn't, I think, particularly like my music and never forgave me for not being British.[4]

Rózsa was being diplomatic. Mathieson was vehemently against the scoring of British films by foreign composers, and was never timid in expressing his opinions.

Mathieson's feelings aside, it is understandable that there should have been a general dissatisfaction that the British film industry had been revived by a Hungarian, however much of an Anglophile he may have been. Korda's productions have an unmistakably cosmopolitan feel to them. For this reason Korda's output of films made at Denham do not serve as any sort of model for an establishment of the British picture as a genre. Korda had always worked

---

[3] Muir Mathieson, quoted in Towers and Mitchell (1947), 61.
[4] Rózsa (1984), 69.

with one eye on the overseas market, especially the American market, and as we shall see, this tendency to 'angle' a film for its potential customers was to prove disastrous for the British film industry. Attempts by subsequent producers in Britain to emulate Hollywood were akin to an unarmed contest between David and Goliath, and it was not until the qualities that are unique to the British people were exploited that the industry in this country came of age.

All writers on the subject of film music are in agreement that it was the score of *Things to Come*, the futuristic fantasy film which Korda released in 1936, that put British film music on the map, and set a standard for others to emulate. Unfortunately, the advantageous conditions that Arthur Bliss experienced during the making of the film were not to be the common lot of composers in this country, and still less in Hollywood. Bliss was a composer of undoubted eminence, and he was accorded a status in the making of *Things to Come* which was not to be enjoyed again by a British composer until 1941, when Mathieson persuaded Vaughan Williams to score *49th Parallel*. Because of the respect shown to Bliss, he was able to make a far greater contribution to the film than is usual for composers. While it was common for the music to be considered as one of the last components to be added to a film, in this case Bliss became a close collaborator of both H. G. Wells and the director, William Cameron Menzies, from the early stages of planning. Wells was given complete artistic control of the film (a situation that Korda was to regret), and it was at his insistence that the music was recorded before the shooting of the film. Thus the music became an inherent part of the structure of the film, and many of its most famous visual sequences were shot and cut with the music as the motivating force. In addition to a full symphony orchestra, Bliss was able to use an extra percussion orchestra to create some of the special noise effects in the industrial sequences, and a large chorus for the opening and closing sequences of the film.

It was not only the colossal budget for the fourteen full recording sessions involving these forces that put *Things to Come* well outside the pale of normal practice in film music, but the whole nature of the film itself. The impressive sets created by Vincent Korda, the large number of extras and the long purely visual sequences all served to encourage the composition of a score on an epic scale. Even the extraordinary, grand rhetorical style of the actors' delivery, which strikes the ear so comically today, gives an opportunity for a far more extravagant underscoring than would be possible for most dialogue scenes even from that period of British film making, when vocal inflection was generally less realistic than it came to be in subsequent decades. So although the score for *Things to Come* is undoubtedly a milestone in British film music, the conditions that helped to shape its greatness were, unfortunately, far from routine in the industry, and it would take some years before the promise it offered could be fulfilled.

What separates *Things to Come* from the majority of British pictures to be scored by established concert composers is, of course, the simple matter of money. The sad history of the British film industry is dominated by the continuous problem of financial constraint and huge errors of judgment from a generally, though not invariably well-meaning government. In this respect Korda's 'revival' of the industry in this country was misleading in that it did not create a precedent that could be followed by other film companies, because they did not enjoy similar financial backing. Tight production budgets obviously had a direct bearing on the type of subject or storyline that could be treated by British film makers. Epic themes, especially those requiring thousands of extras, were automatically out of bounds except on rare occasions. Outdoor or location filming incurs additional expenditure, and the scale of the British Isles themselves has an inhibiting effect. Our culture, including our native literature, our very way of viewing ourselves, is deeply influenced by the unconscious recognition that we inhabit a very compact and relatively unthreatening terrain. We have no understanding of the American psychological inheritance resulting from the background of continuous battling with the unimaginably vast and hostile landscape that is the lot of many Americans. These differences inform every aspect of our lives. Our individual relationship to the space around us affects our attitudes to physical movement. The less space each one of us can claim, the more we must become aware of encroaching on the space of others. If the British are notorious for their reserve and tendency to understatement, it may well be the result of living in each other's backyards for so long. By contrast, Americans often seem to be communicating by semaphore; their metaphorical backyards being so much further apart.

Such oversensitivity to the awareness of others as an ingredient of the British personality has had its advantages, as our literary and dramatic traditions prove. It may seem obvious to us that both these media should treat the developing relationships between protagonists as a major theme, but a glance round the literature and drama of other cultures will show that this is not a universal preoccupation. It was not, therefore, solely financial considerations that cast British films into a generally wordy, static, claustrophobic, studio-bound mould, but something to do with how we came to expect our lives to be represented to us. In a similar vein, the grand spectacle scenes or 'money' shots that are so patently absent from the run of British films, causing them to fail in the requirement that they be cinematic entertainment, are in some way alien to that puritanical part of the British character which deplores ostentation.

If we can safely assume that the primary function of music in film is to assist in the conveying of certain emotional truths inherent in the message, underlying or otherwise, of that film, then the task of the composer is circumscribed by that message. It can be readily seen, then, that the general tendency of British films away from the epic scale, the grand gesture, towards the theatrical inheritance of plot development by dialogue, would have a very direct bearing on the nature and scope of the music written for them. Bliss was indeed fortunate to have been given the opportunity to score *Things to Come*. The relatively few epic pictures that were made in this country were more often than not scored by foreign composers, possibly because British composers were not considered sufficiently flamboyant.

If temperamental suitability was the rationale behind such choices, it is difficult to understand why Georges Auric, whose music is characterized by Parisian urbanity, was chosen to score some of the most idiosyncratically British of all films. In referring here to the three Ealing films that spring most readily to mind – *Passport to Pimlico, Hue and Cry* and *The Titfield Thunderbolt* – it is a delicate necessity to mention that the term 'British' is hardly applicable. These three comedies are patently about the English, as the separate and distinctive race that they are generally perceived to be. The whole subject of the Britishness of films is a thorny one, given that the film industry, certainly the feature-film industry, was so firmly centralized in the area around London. With the wonderful exception of *Whiskey Galore*, that masterpiece of parody on many levels, the treatment of racial differences within Britain is as about as subtle as any joke beginning: 'There was an Irishman, a Scotsman and a Welshman', with all the accompanying stereotypical banalities. Perhaps it is wisest to admit that 'British' is a generic term that has no substance in reality, and that the focus in British films was generally extremely localized.

There is evidence, however, that care was taken to match composers to the films they were to score with the same criteria of suitability that applied to the casting of leading actors:

> When Ealing studios decided to make Scott of the Antarctic everybody agreed that, if Dr. Vaughan Williams could be interested, he was the one man in the world to write the score.[5]

Considering some of the wild miscasting of actors that has inadvertently added so much to the entertainment of audiences over the years, it would seem that the choice of composers has generally been more successful. In other cases there were still many remedies at the disposal of skilful musical directors to obviate the blunders of composers before it became necessary to throw them off the picture altogether, and a great deal more care has been taken to avoid that contingency in this country than in Hollywood, where such instances are legion.

The working conditions for composers in Britain were altogether in contrast to those that existed in Hollywood. The subject is so extensive, and was to have such far-reaching implications for the whole development of film music on opposite sides of the Atlantic, that its significance can only be referred to here, and will be treated more fully at a later stage. For the moment suffice it to say that composers working for British films generally enjoyed considerably more respect and artistic freedom than their American counterparts – although it would be misleading to imply that this was invariably the case.

If the flagging British film industry was revived by the work of Alexander Korda, it was transformed by the Second World War. Since the earliest days of cinema the British government had been aware of the enormous potential for propaganda inherent in the medium. Finance was now forthcoming, not only for the numerous shorts designed to encourage and unite the people on the home front, but for feature films that were considered to be delivering the

---

[5] Irving (1959), 175.

appropriate messages. With their very way of life under threat, the British people turned to a form of entertainment that would reinforce their sense of national identity. While the actual number of British feature films dealing directly with the subject of war made between 1940 and 1945 was surprisingly low (50 films from a total of 278), the overall tone of patriotism, upholding the British way of life, was unmistakable, whether in comedy, crime or drama.

The war also served to increase the number of British composers involved in feature films. Many concert composers such as Alan Rawsthorne and Brian Easdale began writing for documentary shorts as an introduction to the film business, and then went on to write for feature films. Also it was natural that film makers should choose to use more native composers at a time of national turmoil, and the crisis brought out a dormant patriotism in the composers themselves. While in calmer days they may have reacted negatively to what they perceived as the jingoism of some of Elgar's more popular works, the exigencies of the times called forth more than an echo of the great master from them.

British composers in this instance may have tempered their style to suit the occasion, but on the whole they retained far more of their individual styles when writing for film than did their American counterparts. This is partly due to the absence of an expected 'house style' concomitant with the American studio system, and the greater artistic freedom accorded them by their reputations. Their excursions into the film business were motivated by a variety of considerations. While some were attracted by the opportunity to earn substantial sums comparatively quickly and easily, others, among them Vaughan Williams, recognized the enormous possibilities that could be realized under the right conditions. Vaughan Williams, who came to the medium late in life, was very attracted to it, and although his approach was somewhat unorthodox, he was quick to draw parallels between Wagner's dream of the total art-work and the as yet unattained ideal of the perfect fusion of all the elements of film.

As a result of the efforts of Muir Mathieson, and later of Ernest Irving at Ealing studios, most of Britain's leading concert composers tried their hand at scoring films, with varying degrees of success. A crucial factor was the extent of their natural affinity and sympathy for drama. Walton is a supreme example of one who instinctively understood the needs of a given dramatic situation, while others were not similarly gifted. Composers were often wary of the stigma attached to working for films. Some of our concert composers who wrote a substantial number of film scores were to pay the price for their affiliation to such a questionable medium. The musical establishment has consistently undervalued the contribution of William Alwyn, Malcolm Arnold and Benjamin Frankel – all notable symphonists – to the concert repertoire.

Whatever the musical establishment may have felt about the involvement of so many of Britain's leading composers in the film world, there is no doubt that by the late 1940s it had become recognized by film critics in France and America, as well as in this country, that British pictures were producing some of the finest scores. In 1948, the Academy Award for the best original film score was won for the first time by a British composer. In a year that could have seen the award going either to Walton, for his masterly score of *Hamlet*, or to Vaughan Williams for the monumental score of *Scott of the Antarctic*, it was the comparatively unknown composer, Brian Easdale, who triumphed with *The Red Shoes*. Leaving aside for the moment any doubt as to the value of such an award, which a perusal of the list of winners may evoke, it is worth noting that each of these three scores was the product of a particularly significant and creative personal relationship. The close collaboration and understanding between Walton and Olivier, Vaughan Williams and Ernest Irving, Brian Easdale and both Powell and Pressburger, were key factors in the success and effectiveness of these and other scores.

The golden age of British cinema, which had been mainly brought about by the conditions in Britain resulting from the war, was not long to survive the advent of peace. The reasons for its decline in the 1950s are sociologically far more complex than the rising popularity of television, or any other single factor. The decline of an artistic medium will naturally have a direct bearing on all its constituent parts, but the consequences to the music composed for a waning British cinema were not immediately apparent. It was not until towards the end of the decade that the great period of British film music drew to a close.

1. Differences between British and American films: a historical perspective

When writing for film, the composer is faced with a seemingly limitless number of circumscribing factors and impositions which arise directly from the medium. Each national cinema evolved into a distinctive and easily identifiable product whose indebtedness to its own cultural heritage can be observed. The composer for British films is, therefore, a sometimes reluctant heir to a cultural tradition which, by its very nature, has often been accused of working against the best interests of cinema. An understanding of the various factors which have shaped that tradition is needed in order to appreciate the strongly idiosyncratic nature of British films, and how they in turn were responsible for the development of all that distinguishes the British film score.

It is a sad fact that British films are not generally regarded with respect by the international film fraternity. In a poll taken in 1992 by *Sight and Sound* magazine from 233 critics and directors who were asked to name their choice of ten top films, British films accounted for less than 6 percent of those chosen.[1] The British are considered to be by nature unsuited to film making, particularly to the use of the camera. While Charles Barr quotes the words of Satyajit Ray to that effect for the opening of his chapter in *All our Yesterdays*,[2] he might have looked closer to home for an equally damning indictment. Graham Greene worked as a film critic from 1935 to 1941, principally for *The Spectator*, and brought all his renowned penetration and acerbity to the task. Well known for his dislike of all things American, he was no more lenient in his dealings with the British cinema:

> Nothing, a novice might think, could be easier than to catch reality with a camera, and yet this shy bird evades almost every English director.[3]

There can be no doubt that a basic lack of affinity with the camera strikes at the very roots of cinema's fundamental identity. The British director John Paddy Carstairs is stating the obvious when he says

---

[1] *Sight and Sound* (December 1992), 20–30.
[2] Satyajit Ray, quoted in Barr, 'Amnesia and Schizophrenia', in Barr (ed.) (1986), 1.
[3] Graham Greene, 'Sensation: Mazurka', *The Spectator*, 5.2.1937, in Parkinson (ed.) (1993), 172.

Action should be the first consideration in pictures; everything else should fall in line after this has been accomplished.[4]

Yet the obvious seems to have been overlooked in altogether too many British pictures. Certain aspects of the British character are directly challenged by the intimacy of the camera. It arouses an uneasiness, a mistrust born of inherent reticence, of the horror of emotional display:

The camera forces one to face facts, to probe, to reveal, to get close to people and things; while the British nature inclines to the opposite; to stay aloof, to cloak harsh truths with innuendoes. You cannot make great films if you suffer from constricting inhibitions of this sort.[5]

The notorious British reserve was not the only or even the chief culprit:

British cinema was traditionally hampered by the defection of native artists like Chaplin, by the country's lack of a strong financial base sufficient to support a broad-based film industry, and by a drearily conservative, unimaginative financial outlook. Also contributing to the lack of vitality in the British cinema was the snobbish theater-oriented tradition in England.[6]

What Chaplin might have achieved in the British film industry can only be a matter for conjecture. That he became one of popular cinema's greatest directors is indisputable. What the consequences would have been if that other great defector, Hitchcock, had chosen to remain in Britain is equally open to speculation, but the loss to British cinema of such talent is considerable. Britain has also lost a steady stream of experienced screen actors to Hollywood over the years.

Of the other two enemies of British cinema – financial constraint and the 'theater-oriented tradition' – it would be difficult to determine which was the more destructive. So insidious was the influence of the theatrical tradition on every aspect of British cinema and its history, that a serious writer on the subject could hold the opinion that

Dismissal of such work as merely 'theatrical' or 'literary' can only emanate from an arbitrary idealization of film.[7]

Even more alarmingly, a British director, when asked whether the British stage tradition had worked against the cinema's interests, replied, seemingly without concern: 'They more or less worked hand-in-glove.'[8] Such a cosy acceptance of a situation which has done more than anything else to stultify British cinema indicates how the medium itself was fundamentally misunderstood and misused:

---

[4] Carstairs (1937), 19.
[5] Satyajit Ray, quoted in Barr, 'Amnesia', in Barr (ed.) (1986), 9.
[6] Giannetti and Eyman (1986), 202.
[7] Williams, 'Perspectives', in Curran and Porter (eds) (1983), 18.
[8] Muriel Box, quoted in McFarlane (ed.) (1992), 42.

Thus majority cinema, in both the silent and the sound periods, can be reasonably seen as the flowering of a whole body of drama, theatre and entertainment which in its essential interests and methods preceded film but was then at once enhanced and made much more widely available by it.[9]

Film had become a vehicle for the dissemination of other dramatic forms, its unique capabilities of expression debased and disregarded. If film enhanced a 'whole body of drama, theatre and entertainment', the favour was certainly not returned. In the earliest days of cinema, Britain was in the forefront of the technical pioneering that was creating and developing a new medium at almost unbelievable speed. For a brief time at the turn of the century, Britain could compete with America and France in its experimentation with the techniques of film, but by the end of the First World War, America, which had suffered substantially less than Britain and France through its involvement, was in a dominant position. British production had fallen to around 18 percent of its immediate pre-war output, and the weakened markets of Britain and France could not stem the flow of films that poured in from America.

At the time that Britain was incurring a catastrophic debt from which it has never recovered, and which, through a long chain of consequences, have prevented it from ever competing realistically with the American film industry, D. W. Griffith was creating two films which were symbolic of everything Britain could never hope to achieve in film. With *The Birth of a Nation* (started at a time when Britain was making yet another silent version of *Hamlet*) and *Intolerance*, Griffith had brought to the screen not just breathtaking spectacle and grandeur, but, through his innovative approach to editing and his gift for the visual unfolding of a plotline, a realization of film's potential which to this day is rarely matched.

The flooding of the British market with American products after the first world war gave British audiences a taste for American films, and, save during the second world war, a preference for them rather than British films which has persisted to the present. The audiences cannot be blamed. With regrettably few exceptions the films made in Britain between the wars simply will not bear comparison with them. Through film, Britain was in thrall to American culture, while America found reciprocation easy to resist. The history of the British cinema is dominated by the effects of American distribution and the series of measures, mostly disastrous, taken to try to ensure the showing of a higher proportion of British films. Korda's attempted competition with the American market, and Rank's obsession with breaking the American stranglehold on the British market, only seemed to ensure that British films would be locked in a futile struggle, condemning them to a perpetual comparison with American films which could never be to their advantage.

The sharing of a common language and the forging of a 'special relationship' through a sometimes ill-starred history have tended to obscure the fundamental

---

[9] Williams, 'Perspectives', in Curran and Porter (eds) (1983), 17.

differences of the two nations, and any seriously considered comparison of British and American films will soon reveal those differences. Whether film makers in Britain were trying to emulate the American product, as in the case of Korda, or deliberately attempting to create something distinctively and unmistakably British, in the way that Michael Balcon was to do at Ealing, the resulting discrepancies are of vital importance in establishing exactly what is unique to the British film. As every facet of film had a direct influence on the music written for it, it is necessary to investigate all aspects of those facets in order to understand the true nature of film music.

There are very many reasons why America should have produced a master-piece like *The Birth of a Nation* by 1915, while Britain has never produced anything comparable. It was in the nature of the American people to embrace a new art form with an open acceptance and an optimism for its fresh possibilities. America was still a pioneering nation. The last state had joined the Union only a few years before, and much of the territory was still unbroken. While Britain had been effectively tabulated as a result of the Domesday census, so that its society had become localized as early as 1086, America was still in a state of formative flux, with large numbers of immigrants entering the country and sections of the population relocating. While the fixed and relatively stable society of Britain had led to a degree of social sophistication and the development of a strong cultural heritage, the opposite was the case in America:

> The presence of a frontier throughout most of American history has influenced every phase of the American character and activity. The continuing challenge of settling and developing a new continent directed American enterprise into practical channels. There was little time or energy for any of the arts.[10]

The result of this was that America, predominantly East Coast America, remained dependent on Europe, on England in particular, for its cultural direction. The theatre was a notable case in point:

> Even after political independence was won, British actors, playwrights, managers and stagecraft continued to dominate the American stage and to claim a vast superiority over anything of native origin. Despite the aggressive patriotism of many citizens of the new nation, most Americans accepted the claim of British superiority and felt a deep sense of cultural inferiority.[11]

This sense of cultural inferiority is at the root of the extraordinary ambivalence Americans feel towards the British. Like a rejected child assuming indifference, they can never rid themselves of a covert desire to belong. 'The name of England is so frequently on the characters' lips that we recognize at once an American picture.'[12]

---

[10] Wilson (1973), 55.
[11] Ibid., 54.
[12] Graham Greene, 'Generation of Conquerors: Lloyds of London: The Gap: Glamorous Night', *The Spectator*, 7.5.1937, in Parkinson (ed.) (1993), 198.

If the development of a native American theatre, therefore, was severely restricted by the dominance of British theatre, it was ultimately to be to the advantage of the new art form of cinema, because the Americans could not automatically turn to their dramatic heritage, as British film makers were to do when faced with the challenge of forging a new dramatic medium.

There was one particular form of drama that Americans had eagerly absorbed from Europe. At the beginning of the nineteenth century, playwrights in England, Germany and France had begun to exploit melodrama, and Americans had found the new genre very much to their taste. Typically, melodrama simplifies the motivations and emotions of its characters. Villains and heroes become polarized to extremes of evil and virtue. The moral code becomes rigid and inviolable. With characters reduced to puppets, the playwright is forced to resort to

> the invention of surprises, mysteries, and sensations. Instead of character development in complex moral situations, the dramatist substitutes contrived thrills and heightened emotionalism. Instead of the suspense which comes from internal conflict, the dramatist presents struggles between good and evil whose outcome is foreordained.[13]

It was precisely these divergences which were to mark the separation of American and British cinema. Britain was to retain the dramatic inheritance of 'character development in complex situations' and 'the suspense which comes from internal conflict', while American cinema moved towards 'surprises, mysteries and sensations'.

Melodrama appealed to the American temperament for a number of reasons. Its sweeping gestures and simplification of character made it easier to understand for a population with an increasing proportion of immigrants limited in understanding of the language. The more emphatic style of acting was better suited to the large auditoria, seating up to 4,000, that had developed in the East coast towns. Improvements in stage machinery had encouraged the use of more visual pyrotechnics and had enhanced the status of spectacle on the stage. The black-and-white approach to morality was admirably suited to the strong Puritan ethic, and the emergence of the ordinary man as hero appealed to the democratic nature of the American people.[14]

It would be misleading to imply that melodrama, while being so obviously suited to the American taste on a broad base, was beneath the dignity of British audiences. On the contrary, although the educated classes eschewed melodrama, preferring conventional theatre or public lectures,

> The drama, to the simpler, unsophisticated audiences of the new industrial democracy, meant melodrama . . . They wanted, as such audiences have always done, the same things – love, passion, lust and blood. The naïve spectator,

[13] Wilson (1973), 105–6.
[14] Ibid., 107–8.

uneducated to demand a rigorous causal logic in the theatre, untouched by modern cynicism, untrained in the appreciation of subtlety of characterization or acting, to whom the very word psychology was still unknown, shamelessly bedewed his whiskers with tears of genuine emotion . . . These plays were not literature; they were only a primitive kind of drama.[15]

It is easy to see from this extract why the 'unsophisticated audiences' of our present society are so addicted to television soap operas. They bear all the hallmarks of melodrama. Similarly, while it is far too simplistic to describe the mass audiences of popular British cinema as predominantly of the working class,[16] it was this audience which responded to the elements of melodrama in American films.

Once the notion of using film for entertainment, rather than for instruction or simple representation, had occurred to the pioneers of the film industry, it was natural that they should initially choose existing forms of dramatic entertainment for their material. While all the familiar forms of stage entertainment were used – the stage play, melodrama, music hall, vaudeville and burlesque – it was apparent that 'motion pictures from their very inception, built a large measure of their appeal on melodrama'.[17]

Melodrama, by the very elements that separate it from serious drama, is peculiarly suited to the screen. The avoidance of character development and complex emotional or psychological nuances in favour of strong, simple passions make it easier to represent a plotline on a visual basis. Unencumbered by moral dilemma requiring lengthy discourse, the conflict of good and evil is free to be expressed on a physical level. The shocks, thrills and sensations are all grist to the mill of cinematic necessity for movement. There is semantic evidence that Americans have always understood the basic concept of cinema. Whereas the British refer to 'films', for the American they have always been 'motion pictures' or 'movies'. John Paddy Carstairs puts it with refreshing simplicity:

> what a difference that one word makes – that little word 'motion': which probably accounts for that extra little something in American pictures that the others have not yet got![18]

Movement is the crucial issue when contrasting British and American films. Freedom of movement implies a lack of inhibition not immediately associated with the British character. Long centuries of structured socialization had led to an interactive sophistication based on non-revealing constraint. The American had a different historical conditioning:

---

[15] Hudson (1972), 25.
[16] For a detailed consideration of British cinema audiences, see Corrigan, 'Entertainment', in Curran and Porter (eds) (1983), 24–35.
[17] Wilson (1973), 55.
[18] Carstairs (1937), 19.

> The American of mid-[nineteenth] century was restless, thanks to the invigorating climate and the continual challenge of tremendous tasks. He was always 'a-doin'' and always on the go. Even when he tried to relax he was whittling, chewing, jiggling and rocking.[19]

The lack of linguistic complexity also made melodrama an ideal vehicle for cinema in a country that was increasingly made up of immigrants unfamiliar with English. Language was no longer the primary means of expression. That had now passed into the realms of the visual. By contrast, language in British films was, after the coming of sound, hardly ever to relinquish its dominance.

The contrasting backgrounds of the early film makers were a decisive factor in the disparate approach to cinema of America and Britain. In America:

> The movie industry from the very start grew and flourished without the leadership of people experienced in the ways of the legitimate theatre. A few of the early actors, directors and producers had some stage experience, but in general, the founders of the movie industry were true pioneers. They came without pre-conceived notions or past experience in the field of entertainment and they worked with a brand new medium.[20]

In Britain, however, it was a different story:

> Theatre's grip on British cinema started very early. Early cinema looked to the London stage for expertise in acting . . . The stage could also supply ready-made characters and plots, bred from 19th-century realism.[21]

One of the main reasons for this divergence in approach was that the majority of the early film makers in Britain were from the educated classes. For them, inevitably, their notions of entertainment were coloured by an urge, inculcated since childhood, towards instruction and improvement, rather than titillation. The educational use of film is an admirable one, but British cinema was to suffer from the consequences of trying to smuggle education into popular entertainment films. American cinema, never burdened with the benevolent paternalism that permeated entertainment in Britain, was generally content to exploit, excite and horrify its audiences, without feeling an obligation to educate them at the same time.

It is impossible to overestimate the influence of BBC radio on the British public's attitude to entertainment. It seems extraordinary in hindsight that it exercised a monopoly on broadcasting for over thirty years. The first complete programme was broadcast on 23 February 1920, and from the beginning the aims of the BBC were clear. The essentials of its constitution were that it should be

> a public corporation with a monopoly of broadcasting controlled by part-time Governors responsible for seeing that broadcasting is carried on as a public

---

[19] Wilson (1973), 130.
[20] Ibid., 352.
[21] Brown, 'Sister', in Barr (ed.) (1986), 145.

service in the national interest for the information, education and entertainment of the people.[22]

Public service radio meant that entertainment was to take third place after information and education, and listeners were even to be educated in their enjoyment:

> The BBC must not only give its listeners what they like best, it must also afford constant play for the development of liking. Only so can the level of taste be raised and the quality of listener's enjoyment intensified.[23]

While the Ullswater report of 1936 was aware of 'the influence of broadcasting upon the mind and spirit of the nation',[24] it was not until the committee of enquiry was set up under Lord Beveridge in 1950 that the desirability of that influence came to be challenged. Witnesses in the enquiry found that 'the monopoly was dangerous to the public interest because it involved the steady influencing of the public mind in an arbitrary way',[25] and that the BBC was probably 'the biggest single bureaucracy in the world concerned with the propagation of ideas'.[26]

The BBC's plans for the Home Service sound innocuous, if patronizing:

> The Home Service, in all its Regional variants, is a carefully balanced programme, designed to appeal to all classes, paying attention to culture at a level at which the ordinary listener can appreciate it; giving talks that will inform the whole democracy rather than an already informed section; and generally so designed as to help in raising the standard of taste, entertainment, outlook and citizenship of the British people.[27]

But some saw it in a different light:

> One's gorge rises – there is an arrogance in the assumption that one man knows what is good for others – there is a sultriness as of a Fascist authoritarianism in the air.[28]

So oppressive did this speaker, the former Director of Talks, find the monopoly of the BBC, that he found it necessary to embrace American citizenship and the dubious delights of its broadcasting system. With good reason the Crawford Report of 1926, set up to investigate the continued viability of the BBC in its existing form, had

> rejected the United States system of commercial broadcasting as unsuited to this country and felt that no body constituted for profit could adequately perform the broader functions which were then beginning to emerge.[29]

---

[22] Wythenshawe (1953), 23.
[23] The BBC's report to the Beveridge Committee, in Wythenshawe (1953), 79.
[24] Wythenshawe (1953), 30.
[25] Account of the Beveridge report, in Wythenshawe (1953), 30.
[26] Ibid.
[27] Wythenshawe (1953), 78.
[28] Charles Siepmann, 'Radio's Second Chance', quoted in Wythenshawe (1953), 211.
[29] Wythenshawe (1953), 29.

American radio had little interest in performing these 'broader functions'. Its system of commercial broadcasting ensured that the concept of service to the public was limited to that of keeping it informed of the latest available products. By 1948 there were nearly 2,000 stations broadcasting in America, of which fewer than half were affiliated to one of the four national networks. All the stations ran on a system of sponsorship whereby a commercial interest could buy air time in the form of sponsored programmes to promote its products. The result was that 'The advertisers control radio. Radio's primarily a means of selling goods. Everything must be subordinate to that.'[30]

Americans were well aware of the shortcomings of the nation's broadcasting:

> it is obviously a fact that a very large part of America's radio fare (most soap operas, quiz programmes, audience-participation shows, gag-comedy acts, juke-music sessions, commercial announcements) would affect any person of modest discrimination somewhere in the range between complete indifference and acute illness.[31]

While these descriptions give a vivid impression of the contrast between British and American radio, the most significant difference is in the relative importance of the radio play. For Americans, the radio play over one hour in length was practically unheard of; drama meant soap opera. The continual breaking-off for commercials rendered serious drama impossible. The BBC, on the other hand, had a deliberate policy of building up the audience's concentration:

> Gradually over the years a mass audience which must include more than half the population of the country has learnt to listen to plays of one and a half hours length. This involves sustained attention of a kind which the great majority of the listeners have learnt only by listening to BBC plays.[32]

The popularity of radio plays in the 1950s rivals that of television soap operas today. In 1951, the BBC broadcast 360 plays, of which 200 were over 90 minutes long. Saturday Night Theatre attracted audiences of 10 million, while the even more popular Wednesday evening play on the Light Programme had up to 13 million listeners.

That such large numbers of people chose to listen to a play on the radio instead of visiting the local cinema says much about the perception of what constituted dramatic entertainment in Britain. Their long love affair with the theatre was the main reason why the British could seldom make the separation between a new medium of narrative, dependent on visual means for its best expression, and the tradition of dramaturgy. For the British, narrative is inextricably bound to the word, and to the traditional forms that enshrine it:

---

[30] Wythenshawe (1953), 221.
[31] *Fortune* (March 1947), quoted in Wythenshawe (1953), 22.
[32] Wythenshawe (1953), 96.

The continued prestige of 'theatre', as opposed to 'film', is remarkable after a half-century in which it is quite clear that film has produced much more important new work. Moreover, deference towards the forms and styles of the established culture seems continually to re-establish itself within cinema, for predominantly social rather than artistic reasons.[33]

Exposure to the radio play further encouraged British listeners to move away from the visual interpretation of narrative to a world of interiority:

One of radio's greatest assets is that in the exploitation of evocative sound it can create dramatic atmosphere far surpassing that which is possible on the stage or even on film or television – and that because of the fact that in the highest expressive arts the artist asks us to perceive his truth not through *all* our senses but only through *some*, upon which we concentrate in an imaginative way.[34]

This concentration of the imagination through aural perception alone is immortalized in the anecdote of the listener who preferred radio to television because 'the scenery is better'. It also accounts for the tedium so often experienced when watching films that depend too heavily on the spoken word. Realistic representation on the screen forestalls the imaginative recreation of the scene evoked by the words, and the substitution is rarely a fair exchange.

It was precisely this collision of the senses, resulting from the coming of sound, that had caused such a disruption to the natural flow of film:

When the images are given another human attribute, an appeal to the ear, the artificial convention on which their reality depends is broken down, another reality is superimposed, and they appear as the flat photographs they are.[35]

Theorists argue to this day whether the damage inflicted on the heart of film by the introduction of sound has ever been justified by subsequent developments. That cinema was reaching a peak, if not the pinnacle, of its expressive potential can be affirmed by viewing such masterpieces of the medium as the 1927 version of *The Wind*. In discussing another classic of the silent era, *The Son of the Sheikh*, Graham Greene gives an insight into not only the prevailing attitudes of the time, but also the unique appeal of the silent film:

There was a time when many of us thought the talkies were going to be the end of true cinema. It may seem silly now, but if you see this film you will realise why we felt that. There is an inexpressible charm in the silence: the characters fighting, loving, hating, move to music only, the music probably of one rather out of tune piano: their gestures are ritualised. It is all a kind of dance.[36]

---

[33] Williams, 'Perspectives', in Curran and Porter (eds) (1983), 19.
[34] Wythenshawe (1953), 98.
[35] Graham Greene, 'A Film Principle: Sound and Silence', *The Times*, 10.7.1928, in Parkinson (ed.) (1993), 172.
[36] Graham Greene, 'The Cinema', BBC National Service broadcast, 29.8.1937, in Parkinson (ed.) (1993), 512.

The coming of sound resulted in the complete stultification of film for five or six years on both sides of the Atlantic. With few exceptions – the most notable being the case of Chaplin, who recognized that the whimsical charm of his style of visual comedy could not survive the translation to sound – the film companies rushed into production of the new talkies. Initially, America and Britain were equally guilty of misusing the new medium:

> Having sound unwillingly thrust upon them, the producing companies, in a frantic agony of competitive desperation, immediately bethought them of the treasures of the stage. A play had action and words, they argued; the new sound film had action and words; therefore it seemed reasonable to suppose that herein lay material ready for cinematic exploitation.[37]

The introduction of the spoken word led to an immediate cinematic paralysis. Everything slowed down or stopped altogether in order to focus attention on the novelty. Some silent stars found themselves redundant in the face of 'the prestige weapon of the educated English voice'.[38] It would seem that, even in Hollywood, an Oxford accent was required:

> The army of British actors in search of a job was enormous, their accents almost as embarrassing as some of the American stars' attempts to prove that English was a push-over! . . . Everybody with an English college tie or a broad 'a' accent cashed-in whilst the cashing was good: and who was to blame them?[39]

The ebb and flow of fashion in British acting since the days of the Globe, although it had laid differing emphasis on physicality, had never abandoned the basic precept of the beauty of the voice as a first essential in dramatic delivery, and it was not to do so until the realism of the late 1950s. The American talking picture, after its initial hiatus in the early years of sound, was characterized by its far more natural style of delivery which eased the flow of the action. Reverence for the beautifully modulated tones of the theatrically trained British actor was partly responsible for the weighting in favour of the word which so becalmed British films. Four of Britain's most distinguished stage actors, who all possessed voices of immense power and flexibility of expression, made an incalculable contribution to cinema. Although the interest and commitment of Laurence Olivier, Michael Redgrave, Ralph Richardson and John Gielgud to the medium may not have been equal,

> These actors are evidence of the abiding interconnection in Britain between cinema and theater, which affects the kinds of roles they play . . . Their theater connections give them a certain legitimacy, in contrast to those stars who are associated exclusively with the cinema. Much more than the Hollywood cinema, British cinema has always maintained a strong link with the theater, not only through its use of actors from the theater but also in its dependence on stage plays.[40]

[37] Nicoll (1972), 124.
[38] Barr, 'Amnesia', in Barr (ed.) (1986), 12.
[39] Carstairs (1937), 24.
[40] Landy (1991), 39.

Two other contrasts between American and British actors had an important effect on the treatment of the material for film. The American star system dates back to the theatre of the nineteenth century, when the importation of big names from Europe, and the emergence of a number of strongly charismatic American actors, had encouraged early development of the 'star vehicle' system whereby plays were chosen or especially written as a show-case for the individual actor. So intense was public adulation of these stars that a rivalry between the American Edwin Forrest and the English actor William Charles Macready, led to the death of twenty-two supporters in riots outside the Astor Place Opera House on 10 May 1849.[41] This compares with the hysterical scenes that attended the lying-in of Rudolph Valentino in 1926, when riots resulted in scores of injuries. British cinema never really operated on a star system, except in the films designed for Gracie Fields and George Formby. It is rather revealing of the British personality that George Formby was the greatest box office success of the early 1940s. Even more revealing is the contrast between British and American leading actresses. While America had produced a number of female stars who to this day remain sexual icons, Britain gave its audiences Margaret Lockwood, Phylis Calvert and Patricia Roc – actresses notable for their lack of any comparable appeal. As the French critic Jean Quéval amusingly put it:

> An utter lack of pulchritude clearly distinguishes Great Britain at large, but, whether one likes it or not, film audiences fall for pulchritude the world over. Even British audiences do. Unfortunately, they go wrong: they mistake Miss Lockwood for pulchritude; we prefer Rita Hayworth.[42]

It was common for screen-plays to be created to fit the American star, or to be transferred to a different historical period in order to flatter the figure with a more becoming costume. In Britain, except in the case of musical comedies, it was not the custom to create a film for a given star. When asked if the knowledge of who was to play the lead had any effect on his writing for the screen, Graham Greene replied

> In almost all cases I have known who was to play the lead, but I don't think I have ever altered the emphasis of a film to fit the star. It usually happens the other way round; one chooses the star to fit the film.[43]

The second contrast between British and American actors is connected to the differing emphasis on the star system. One of the more positive outcomes of the dependence of theatre in British cinema is the extraordinary depth of its supporting roles, provided by a wide range of brilliant character actors. The American system called for a handful of stereotypes to support its star, but the

---

[41] For a full account, see Wilson (1973), 85–6.
[42] Quéval (1950), 200.
[43] 'The Screenwriter' (Graham Greene interviewed by Ivan Butler), in Ivan Butler, *The Making of Feature Films: A Guide* (London, 1971), quoted in Parkinson (ed.) (1993), 524.

British film relies on a sometimes large cast of strongly individual secondary characters.

America and Britain had both turned automatically to the stage play as material for their films with the advent of the talking picture. Initially, both were guilty of being content merely to reproduce the play as if the camera were a member of the audience. Graham Greene, writing of Max Reinhardts's production of *A Midsummer Night's Dream*, complained that

> At every passage of dialogue we are back before footlights and the camera is focused relentlessly on the character who speaks. The freer, more cinematic fairy sequences are set to Mendelssohn's music, and this is the way Shakespeare's poetry ought surely to be used if it is not to delay the action. It must be treated as music, not as stage dialogue tied to the image of the speaker like words issuing from the mouth of characters in a cartoon.[44]

In the theatre, the stage characters are 'the carriers of all the meanings a theatrical plot involves'.[45] We are accustomed by the theatrical tradition to expect the unfolding of a narrative to be presented to us by the interaction of the characters to the virtual exclusion of all other means. When film is used to its best advantage, the centrality of the characters' position is challenged:

> The film actor is not necessarily the nub of the narrative, the carrier of all its meanings. Cinematic action is always likely to pass through regions which, should they contain human beings at all, yet involve them only in an accessory, unspecified way.[46]

The film actor, instead of maintaining the recognized position and stature of a stage character, in relation to his audience, may be reduced to a small component in a film dominated by the landscape, by natural forces or even by an object or creature such as a train or a giant gorilla. Under such circumstances, dialogue assumes a completely different role:

> Cinematic dialogue must be much more economic in its effects than dialogue in a play, that we expect in it not the complete development of a conversation from beginning to end but a series of suggestions concerning the conversation's course.[47]

To the viewer's cost, many British directors seem to have overlooked a simple point:

> while dramatic dialogue must always be directly presented, filmic dialogue may be introduced in a variety of ways, of which by far the least interesting is that which shows persons speaking.[48]

[44] Graham Greene, 'A Midsummer Night's Dream', *The Spectator*, 18.10.1935, in Parkinson (ed.), 48.
[45] Kracauer (1961), 96.
[46] Ibid., 97.
[47] Nicoll (1972), 149.
[48] Ibid., 136.

The novel may seem closer to the nature of film, with its dramatic possibilities only limited by the author's imagination, but in some ways its use is as problematic as that of the stage play. Graham Greene, who was experienced in adaptation, knew only too well that 'my books don't make good films. Film companies think they will, but they don't.'[49] He was aware of the problems of translating one medium into another: 'What has the right rhythm in the book because of the surrounding paragraphs may seem unreal on the screen and must be modified.'[50] The novel presented as much of a challenge to the writer of screen-plays as did the stage play:

> Undoubtedly the freedom of the film brings it nearer in structure to the novel than the drama, where a conventional limitation and restriction is demonstrably essential; but simply to follow the plan of a novel in the preparing of a screen-play is as erroneous as the faithful reproduction on the screen of dramatic form.[51]

While it would be impracticable to dismiss all adaptations on the grounds that 'there are no genuinely cinematic literary forms',[52] because to do so would be to dismiss almost half the films of the period under consideration, it would also be unwise. Although the ideal film script is obviously one that has been conceived entirely in cinematic terms, in reality the situation is more complex. American producers and directors realized that they had taken a wrong direction for film in the early years of the talkies, and began to produce films using the potential of cinema that were as far removed as possible from the reproduced stage play. *King Kong*, which had enormous significance for the history of film music, was released in 1933, and liberated American cinema from the grip of theatrical dialogue. The spoken word has minimal significance in this film, and could easily be dispensed with. British films, however, continued to

> lag miserably at the heels of novelists and dramatists, attempting to do what they can never do so well as their seniors in fiction, instead of exploring the territory that is proper to themselves.[53]

The problems lay not so much in the source material as in its treatment. In skilled hands, the stage play or the novel can be transformed into a screen-play that is more cinematically successful than one originally conceived for the screen. Although Graham Greene maintains that film is 'a director's art, neither an author's nor an actor's',[54] everything depends on the quality of the screen writing:

---

[49] 'Graham Greene at 77' (Graham Greene interviewed by Mort Rosenblum, in *St Louis Post Dispatch* (12.9.1982), quoted in Parkinson (ed.) (1993), xxxii.

[50] 'Graham Greene on the Screen' (Graham Greene interviewed by Gene D. Phillips, S.J., in *The Catholic World* (USA, August 1969) and also *The Month* (UK, June 1970), quoted in Parkinson (ed.) (1993), 136.

[51] Nicoll (1972), 160.

[52] Kracauer (1961), 245.

[53] Graham Greene, 'Film Aesthetic: Its Distinction for Drama – The Province of the Screen', *The Times*, 19.3.1929, in Parkinson (ed.) (1993), 395.

[54] Graham Greene, 'Anna Karenina: The Informer', *The Spectator*, 11.10.1935, in Parkinson (ed.) (1993), 35.

Gradually the British studios have managed to creep steadily forward until they are, again, turning out a number of pictures that are on a par with the more experienced Hollywood product. But, despite the fact that the direction, camera work, settings and general production polish have now reached a high level, still the most important department of any studio – the story department – is left in a pretty sad state of non-existence! . . . Too many second- and third-rate writing brains have been allowed to wreck what might have been entertaining British productions.[55]

Among Britain's great cinematic successes original screen-plays are conspicuously absent. With the exception of the films produced by Ealing studios, most of Britain's best-known films are literary or theatrical adaptations. In the late 1940s British cinema was looking for a new direction, and yet

> there is in each year of this period scarcely a handful of either critically or commercially significant films based on original screen-plays.[56]

America drew heavily on the British novel and play for its films, but the studios there had a large number of experienced writers to choose from. They were often ruthless in their treatment of these treasures of literature in pursuit of a suitably cinematic screen-play, but their ruthlessness, sometimes tantamount to butchery, was often effective. With British screen-plays the problem was generally one of too much reverence for the source:

> There has not often been a radical approach to the original material but, rather, a characteristic tendency to be awed by or to trade on the prestige and popularity of the source novels and the result has often been to contribute another unadventurous element to the British cinema at large.[57]

This reverential attitude did not just apply to the much-plundered Shakespeare, Dickens and other literary legends. There was too much use of well-known contemporary writers such as Somerset Maugham and George Bernard Shaw. The ridiculous pandering to Shaw, who insisted on 'faithful reproductions of the plays as written and designed for ordinary theatrical representation',[58] led to a series of cinematic disasters, culminating in the fiasco of *Caesar and Cleopatra*. The impossibility of treating Shaw cinematically on these terms is neatly expressed by Graham Greene:

> In the theatre Mr Shaw explains and explains, and we take away not the long discussions, but a few vivid images. The thought, which takes pages to express, arises from one sharply focused picture in the mind. The object of the film should be the translation of thought back into images.[59]

---

[55] Carstairs (1937), 54–5.
[56] McFarlane, 'Literary', in Barr (ed.) (1986), 132.
[57] Ibid., 120.
[58] George Bernard Shaw, quoted in Brown, 'Sister', in Barr (ed.) (1986), 152.
[59] Graham Greene, 'The Province of the Film: Past Mistakes and Future Hopes', *The Times*, 9.4.1928, in Parkinson (ed.) (1993), 388.

While Shaw transparently had no conception of the basic function of cinema, other contemporary literary figures were under the misapprehension that they were better informed. The British director John Paddy Carstairs was unimpressed by their knowledge of the medium:

> You can name this famous writer or that clever playwright who is doing a story for such-and-such a film company, but in none of these cases are any of these writers being taught to write for the MOTION PICTURE. They glibly talk of long shots and close-ups and wipes and mixes, but they do not know the real uses and significances of these cinematic devices.[60]

Although Carstairs is writing of the situation in 1936, British cinema continued to use established writers in the 1940s and 1950s. The passing of time had done little to improve things:

> Some writers eventually found the means to step beyond the studio floor barrier, blending and expanding their established style with the methods of the cinema, but they were few.[61]

Much of the often unsatisfactory nature of British films can be attributed to the fact that their screen-plays, whether adaptation or original, support the centrality of the human protagonist. While America had discovered the cinematic advantages of displacing its characters in favour of dominating terrain and large animals, Britain persisted in the theatrical tradition of subordinating everything to the importance of character interaction as the means of narrative exposition. As a result, the use of the symbolic object, one of cinema's greatest weapons, had little place in British films, where an object rarely transcends the status of a stage-prop. By a curious national quirk, the train, an archetype of the cinematic symbolic object, is rendered by British films into an honorary character. The British obsession with steam railway has led to a number of films in which an engine appears to have become anthropomorphized.

The natural environment plays all too small a part in British films. The wonderful exception of *Black Narcissus* serves to demonstrate the opportunities that have been lost. In this film all aspects of the environment combine to unbalance and overpower the protagonists. It is ironic that in this visually ravishing film, the scenery is in reality painted glass. If exterior shots are not always necessary to convey the power of natural forces, neither do their presence automatically ensure good cinema. British films are riddled with examples of a director's belief that a few establishing shots will somehow alleviate the staginess of their film. Kracauer must have had British cinema firmly in mind when he wrote

> In sum, films which aim at the straight implementation of a theatrical story have the following, easily recognizable features in common. They emphasize the actors

---

[60] Carstairs (1937), 57.
[61] Brown, 'Sister', in Barr (ed.) (1986), 148.

and their interplay. In keeping with this main concern, they further coincide in assigning to inanimate objects and environmental factors a subsidiary role. Finally and most important, they include practically no image that would not serve the ends of story construction.[62]

The British public, largely unaware of the shortcomings of its national cinema, especially in the 1930s, accepted them with complacency. Conditioning had led to the expectation that the cinematic experience would be wordy, stagey and moribund, and British audiences were satisfied as long as the words were beautifully enunciated and the story was good. There may be more than a grain of truth in Kracauer's theory that 'the theatrical film appeals to adults who have suppressed the child in themselves',[63] since the British are notorious for repressing anything that is potentially embarrassing, disruptive or inconvenient – such as sexuality. If it is true that 'the British mind is never at home with symbols',[64] then it is no surprise if British audiences bore the lack of symbolism in their films with equanimity. What they most wanted to see was themselves – their community, their society – reflected back at them. This reflection, however, must be selective, not comprehensive. The less palatable, the 'real' side of life, was approached, if obliquely, by the documentary movement, but in this period was firmly ignored by feature films.

The British Board of Film Censors had often been blamed for the super-ficiality of the majority of films made in the 1930s, but British audiences of the time were content to be denied films that challenged the political system:

> Bodies like the BBFC had little to fear from the British cinema of the 1930s. And it is perhaps not surprising that the British cinema was, for its own part, and without much prompting, a further significant factor in contributing to the remarkable stability of British society during this period. It reflected and reinforced the dominant consensus and sought to generate adherence to the idea that society should continue to remain stable and cohesive as it changed over time.[65]

This stability of British society was in large part due to the fact that the most recent foreign invasion had taken place nine centuries before, and that, except during one brief aberration in the seventeenth century, the British people had generally been content with a class-dominated system, based on feudalism and the fusion of monarchy and parliamentary democracy, since 1265. The consensus of approval had crystallized into what amounts to a national obsession with maintaining the status quo, and this obsession, this religion, has even had an effect on the structure of dramatic narrative. For the British, there is one particular narrative pattern which feels peculiarly right and reassuring, and it can be seen in countless British films. Characterized in

---

[62] Kracauer (1961), 223.
[63] Ibid., 222.
[64] Hudson (1972), 199.
[65] Aldgate, 'Containment', in Curran and Porter (eds) (1983), 270–1.

music by the A-B-A-plus-coda pattern, it typically presents the status quo as a group of people or a society in a relative state of equilibrium. The status quo is then challenged by a threatening force, often in the shape of the 'outsider', which results in the society pulling together, either to defeat the threat or to assimilate it. The return of the status quo is accompanied by some element of transformation; either the society is enhanced by the experience, or the outsider has developed through acceptance of the group norm.

While this pattern conforms to a type of narrative common to many cultures, its significance lies in its insularity. The basic instinct of the British is to stay at home. Unlike the American of popular fiction, they do not go off on quests. Their impulses are directed inwards, not outwards. If the determination to protect the status quo at the expense of all chance of risk, of unexpected good fortune, of creative possibilities, leads to very dull lives, it also leads to very dull cinema. Of course, not all Britons have been content to spend their lives shut up in their castles. There have always been the more adventurous among them who have found the British Isles too confining. But it was from these trail-blazers, the ones who built an empire covering a quarter of the earth, that the 'jiggling' American of the nineteenth century evolved; it was the shopkeepers who stayed behind, and spawned playwrights.

Ultimately, it is the fundamental divergence of primary motivation between the British and the Americans which is the dominant factor in their comparative affinity with the cinematic medium. The inwardly directed impulse of the British, manifested by their reticence and inhibition, contrasts with the undiscriminating self-aggrandizement of the outwardly directed American. The consequences of these temperamental differences were vividly summed up by John Paddy Carstairs in 1936:

> One of the chief reasons of successful screen story-writing, I think, is the American national characteristic of self-dramatization. This dramatizing of themselves is, indeed, a most useful thing – from the screen point of view, because in all sorts of situations, it helps many suspenseful and coloured moments in life, in a film drama, moments when we would here, through no fault of our insular selves, be inclined to choke back the inevitable sob and 'carry on'. This famous British tradition of non-reaction is by no means helping our film industry.[66]

A film industry that aims to serve the majority of the population can never hope to produce anything that transcends the limitations imposed by that society's formative influences. If those influences render the nation unreceptive to the true expression of a particular art form, then that art form becomes something other, something less:

> A mass medium like the film is bound to yield to the enormous pressures of social and cultural conventions, collective preferences, and ingrained habits of perceiv-

[66] Carstairs (1937), 70.

ing, all of which combine to favor spectacles which may be high-level entertainment but have little to do with films.[67]

British films may seldom be worthy of the title, but they have not been completely without success. The very ways in which they fail to be good cinema reveal as much about the British character as any attempt to portray it directly. If British screen writers have been too deferential to their sources, then their very deference has brought some of our finest literature unsullied to the screen. If the grip of the theatrical tradition has been too strong, then we are compensated by the preservation of some of our greatest actors' best performances. If our eyes are wearied by the excessive use of the shot/reverse-shot, then we can close them, and feast on a variety of beautiful speaking voices. The shortcomings of our cinema have resulted in the loss of many creative possibilities for the composer of film music in this country, but those shortcomings have been responsible for defining the parameters of a unique product – the British film score.

[67] Kracauer (1961), 230.

2. Formulae in the classical Hollywood score

The score of a feature film, while serving many different functions, has primarily to act as an interpreter, to guide the audience through the narrative by the systematic use of easily identifiable cues. The majority of these cues relate directly to the overall emotional tone of a given scene, and music in feature films is predominantly used to indicate to the audience how they should react to different situations on the screen. This role becomes particularly important when a scene is emotionally ambivalent. The power and subtlety of music is such that it can advise an audience of the underlying emotions that are not being projected by the images or the dialogue. An audience will instinctively respond to the musical prompt to laugh in an apparently serious situation, or to reach for the tissues despite the brave smiles on the screen.

With such an effective weapon there is obviously the inherent danger of its potential misuse. If music can override the evidence of our eyes, then it can with the utmost facility endorse what is already present on the screen, and with overuse, a very real problem of redundancy can result. The greatest contrast between British and American film scores centres on this issue. The differences in the use of music in feature films between the two countries is an inevitable reflection and consequence of the differences – cultural, geographical, historical and temperamental – already discussed.

After the upheavals and uncertainties following the introduction of the talking picture, Hollywood quickly recovered its composure, and within a few years had brought its films to a very high polish. By the mid-1930s, what has become known as the classical Hollywood film's golden age was firmly established, and its characteristics were easily recognizable. While there was significant variation between the major studios, the classical Hollywood film came to be epitomized by certain common features. These included high production values, with meticulous attention to detail paid by specialized staff in all departments. Time and money were lavished so that the studio stars could appear flawless in their carefully researched and created wigs, make-up and costumes, with their best profiles lovingly lit and shot after endless preparation. There is a seamless, narcotic pseudo-reality about the films of Hollywood's golden age, and this is due not only to their technical sophistication, but in large measure to their scores.

If the classical Hollywood film had soon settled into an easily definable product that was both idiomatic and formulaic, the same was also true of the classical Hollywood score:

> Its form was based upon a set of conventions for the composition and placement of nondiegetic music which prioritized narrative exposition. These conventions included the use of music to sustain structural unity; music to illustrate narrative content, both implicit and explicit, including a high degree of direct synchronization between music and narrative action; and the privileging of dialogue over other elements of the soundtrack. The medium of the classical Hollywood film score was largely symphonic; its idiom romantic; and its formal unity typically derived from the principle of the leitmotif.[1]

In short, the classical Hollywood score was a curious anachronism, a hangover from the late nineteenth century, and in many instances a grotesque parody of the more obvious techniques of the three great musico-dramatists of that era: Wagner, Strauss and Puccini. How did such a musical idiom come to be established as the norm, as the accepted accompaniment to an art form so recently created? How did the relics of an alien musical culture come to be so closely woven into the fabric of a medium to which Americans had prided themselves on being so uniquely adapted? What had happened to the pioneering spirit?

During the 1920s and 1930s much of the pioneering spirit of Hollywood had been tempered by a huge influx of Europeans. These writers, directors and musicians were mostly Jews from Austria and Germany who had left their countries because of rising anti-Semitic feeling. Hollywood music departments became a curious mixture of varied indigenous talents and sophisticated European composers trained in the Viennese operatic tradition. Often the departments were run by musicians from theatre pits who had no time for the less practical application of music. In his account of the musical scene in the American film studios, *The Composer in Hollywood*, Christopher Palmer neatly conveys the prevailing attitudes of those in control:

> As for the heads of the studio music departments, in the early days some of them were barely even musically literate, and even for those who were, 'Carnegie Hall' was still a term of abuse.[2]

If this view seems extreme, it is endorsed by Hanns Eisler, who also had first-hand knowledge of working in Hollywood:

> Motion-picture music, however, suffers from a particular handicap: from the very beginning it has been regarded as an auxiliary art not of first-rank importance. In the early days it was entrusted to anyone who happened to be around and willing – often enough to musicians whose qualifications were not such as to permit them to compete in fields where solid musical standards still obtained. This created an affinity between inferior 'hack' musicians, busy-bodies and motion-picture music.[3]

[1] Kalinak (1992), 79.
[2] Palmer (1990), 22.
[3] Adorno and Eisler (2/1994), 46.

Such a situation was not without parallel in British film music, although it was very much the exception. Louis Levy, whose background was light music and silent movie music, was for years the musical director at Gaumont British. Many of the films produced in the 1930s bear only his name in the music credits of the main titles, while the various composers he subcontracted, sometimes several for the same film, go uncredited. Roy Douglas said of him

> I was always given the impression that Louis Levy wasn't capable of putting any notes on paper at all. It was all composed by either Charles Williams or Hubert Bath.[4]

In fairness to Levy, he was later to bring into films some important contributors, such as Leighton Lucas, and the practice of mis-accreditation was largely, though never quite entirely, phased out.

Chief among the Europeans who emigrated to Hollywood were Max Steiner, Franz Waxman and Erich Wolfgang Korngold, all of whom brought with them the baggage of the late-romantic symphonic tradition. Collectively their music came to epitomize the opulent lushness of the classical Hollywood score. Aficionados of their music are at pains to point out the distinguishing features of their scores, but to the less well-informed they all sound remarkably similar. Whereas an educated musician could be expected to identify a Walton score, or one by Vaughan Williams or Rawsthorne, the same does not apply in the case of a classical Hollywood score, where differences of style were far harder to distinguish. The exception is, of course, the music of Bernard Herrmann. With his first film score, for *Citizen Kane* in 1941, he rewrote the rules, and continued, throughout his film career, to be both a maverick and an inspiration to future generations of composers.

Part of the initial acceptance of the anachronistic idiom of the classical Hollywood score is a result of the expectations engendered by the silent film era. Audiences had become familiar with an assortment of nineteenth-century romantic pot-boilers doing service as emotional cues:

> The classical Hollywood film score developed an idiom for its expression based on musical practices of the nineteenth century, particularly those of romanticism and late romanticism. The silent film score's reliance upon these practices offered a clear precedent for their use in the sound era, and composers in the crucial decade of the thirties, themselves trained in the late romantic style, reinforced the connection.[5]

The system of emotional prompting had already been set up, no matter how crudely, by the juxtaposition of mood pieces to the appropriate scene. In this respect, the very success of the American silent film of the 1920s already inclined the industry towards the use of a musical language chiefly employed as an

---

[4] Roy Douglas, in conversation with the author. See Appendix A, p. 193.
[5] Kalinak (1992), 100.

encoder of information, while the British film industry, which had all but collapsed during this period, had set itself no such pattern to follow.

The golden age of Hollywood transformed the feature film from an unclassified and unpredictable art form into a glossily packaged product that could guarantee a good box-office return. The music, along with all other aspects of film production, conformed to the standardization of the product, in order that the consumer should enjoy the confidence of familiarity. Although the British film industry prior to the Second World War operated while glancing over its shoulder across the Atlantic, its films never became predictable, uniform products as though from a conveyor belt, and consequently none of the ingredients, including the music, were circumscribed in quite the same way.

One of the expectations of the consumer of the Hollywood product was that they would be made to feel good, that they would be transported to another, better world, where the minimum of reality would intrude. In accordance with this expectation, there should be no threat that they might be challenged to think. The narrative must be clearly unfolded, and the task of interpretation undertaken for them:

> The core musical lexicon had tended to remain conservatively rooted in Romantic tonality, since its purpose is quick and efficient signification to a mass audience.[6]

Hollywood's adoption of a musical idiom so incongruous with the image of the great American West has another, paradoxical explanation. If the nature of the country, its terrain, climate and the vast human endeavour to tame it, seems aptly echoed by the music of the pioneering indigenous composers, such as Henry Cowell and Charles Ruggles, it must be remembered that Hollywood itself was a small, enclosed community that became increasingly cut off from its own social environment. In Britain, the film studios, situated close enough to London for actors to pursue their stage careers simultaneously, were much more integrated with the local community. At the end of the day the studio workers went home to London or the Home Counties; they did not, as did their Hollywood counterparts, live virtually on the set. In this respect the accusation of insularity is far more appropriately levelled at Hollywood than at its more traditional target:

> It has, after all, always been a Los Angeles speciality to insulate itself from the rest of the world, to create its *own* world, one which in many ways has little enough contact with life's realities understood elsewhere. This musical isolation was wholly typical: the 'real' world would have decried the music of Korngold, Newman and Steiner as anachronistic and refused it a place, whereas the 'fantasy-world' of Hollywood not only wanted it but encouraged its procreation in vast quantities. 'Romantic' music, music of romance, of fantasy, dream, illusion: what more logical than that it should find a final refuge in the real world's dream-factory?[7]

[6] Gorbman (1987), 4.
[7] Palmer (1990), 23.

The music of Korngold, Newman and Steiner could never be equated qualitatively with that of Wagner or Strauss. Any comparison of their music can only be in the loosest of terms. Even similarity of orchestral sound is on the most superficial level. In the final analysis, Strauss's orchestration could never realistically be described as 'sweet', any more than Wagner's music could be called tuneful. The appropriation of the leitmotif by Hollywood composers is the only possible excuse for even mentioning Wagner's name in connection with them. The overall sound of a Hollywood score approximates more to a generalized, *Reader's Digest* idea of the romantic orchestral sound; something like a cross between Tchaikovsky and early Schoenberg.

Thus the classical Hollywood score was characterized by a rich, sweet, 'romantic' orchestral colour, dominated by strings, particularly upper strings. In addition, it would typically be seriously over-scored, at least to British taste. Despite Max Steiner's apparently sensible comment, 'Some pictures require a lot of music and some of them are so realistic that music would only hurt and interfere',[8] the truth was that most Hollywood pictures were so unrealistic that audiences were seldom treated to a lightly scored film. Steiner himself was notorious for his excessive use of music, though this was largely to satisfy the demands of Jack Warner, the studio head. The size of his scores for *Gone with the Wind* and *Now Voyager* amply justify the much-used epithets 'saturated score' and 'wall-to-wall scoring'.

Hollywood composers frequently resorted to the use of borrowed music to hammer home some point already amply demonstrated on the screen. Future analysts will probably reveal that 'Yankee Doodle' is the most quoted tune in the history of the motion picture, since it would seem to be obligatory to accompany every scene involving Unionist troops with a reference to it. Similarly, the British cannot be mentioned without 'Rule Britannia', and 'Dixie' confirms to the audience that the cotton plantation shown on the screen really *is* in the South.

It was not only the direct use of borrowed music that informed the audience:

> Music signifies in films not only according to pure musical codes, but also according to *cultural* musical codes and *cinematic* musical codes. Any music bears cultural associations, and most of these associations have been further codified and exploited by the music industry. Properties of instrumentation, rhythm, melody and harmony form a veritable language.[9]

Hollywood composers used this automatic association of certain musical idioms with geographical locations to signal to the audience. These location signifiers are almost always redundant, unless the view is taken that American audiences were so ill-informed that they were unable, for instance, to identify the French capital from that much-abused indicator, the Eiffel Tower, without the further assistance of music:

[8] Max Steiner, quoted in Manvell and Huntley (2/1975), 225.
[9] Gorbman (1987), 2.

Strangely codified Hollywood harmonies, melodic patterns, rhythms and habits of orchestration are employed as a matter of course in classical cinema for establishing setting. A 4/4 allegretto drumbeat (or pizzicato on bass viols), the first beat emphatically accented, with a simple minor-modal [sic] tune played by high woodwinds or strings, signifies 'Indian territory'. A rumba rhythm and major melody played by either trumpet or instruments in the marimba family signifies Latin America. Xylophone and woodblocks, playing simple minor melodies in 4/4, evoke Japan or China. If one hears Strauss-like waltzes in the strings, it must be turn-of-the-century Vienna. Accordions are associated with Rome and Paris; harps often introduce us to medieval, Renaissance, or heavenly settings. The hustle and bustle of the big city, especially New York, is signified by rhythmic support of a jazzy or slightly discordant major theme played by brass instruments or strings, interrupted now and then by a brass automobile-horn imitation.[10]

A European mind may well shrink from such blatant stating of the obvious. Parallel examples are mercifully rare in British film scores, being mainly confined to that category of film which has its origins in music hall or melodrama, where such practices originated. Americans, on the other hand, have seldom been subject to the inhibition of embarrassment at their affinity with the obvious. This in part explains the prevalence of the practice in American film music that came to be known as 'Mickey-Mousing'. A moment's reflection will serve to conjure up images of cartoon animals whose every action is caught and illustrated in sound with absolute precision. The skill needed to synchronize music and image in this way is to be admired, and in this context the practice is wholly appropriate. Its use in the feature film, however, calls into question the whole relationship between the film maker and his audience. If a small animal in a cartoon droops its shoulders in dejection, we are accustomed to the accompanying downward string glissando, but any such pictorial use of music to reinforce body language in a feature film can only cast doubt on the ability of its actors and on the integrity of its director:

> Max Steiner developed this style of dramatic scoring very early in his career, frequently emphasizing each action on the screen and each shift in emotion. Steiner explained why his music so often hit the action. 'When a scene is weak – for example, if an actor raises his eyebrow in shock and looks like the very devil, my music helps get that shock idea across.'[11]

Outward expression of all kinds, from a turn of the hand to extremes of movement, can and must be conveyed to the audience by the magical fusion of cinematic techniques, *without* reliance on music, if the audience is not to be patronized. The use of music to illustrate that which is already visible reduces cinema to the level of the newsreel or the educational film. In this context it is particularly important to separate the two main types of music used in the feature film. While these two types have a varied nomenclature in the literature

---

[10] Gorbman (1987), 83.
[11] Karlin (1994), 79.

of film music, they will consistently be referred to here as 'illustrative' and 'atmospheric'. It is illustrative music that suffers the most danger of redundancy by being pressed into the service of duplicating or reinforcing the images on the screen. Atmospheric music, which enhances and interprets an image without resorting to sledge-hammer unsubtlety, can, in nearly all instances, be used to better effect. Thus, many establishing shots of locations, instead of being reinforced by some trite musical code, would be far more effectively supported by the use of atmospheric music. The supreme example of this is to be found in Vaughan Williams's score for *Scott of the Antarctic*, which, mainly through its use of orchestral colour, not only echoes the grandeur of the landscape, but literally strikes a chill in the viewer, although Vaughan Williams would, admittedly, have been hard-pressed to find an equivalent Hollywood-style cultural encoder to represent the Antarctic, had he been so inclined.

It was wholly in keeping with the preference for illustrative music shown by the composers of the classical Hollywood film score that the use of the leitmotif should have become their virtual trademark. The more superficial applications of the leitmotif technique bear all too graphic a witness to the essential pointlessness of spelling out musically that which is already visually lucid. At its most primitive, the use of the leitmotif in film is slightly less effective than the old system of intertitles. It was not considered necessary in the silent era to point out to the audience which character was on the screen at any given time, but in many instances the leitmotif does little more than this. If each main character has a theme, which must be trotted out every time he or she appears or is discussed or thought of, then the result is a ragbag of motivic shreds tossed about incoherently. There were other reasons why a composer constrained by deadlines might resort to its use:

> Cinema music is still patched together by means of leitmotifs. The ease with which they are recalled provides definite clues for the listener, and they also are a practical help to the composer in his task of composition under pressure. He can quote where he otherwise would have to invent.[12]

Although the leitmotivic technique had been used for cinema as early as 1915 in the score intended to accompany *The Birth of a Nation* compiled by Carl Joseph Breil, it was never successfully transferred from music drama, where it had been used to such effect. While it might have appeared, by virtue of its unifying qualities in relation to a very fragmented medium, to be a solution to the problems of structure inherent in the film score, the repetition of motifs, even if developed and subject to variation, does not ultimately create a satisfying structure if its material is manipulated through the exigencies of diegesis, or crudely, through the whim of the editor rather than by the process of organic growth generated solely by the composer. Of the Hollywood composers, it was Max Steiner who took the use of leitmotifs to extremes:

[12] Adorno and Eisler (2/1994), 4.

A Steiner score accompanying an eventful sequence can sound like a hodgepodge of mixed thematic material, rapidly changing dynamics and orchestral texture, and rapid modulations, in its tendency to provide hyperexplicit, moment-by-moment musical illustration.[13]

This is a far cry from Wagner's conception of the aesthetic possibilities of the leitmotif:

The Wagnerian leitmotif is inseparably connected with the symbolic nature of the music drama. The leitmotif is not supposed merely to characterize persons, emotions, or things, although this is the prevalent conception. Wagner conceived its purpose as the endowment of the dramatic events with metaphysical significance.[14]

While metaphysical significance was in fairly short supply in the classical Hollywood film score, there were instances of extremely subtle use of the leitmotif to convey complex or delicate ideas to the audience. Korngold's score for *Anthony Adverse*, in which eighteen major themes have been identified,[15] provides examples of motivic use to provide information not otherwise divulged by the screen:

Preceding the first love scene Korngold provides a fine example of a premonitory musical motive. Maria (Anita Louise), awakened by her maid, is given a note . . . 'Denis' [theme] in the orchestra tells us who the note is from even before Maria opens it . . . When we learn that a meeting with Maria is requested, 'Anthony' [theme] appears. With this sequence of themes – father to son – we are told that the forth-coming meeting will lead to conception, an idea that Hollywood in 1936 could not treat in visual or verbal terms.[16]

Obviously, it would take an audience of extreme sophistication and musical perception to grasp a narrative hint so cryptically conveyed. Although such an example of motivic manipulation is still far from the esoteric complexity of psychological motivation demonstrated by Wagner in the first act of *Tristan*, it should not be forgotten that Korngold had received international acclaim at the age of twenty for his opera *Die tote Stadt*, and that he left Hollywood in 1946 to return to serious composition. Korngold may have been a distinguished composer in his own right, but the demands of Hollywood had ensured that he conformed to a stereotypical treatment of music for film:

While the toxic effect of the more discreditable Hollywood music cannot be overestimated, the aesthetic value of the more competent Hollywood music can hardly be underestimated. 'Hollywood music' – is this not an unwarrantable generalisation? Admittedly generalisations about what people produce are unjustified when each man produces according to his individual character. But

---

[13]   Gorbman (1987), 87.
[14]   Adorno and Eisler (2/1994), 5.
[15]   Darby and du Bois (1990), 162.
[16]   Ibid., 167.

they are justified when all produce in response to a common external demand. This, exactly is the case in Hollywood.[17]

It was principally the comparative freedom to produce 'according to his individual character' that separated the British composer from his Hollywood counterpart. The studio system, with its rigid departmental codes, had effectively strait-jacketed the Hollywood composer of the golden age into the production of a uniform package that was bound by a system of conventions. On the other hand, it was the vulnerability of the British film industry in this period, its very lack of crystallization, that had ensured a flexible attitude to the nature and function of music in film. The British film score rarely suffered, in the hands of its indigenous composers, from the formulaic stagnation that beset the Hollywood score. Certainly British composers, both experienced and inexperienced in film, dabbled in the techniques of illustrative film music on occasion, but generally they are far better suited to the writing of atmospheric music, which gives greater scope for the preservation of individuality:

> It would, I think, be fair to say that the standard of music in British films is at the present time as high, if not higher, than in any other country. This applies more especially to the serious type of film. Let me hasten to explain that I refer more to the quality of the music than to the technical handling of it. I would say that the technique of the Americans is more advanced, or at least infinitely 'slicker' than ours. Their management of music on the sound-track is brilliant, and their composers seem to have trained themselves to write with a precise care and appreciation of the dramatic significance of each turn in a story. Perhaps because he has been at it longer, the American composer has turned himself more thoroughly into a music dramatist than the British. On the other hand, I think the average score written here has more intrinsic musical value.[18]

It would be unwise to dismiss out of hand the possibility that British composers, especially those more eminent composers already committed to the concert platform, tended to look more favourably on the atmospheric approach to the film score simply because it was less demanding of their time and effort. At first glance, the following extract from Vaughan Williams's article in the *Royal College of Music Magazine* would seem to bear out this possibility:

> There are two ways of viewing film music: one, in which every action, word, gesture or incident is punctuated in sound. This requires great skill and orchestral knowledge and a vivid specialised imagination, but often leads to a mere scrappy succession of sounds of no musical value in itself . . . The other method of writing film music, which personally I favour, partly because I am quite incapable of doing the former, is to ignore the details and to intensify the spirit of the whole situation by a continuous stream of music.[19]

[17] Keller (1947–8), 168.
[18] Muir Mathieson, quoted in Huntley (1947), 186.
[19] Ralph Vaughan Williams, 'Film Music', *RCM Magazine* xi/1 (1944), reprinted in Huntley (1947), 178.

First glances, however, can be misleading. Vaughan Williams's sense of humour must not be overlooked. Although approaching seventy when he wrote his first film score, he embraced the new medium wholeheartedly and with an acute awareness of its immense possibilities. A composer who insisted on writing his own foxtrot, when such a task is often undertaken by someone more familiar with the idiom, would not balk at learning a few new tricks. The simple fact is that Vaughan Williams exemplifies all that has been said about the British in connection with drama and the imagination. He freely admitted that he began to compose his film scores immediately *after reading the scripts*. He knew this was the 'wrong' way to go about it, but his inspiration came from the word, from the internalized drama of the BBC radio play, not from the screen images. For someone who turned to the script in order to generate his musical ideas for a film, the notion of tailoring his score to the action in the manner of a circus band was clearly unthinkable.

It should not be forgotten that the very qualities of British film which render it so much less satisfactory in terms of pure cinema in comparison with the American film had a direct bearing on the approach of producers, directors and composers to the music. If they are stage-bound and lacking in movement, then out of the window go all the possibilities of synchronization. If the scenes are longer, there is less call for motivic use. If the diegesis is carried by the word, then the word must be the controlling factor in the use of music. If the acting is of a greatly superior quality, then much of the need for emotional cueing is obviated. If, as has been suggested, the British and the American film were two fundamentally different types of entertainment, then we can begin to see why their scores functioned in such different ways. Walton, despite having composed some of the most brilliant and widely acclaimed film music to accompany rhythmic action sequences, evidently was thinking in dramatic terms based on the English theatrical tradition when he wrote

> The value to a film of its musical score rests chiefly in the creation of mood, atmosphere, and the sense of period.[20]

The differences in the fundamental approach to cinema between Britain and America should not be laboured to the point where the former is equated with, say, *The Night of the Party* (an early Michael Powell offering of such moribund wordiness as to make the intrusion of music a virtual impossibility), and the latter with any example of Errol Flynn's irrepressible exploits on the screen. Britain and America share innumerable cinematic clichés which serve to demonstrate the difference in attitudes to scoring based on aesthetic standards. In nearly all matters of artistic taste Britain traditionally stands firmly with Western Europe against America. The proper application of film music is no exception. Maurice Jaubert's article in *Footnotes to the Film*, written in 1938, is virtually a blueprint for the approach that was to be taken

---

[20] William Walton, quoted in Manvell and Huntley (2/1975), 93.

by the majority of British composers. His critique of the illustrative Holly-wood score is unequivocal:

> The closing of a door is emphasised with a chord; footsteps are accompanied with a march rhythm, etc. In *The Informer*, where this technique is carried to its highest pitch of perfection, the music has actually to imitate the noise of pieces of money falling on the ground, and even, by a roguish little arpeggio, the trickling of a glass of beer down a drinker's throat. Apart from its childishness, such a procedure displays a total lack of understanding of the very essence of film music . . . [Americans] seem to be satisfied with a musical style which – in itself scarcely defensible – surrounds a film with an unbearably antiquated atmosphere. How many fine films have been botched in this way by the over-emphasis and lack of taste of their musical accompaniment![21]

Jean Cocteau points out another problem with this kind of scoring:

> Nothing, it seems to me can be more vulgar than music synchronism in films. It is, again, a pleonasm. A kind of glue where everything gets stuck rigid, and where no play (in the sense of 'play' in wood) is possible.[22]

In other words, the practice of tying the music to events on the screen in slavish imitation precludes the possibility of interpretation on a deeper level, unless the music can be made to serve both functions simultaneously:

> Pictorial music as such is totally unnecessary in an art form that is itself pictorial. If a company of soldiers is seen marching down a road, it is not necessary for music to begin marching with them, unless the particular march plays an essential part in the emotional structure of the film and the music intensifies the audience's response.[23]

This extract is a good indication of the attitude taken by many British composers in relation to film scoring. However, every facet of film making in this country was influenced by American practices. How could the situation be otherwise when American films had overpowered the market since the end of the First World War? The Hollywood film was the yardstick which British producers were obliged either to match, or, in pursuit of a more national cinema, to shun deliberately.

British composers, often novices in the art of film scoring, had unconsciously assimilated many of the techniques of the Hollywood composers. The significance of these techniques, however, lies in their very different application in British films.

---

[21] Jaubert, 'Music', in Davy (1938), 108, 110.
[22] Jean Cocteau, quoted in Manvell and Huntley (2/1975), 91.
[23] Cockshott (1947), 1–2.

3. A comparison between British and American composers in their approach to film scoring

In order to appreciate how British composers differed in their use of the techniques that had been established by the Hollywood composers, it is necessary to understand the extent to which their widely contrasting circumstances affected their approach to film scoring. Two factors may be singled out as contributing most directly to the dissimilarity in their aesthetic and technical handling of the task. The first of these factors is the inequality in the degree of evolution of British and American films, and the second is the contrasting significance that film scoring bore in the lives of the individual composers. A third factor, which links these two closely together, is the disparity in the conditions that were experienced by composers when working for film.

It was highly appropriate that during its golden age, Hollywood should commonly be known as 'the dream factory', because the whole business of film making in America had taken on the characteristics of an assembly line. Once the formula for producing films that appealed to a wide audience had been established, there seemed little point in deviating from it, or indulging in risky attempts at experimentation. The product had proved to be a financial success, so there was every reason to continue turning out a succession of films which bore the same hallmarks. The American film industry, unlike its British counterpart, was indeed a true industry. Each employee was assigned an exact role, a specific function with little scope for independence. Mass production as a whole in America had resulted in the human cog being reduced to a minimum of autonomy in order to achieve the maximum efficiency. While this analogy can be carried too far in discussing what is, in theory at least, an artistic endeavour, the basic premise of acute specialization operated in all departments of film making in America, the music department being no exception:

> The studios needed composers, orchestrators, arrangers, conductors, copyists, musical administrators and performing musicians who, like other technicians and artists, would be under permanent contract to work on any film in production, would ask no questions and be told no lies.[1]

---

[1] Palmer (1990), 24.

In Hollywood's studio system, music was simply one more component of the standard product. It had to conform to the requirements of that product in exactly the same way as did every other detail of its intricate construction. Composers, no less than any other contributor to this commodity, were expected to deliver goods that accorded with the corporate ideal. If that ideal had been hit upon by a process of trial and error, then, again, the musical contribution was no exception:

> The character of motion-picture music has been determined by everyday practice. It has been an adaptation in part to the immediate needs of the film industry, in part to whatever musical clichés and ideas about music happened to be current.[2]

Perhaps the most damaging result of working in the studio system was the 'jobsworth' mentality that it engendered in composers, who were obliged to cut their cloth not only in respect of the specific demands of the Hollywood product, but to stay in favour with those who controlled their financial destiny:

> The typical Hollywood composer is concerned not with the reaction of the public, as you might think, but with that of the producer. It isn't surprising, therefore, that all film music originating in Hollywood tends to be very much the same. The score of one picture adds up to about the score of any other. You seldom hear anything fresh or distinctive partly because everyone is so intent upon playing safe. A pleased producer means more jobs. That alone is sufficient to explain the Hollywood stereotype of music.[3]

The fundamental difference in conditions of employment experienced by British and American composers writing for film was of great significance in its effects on their output. To begin with, there was not the same system of salaried composers writing for British films, as each score was generally assigned to an individual under separate contract. Of the three major musical directors on permanent contract; Mathieson, Levy and Irving, only Irving ever scored seriously for film, and that on a very irregular basis. There was never the situation in this country of composers clocking in day after day, year in, year out, as there was in Hollywood. For those composers in Hollywood who did not sufficiently stifle any inspiration and individuality in their film writing, the consequences of corporate disapproval could be severe. Under such repressive conditions it is not surprising that freshness was a quality almost completely lacking in the approach to composing for film in Hollywood.

For the British composer, however, whose drudgery was to be found in quite other directions, the opportunity to score a film must have come as a welcome respite. Accustomed to supporting the indulgence of serious composition by all the less glamorous jobs available to the musician, British composers were generally delighted to have the opportunity to work in a medium which they perceived as offering new challenges and creative possibilities. For those British

---

[2] Adorno and Eisler (2/1994), 3.
[3] Aaron Copland, quoted in Keller (1947–8), 168.

composers who had spent their lives working for serious music, their introduction to the world of film meant approaching something completely unknown. If they should fail at the task, then at worst it was a blow to the self-esteem, which they suffered temporarily, before returning to their 'real' work. For most, it was only a small, rather eccentric portion of their working life, which could quickly be put in perspective if necessary. It was a freelance option, to be taken up if desired.

Nothing could be further removed from this position of freedom than the situation in the Hollywood studios, where composers were bound in every way. They were bound by a contract to produce work that was circumscribed by conditions beyond their control. They were bound by the formulae, the clichés that filmic convention had come to impose, bound by the very success of the Hollywood product. They were marooned in a hothouse environment where they were expected to generate almost identical material rapidly and repeatedly. Not all the composers employed in Hollywood found it possible to assume the corporate mantle, particularly if they had enjoyed success elsewhere. If they brought too many attitudes derived from their work for the concert platform into the film studio, they could find their contribution diverted into expedient backwaters:

> Other refugee European composers of note . . . never properly fitted into the system at all; they were given the occasional (generally insignificant) film of their own to compose, but for the most part their activities were restricted to providing utility sequences for use in whatever picture their studio deemed appropriate, to orchestrating, or to ghosting music for other 'composers' who received all the credit.[4]

Ernst Toch in particular had caused offence with his score for *Peter Ibbetson*, because he had been unwilling to compromise his own style. Aaron Copland was only too familiar with the penalties for overstepping the mark in this way:

> On the strength of this job, Toch should be today one of the best known film composers. But unfortunately there aren't enough people in Hollywood who can tell a good score when they hear one. Today Toch is generally assigned to do 'screwy music'.[5]

The fact that Copland championed the score for *Peter Ibbetson* in this way is deeply revealing of the contrast in aesthetic approach to film music between leading composers in America and Europe. Copland, by virtue of the fact that he was a distinguished concert composer, might have been supposed to be nearer the approach to film of other serious composers, no matter from which continent. His experiences in Hollywood had left him in no doubt that the music there was in most cases 'artistically of a low order,[6] and yet he was

[4] Palmer (1990), 24.
[5] Aaron Copland, quoted in Keller (1947–8), 168.
[6] Ibid.

impressed by a score that gave only the illusion of superior value. The French composer Maurice Jaubert certainly did not share Copland's enthusiasm for this score, as is evidenced by his question

> Did not *Peter Ibbetson* – which offered the musician a splendid opportunity to prove his feeling for the right relationships between imagery and music – call forth a deplorable and grandiloquent symphonic poem, whose aggressive mediocrity combined all the worst formulae of a certain type of dramatic music, inexcusable to-day even outside the film?[7]

If Copland had been a more genuinely American composer, instead of being content merely to season his music with 'local-color references',[8] he would have been closer to an understanding of the true potential of music for film. It is to be regretted that composers with the vision of Ives or Cowell did not write for film, for, ironically, such authentically American composers would have been more in sympathy with the European approach. Jaubert's conception of the role that music should play in film exemplifies this approach:

> Music must never forget that in cinema its character of *sound phenomenon* outweighs its intellectual and even its metaphysical aspects. The more it effaces itself behind the image, the more chance it has of discovering new perspectives on its own account.[9]

This preference for 'sound phenomenon' over and against the intellectual basis of music is not altogether surprising in a French composer. The divide between French and German music since the days of Berlioz can at its simplest be expressed as the opposing of colour to form. Given that is was the German tradition that found its way to Hollywood, the priority there of using some organizing principle in the writing of a film score can be more easily understood. Colour, in this context, should not be confused with orchestral sonority, which was used by all Western composers, with varying degrees of priority, since the early days of the nineteenth century. Colour, combined with texture, had for some become sufficient justification on its own, as a compositional basis. The British composer, who for over two centuries had been all but invisible, was now on the brink of validation, thanks to the work of Elgar and Vaughan Williams, just at the time when the film score in Britain was assuming importance. If the British people as a whole had long experienced difficulty in choosing between France and Germany as an ally, the same could be considered true of the British composer, who was in the process of re-establishing some kind of national voice. If our composers held allegiance, however qualified, to one side or the other, then that inclination could influence their approach to film scoring. In other words, those who tended toward formalism might have found themselves more in sympathy with the techniques favoured by Holly-

---

[7] Jaubert, 'Music', in Davy (ed.) (1938), 111.
[8] Greene (1986), 1151, s.v. 'Copland'.
[9] Jaubert, 'Music', in Davy (ed.) (1938), 112.

wood, while those who were more attracted to colour and texture would have had a preference for the use of atmospheric music.

By introducing so many serious composers to the medium, Mathieson and Irving deliberately led the British film score away from the stereotypes of the classical Hollywood score. After all, it could hardly be expected that a composer of the stature of Vaughan Williams would be invited to write a film score on the understanding that he imitate the style and techniques of Max Steiner. A sixty-nine-year-old composer with a towering reputation is employed expressly to bring his own personal style, both in his musical language, and in its technical application to the film. In this respect, the whole concept of the meaning of music for film in this country was far removed from that of Hollywood. Each composer who came fresh to the task brought a different approach; and most serious composers of reputation in this country made some contribution to film.[10]

If the British film producers had been determined to replicate the Hollywood score for their pictures, they would have taken steps to ensure that a pool of hack composers obliged them. Naturally, such scores would have been unsuitable for British films, or rather, those films that were truly British, because of the numerous differences that separated them from the Hollywood product. Because British films never settled into the formulae that are concomitant with commercial success (at least until the 1960s, with such series as the *James Bond* and *Carry On* films), scores in imitation of the formulaic Hollywood score would have been inappropriate. British composers, by their very inexperience in the field of film writing, were in many cases to serve British pictures well. Although it would have been impossible for them to come to the task in complete ignorance of the Hollywood score, because exposure to it would have been inevitable unless they had deliberately shunned the cinema, they did not generally feel constrained to take it as a model. It is revealing that William Alwyn, who wrote prolifically for film, should have said in 1951

> The film is a new medium for the musician and, unlike opera and ballet, it is as yet untrammelled by tradition.[11]

From this it would seem that he had not felt in any way impelled to follow the 'tradition' that had been established by the classical Hollywood score. Alwyn had a wide knowledge of films, and his commitment to the task of film scoring is clear:

> I am passionately fond of films, and I think all good film composers are. You must believe in pictures, have faith in your artistic medium, and you can produce good scores. I like going to the pictures and I like doing music for the pictures.[12]

---

[10] In his article on British film music in the fifth edition of *Grove*, Keller refers to Rubbra as the only leading contemporary composer who had made no contribution to film. Arguably there were others, such as Howells and Brian: but presumably Keller did not regard them as leading composers.

[11] William Alwyn, quoted in Lindgren (1951), 20.

[12] William Alwyn, quoted in Huntley (1947), 162.

It may seem unlikely that Alwyn, as a musician and a regular cinema-goer, could have been unaware of the practices of the Hollywood composers, even if he refused to acknowledge them as a tradition. Yet Roy Douglas who had much experience in working for film, both as orchestrator and composer, was unaware of the extent to which the leitmotif had been used in American film scores – as he made clear in an conversation with the present writer. When asked about it, he replied: '*Was* it used a lot in Hollywood? . . . I hadn't thought of that.'[13] This implies that British composers did not feel under an obligation to use the techniques employed in the Hollywood score. The effects of repeated exposure to American films could and did result in a lot of unconscious assimilation of the part of our composers. The instance of Roy Douglas proves that without a deliberate intention to analyse the score, the power of film could lull the composer in the audience into non-judgmental absorption. Whatever might have been established by custom in Hollywood, Alwyn regarded the subject of film scoring as if it were a clean slate:

> Every film needs a fresh approach. Unless one identifies oneself with the subject it will not be good music.[14]

If Alwyn considered that every film deserved to have a fresh approach, then not only did that show him to be unwilling to adopt the clichés of the Hollywood composers, it also meant that he was unwilling to incur the penalty of formulating any of his own. And if British composers had almost universally taken up the challenge to write for a medium unfamiliar to them without using, at least consciously, the templates cut by the composers in Hollywood, many of them were also to carry the impetus of their fresh approach through each of their successive scores.

By far the most significant of the techniques adopted by the Hollywood composers, by virtue of its wide-spread and pervasive use, and by its almost automatic identification with the American picture, was the technique of the leitmotif. The reasons why composers in Hollywood should have taken to using the leitmotif so extensively in American films have already been touched on. It has been established that many of those reasons related directly to the inclinations and personal histories of the composers themselves, as well as to the characteristics of the Hollywood product.

There was, however, one very specific function which the leitmotivic approach could fulfil, and which was to find common ground with British films because of the perceived centrality of its importance. This was the function of lending unity to a film. If one of the chief requirements of a feature film is that it should be unified (and generally it can be assumed that mainstream film needs unity as much as it needs coherence), then it is understandable that music should be used specifically to assist in providing that sense of unity. Because it is essentially fragmentary in nature, film needs music to bind it in such a way that

---

[13] See Appendix A, p. 206.
[14] William Alwyn, quoted in Manvell and Huntley (2/1975), 225.

the true extent of its disjointedness is disguised from the audience. In those instances where unity and coherence are deliberately eschewed by film makers, music plays little or no part. The film *Jigsaw* (1962), one of the more successful examples of British new-wave cinema, demonstrates how a film totally without music can create an almost unwelcome apprehension of reality. There is no palliative for the sense of alienation which is engendered when the fragmentary nature of film is intentionally left exposed. Without the customary opiate of music, the mind is forced into an uncomfortable degree of attention and concentration that was never the objective of the classical Hollywood film. The illusion of completeness and relatedness which the use of music can conjure up, is most easily accomplished by the use of repetition – which, with or without variation, has the obvious effect of inducing a sense not only of unity, but also of familiarity. It is the reassurance of familiarity – guaranteed to evoke in the audience a feeling of being pleasurably entertained – which is the true motivation of mainstream cinema.

A justification for the use of the leitmotivic technique is, therefore, that it fulfils two purposes, both of which are in accord with the principles that applied to mainstream cinema in Britain at the time in question. This explains why the repetition of familiar material, the use of themes, in fact, seems so natural to the composer writing for mainstream feature films, and why it does no violence to the fundamental nature of British films. However, there is a chasm between the tortuous manipulation of leitmotifs to convey every intricate twist and turn of a story line, as exemplified by the techniques of Korngold in *Anthony Adverse*, and the generalized, atmospheric use of thematic material for unifying purposes which characterized the film scores of British composers. It is, after all, the way in which the music cue is treated within the diegetic context which determines whether it is leitmotivic, or a suitably tempered variation of a theme. If the hero in a particular scene is mustering his courage to fight the enemy, he will usually be portrayed musically by an aggressive treatment of his own theme or motif. If this treatment – quite possibly featuring the rhythmic use of timpani and brass – is merely representative of the feeling it is trying to convey, but contains no thematic material associated with other elements in the film, then it is simply a variation of the main theme with appropriate characterization. If, on the other hand, the music in this scene interlards the hero's theme with a motif that has already come to be identified as signifying 'courage', by its earlier associations in the picture, then the treatment is leitmotivic.

This distinction is what chiefly separates the Hollywood score from its British counterpart. Hollywood composers would quote from their large array of motifs as a means of following the contours of the plot. British composers, on the other hand, achieved the same end by developing a small number of themes, for while they were content to assign themes to the main elements of a film, they baulked, possibly out of sheer embarrassment, at the notion of musically labelling a spectrum of minor ingredients. It is one thing to write themes for the central character of the film, possibly for their love relationship and for the overwhelming hand of destiny, but quite another to identify in this way a whole range of lesser contributions to the plot, both concrete and abstract. If the main thrust of the narrative is to demonstrate how a fundamentally good man may be brought down by one fatal flaw in his character, a fairly popular dramatic notion, then it is sufficient that we hear the theme associated with this whenever the weakness comes over him. From a structural and interpretative point of view this is satisfactory, but it is less satisfactory if the issue is clouded by the introduction of numerous subsidiary motifs heralding the appearance of various minor narrative strands. By using a large number of motifs in their film scores, composers like Korngold tended to obscure the clarity of the diegesis.

It is useful to distinguish here between drama and diegesis. Mathieson may be correct in claiming that the American composers were better music dramatists than our composers, but, as has already been established, it was the narrative that, for historical reasons, had priority in the British psyche. By introducing fewer threads into the thematic tapestry, British composers were fulfilling an imperative to protect the integrity of the narrative. When Alwyn spoke of the necessity for the composer to identify with the subject of the picture, he was referring to the narrative and its emotional direction. For a British composer it is the diegesis which constitutes the subject of a film. When Alwyn said

> I like to read the script and discuss the subject with the director and generally identify myself with the film at its inception,[15]

it is clear that he was thinking of the inner core of the picture, not its external trappings. It is fascinating to compare this with the attitude of the American film composer Hugo Friedhofer, who, on being asked how he identified with the subject of a film, responded by thinking in more immediate dramatic terms:

> I find that style, period and content are all powerful determinants. I do not mean by this that a completely eclectic attitude is indicated, or that it is necessary to compose music for a film dealing with the Crusades in an idiom lying somewhere on the far side of organum.[16]

This question of what constitutes the subject of a film raises the issue of how British and American films differ in their basic nature. For the American composer, the subject of his films can be easily defined by generalities that instantly conjure up an image by the use of a single definition – 'crusade', 'gangster', 'escape' – which all owe allegiance to dramatic action. For William Alwyn, the subject of a film could be the issue of whether (as in *The Fallen Idol*) a small boy will unintentionally incriminate his surrogate father by lying to the police out of misdirected loyalty, or whether (as in *The Winslow Boy*) a father's determination to take on the whole establishment in order to prove his son's innocence was justified in the face of his family's suffering. Intense psycho-

---

[15] William Alwyn, quoted in Manvell and Huntley (2/1975), 224.
[16] Hugo Friedhofer, quoted in Manvell and Huntley (2/1975), 224.

logical drama of this nature, with its strong literary overtones, will quite obviously not benefit from a score with extensive motivic treatment.

One of the most notable features of such films is the uncinematic length of their scenes. In these two examples, dialogue scenes can last as long as 7 minutes, with the whole action and pace of the film, as such, dependent on the development of the narrative. In an action film of the 'escape' variety, the scenes will be short, fragmented, and frequently skipping from one location to another. In such a context, the use of leitmotifs serves to unify, structure and signpost the sequence of events. This technique is totally redundant if our characters are still sitting in the same room at the end of a 5-minute conversation. Franz Waxman's requirements of a motif indicate the problems composers face when dealing with fragmentation:

> Motifs should be characteristically brief, with sharp profiles. If they are easily recognizable, they permit repetition in varying forms and textures, and they help musical continuity.[17]

If the scenes are rapid and disjointed, leitmotivic treatment can give the semblance of musical coherence. Scoring each scene independently would have resulted in a kind of musical schizophrenia, so there is a structural justification for the use of leitmotifs in such instances. For the British composer, longer scenes gave the opportunity for more autonomous musical development, and the use of themes that could be other than 'brief' and 'sharp'. Detailed analysis is needed to ascertain the nature of these themes in relation to the main narrative strands of a film, and to illustrate how their use in British film scores deviates in application and in effect from the use of the leitmotif.

[17] Franz Waxman, quoted in Karlin (1994), 26.

4. British composers' use of themes for narrative development

All the formulae of the classical Hollywood score can be found in British scores. There are examples of Mickey-Mousing, stingers and location signifiers, although their use is considerably less frequent. Of all the techniques employed by Hollywood composers in the golden age, it was their treatment of the leitmotif that differed most from that of British composers. To a composer of Korngold's background it seemed the most natural thing in the world to approach film scoring from a Wagnerian standpoint. Cinema's unique freedom of movement is just one of the features that removes it from the world of opera, but in the eyes of Hollywood composers there were still sufficient dramatic correlations to justify the use of leitmotivic techniques.

Opera was a sensitive issue for British composers, who, until the successful production of *Peter Grimes* in 1945, were not considered capable of creating large-scale operatic works. For the generation of composers who came to film writing in Britain, it was only the Savoy Operas that could be regarded as having any sort of established formula. Whatever the value placed on Gilbert and Sullivan, they hardly serve as a model for musical treatment of another dramatic medium.

British composers did not, therefore, carry a burden of recent operatic imperatives, and this was the main reason why they were never tempted to treat composing for film from an operatic standpoint. While it is easy to assume that the stagebound nature of British films would lend itself more naturally to operatic techniques, such an assumption would overlook the very real difference in the status of text between the two stage genres. After all, many opera-goers attend and enjoy performances given in a language they do not understand. Such a situation in the straight theatre would be something of an oddity. The theatrical tradition that overawed British films has contributed enormously to the way in which they came to be scored, but that tradition is in no way linked to the operatic stage.

For those 'American' composers who were born with the sound of Siegfried's horn ringing in their ears, it was more natural to regard any form of drama in Wagnerian terms. Therefore all elements in the drama, whether human, natural or symbolic, were legitimate targets for leitmotivic treatment. Such treatment may give the appearance of providing a structural unity, but if too many dramatic elements, or threads, are involved, the result is simply the unity of a patchwork quilt.

British composers may have eschewed the kind of leitmotivic technique practised by Hollywood composers, but very few considered the possibility of writing a score that did not in some way interpret or emphasise the main dramatic themes of the film. The most obvious and easily identifiable way of demonstrating a major dramatic element in musical terms is to give it a theme of its own, and British composers did assign musical themes to individual characters in films, also to places, significant objects and psychological complexes in very much the same way as Hollywood composers. The contrast lies both in the nature of those themes, and in their treatment. A distinction needs to be made between the terms 'theme' and 'motif', although the two are frequently used in an arbitrary and interchangeable fashion by commentators. Fred Karlin differentiates them quite simply:

> Although a theme is often a fully developed melody, it can be shorter, or even not completely developed. If it's much shorter, only a few notes, it is called a 'motif', or 'motive'. These themes and motifs not only spring from the concept of the score, but also help to clarify the concept and make it come to life.[1]

The length and pace of a theme is dependent on the method of its future use, as well as on the nature of its intended target. The more a composer uses his themes for vague and general applications, the longer and more expansive those themes can be. If he has no intention of manipulating those themes to suit the exigencies of the drama in very specific and encoded ways, then he is free to sustain and extend them at his own pleasure. This type of theme is in stark contrast to the musical insignia used to portray the eponymous 'hero' of one of the earliest films famous for its leitmotivic score:

> It is worth noting the clever way in which Steiner, by making the theme of the monster a memorable and easily recognizable but also eminently simple descending three-note chromatic motif, greatly facilitates its contrapuntal inclusion in many different contexts.[2]

Christopher Palmer goes on to recount some of the contexts in which this three-note motif is used, and in so doing provides us with a vivid description of the archetypal leitmotivic Hollywood score:

> At one point it becomes the motif of Kong's approach. Later it is transformed into the first phrase of the march played in the theatre when Kong is put on public display in New York . . . A particular subtlety is the way in which at certain critical moments . . . the Kong theme and the Fay Wray theme . . . actually converge and become one, thus musically underlining the explicitly stated parallel between the story of King Kong and Ann Darrow and the old fairy-tale of Beauty and the Beast. Here the music is required, perhaps for the first time in an American film, to explain to the audience what is actually happening on the screen, since the

---

[1] Karlin (1994), 26.
[2] Palmer (1990), 28.

camera is unable to articulate Kong's instinctive feelings of tenderness towards his helpless victim.[3]

It is Kong's very inarticulacy, a quality shared in varying degrees by many heroes of American films, which makes this type of motivic treatment so appropriate. Kong cannot speak for himself, a situation which immediately equates him with a character from the silent movies. Unlike such a character, however, a manipulated puppet is denied most of the powers of physical expressiveness. Kong's progress throughout the film, most of which consists of confronting a variety of adversaries in different locations, is well served by a score which seeks to interpret for and guide the audience.

In contrast, it was not until the late 1950s that the British film industry managed to sever the umbilical cord of middle-class articulacy. *Brief Encounter*, one of the best-known and most respected British films, masterfully portrays the tendency of the British middle class to react to the threat of uncontrollable emotion by instinctively resorting to a highly articulate and generally misleading rationale. It is no coincidence that, by plundering Rachmaninoff's second piano concerto to accompany this most British of all films, a 'score' was devised that was as far removed from the leitmotivic scores of Hollywood as it is possible to be. There is much to be argued on both sides when considering the question of applying borrowed music to a feature film, but the most important issue in this context is that, however apt a piece of music may be on an emotional level, however it may seem to fit the mood of a given scene or sequence, its material is fixed. There are instances of grotesque distortion and manipulation of standard classics in film scores, and the fact remains that a symphony or concerto is created as a unified whole, and when patched onto a soundtrack, can serve only at the most impressionistic level in functional terms.

Forgetting for a moment that Rachmaninoff's work is not a film score by a British composer, there are certain features of the 'theme' and its application in the film that may usefully be compared with those of a particular type of British film score. In a diegesis where action is minimal, and the plot components are few, there is a pervading air of monothematicism about the film. In *Brief Encounter* there are no real adversaries, no cataclysmic events impinging from outside; just two people struggling with their inner selves.

In other British films where there is an absence of black-and-white characters and strong, easily identified dramatic threads, the same type of musical treatment has been applied. Rachmaninoff's concerto is renowned for its cyclic structure, thematic relationships, and most especially for its extended themes. The more monothematic a film is, the more appropriate is the use of the type of development associated with monothematicism in music. If the dramatic pace is slow, then the extended melody comes into its own. *The Winslow Boy* has already been mentioned in connection with the length of its

[3] Palmer (1990), 28–9.

scenes and the complexity of its main dramatic idea. The moral issues of the film are convoluted, and none of the characters is purely good or bad. This is at the opposite end of the spectrum to the simplistic postulates of the melodrama. The adversaries in *The Winslow Boy* are not black-hearted villains, but the faceless bureaucracies of this country: the navy, Parliament, the legal system. Such adversaries cannot be portrayed in strong musical terms. William Alwyn chose to represent the intricacies of this narrative by one theme which, by its use of sequence and extension, is similar in structure to the Rachmaninoff. Nearly all the nondiegetic cues in *The Winslow Boy* are derived from the main theme, and with music cues lasting as long as 4′ 42″ it can be seen why Alwyn used a theme with so much plasticity. Whereas it was common practice to use several themes for the main titles, Alwyn presents his single theme which, after a two-bar introduction on horns and trumpets, extends right through to the opening shot of the film. Alwyn had written this to the original timing of 1′ 45″, but the titles in the film finally ran for only 1′ 25″, and the last seven bars were simply cut.

Example 1. Theme from the main titles to *The Winslow Boy*

William Alwyn, *The Winslow Boy*. Reproduced by the kind permission of the William Alwyn Foundation.

This is a long way from a three-note chromatic motif, but Alwyn was given little alternative to long dialogue scenes in which to develop or treat the theme.

Interestingly, nearly all the scenes that take place outside the main 'setting' of the Winslow home are served by diegetic music cues. This may have been an attempt to help open out an intensely claustrophobic film, or to emphasise a contrast between the world outside and inside the family. This theme, with its aspiring sixths and sevenths, may seem a little too luscious for the subject-matter of the film, but it must be remembered that Alwyn has never been afraid to use lyricism in his serious music. The symphonies, in particular, use soaring, uncompromising themes, which helped to put them very much beyond the pale at a time when recognizable themes of any sort were out of favour. Many British composers were encouraged to develop the lyrical side of their writing through composing for films, thus distracting them from some of the more extreme techniques of contemporary composers. It is ironic that while Alwyn's concert work was considered too reactionary to be taken seriously by the musical establishment in this country, his music was, through his film scores, reaching an audience many times the size of that which was available to more 'acceptable' composers. In the words of Ernest Irving:

> There is one advantage in writing for film music; millions of people have to listen to it whether they like it or not.[4]

The use of themes is an almost automatic response on the part of composers when faced with the responsibility of illuminating the dramatic progress of a film. With rare exceptions, it was always the intention of film makers to unfold the diegesis in an unambiguous way for the audience. In this respect, both British and American films were for decades curiously inflexible on the matter. Experimental cinema has always remained on the fringe, indicating the contentment of mass audiences with the straightforward approach to narrative exposition. For this reason, sweeping aside for a moment all the national differences of cinema with which we are concerned, there is an overall similarity in the fabric of feature films which is universal. In the same way that a Japanese person might have difficulty distinguishing between a British and American film with sub-titles, British composers did not deviate *radically* from the principles

[4] Irving (1959), 161.

of film scoring adopted by the Hollywood composers. The function of music in both cases was broadly the same. It was, therefore, equally true to say of British and American film scores that

> Mysterious as the process may seem, the best film music really comes from the films. The more you become emotionally connected with the film, the more likely it is that the themes will evolve naturally from the drama.[5]

Given such an ideal, the use of a theme tune to promote a film would seem to work against the best interests of the drama. A theme that was written with a view to selling as many copies of gramophone records and sheet music as possible can only loosely represent the drama to which it is attached. That the title song for a film should have become one of the categories for an Academy Award says little for the dramatic sensibilities of the Hollywood film makers. When Dimitri Tiomkin wrote his score for the western *High Noon*, he could not have known how much influence it was to exert on the direction of film scores in America. In his book *Film Music: A Neglected Art*, Roy Prendergast sums up the situation neatly:

> The title song of this fine film, 'Do Not Forsake Me Oh My Darlin'', sung by the late Tex Ritter, became a popular hit in its own right and unknowingly rang the death knell for the intelligent use of music in films.[6]

Leaving aside for the present the issue of the consequences to film music caused by the success of this theme song, there remains the question of which dramatic element of the film Tiomkin was intending to illuminate by its use. Christopher Palmer was, presumably, referring to the score when he wrote

> *High Noon*, like *Gunfight [at the O.K. Corral]*, is virtually monothematic; the tune is the source of practically every bar of the orchestral incidental music, thus a unique musico-dramatic unity. Tiomkin intuitively realized that the film's thematic *idée fixe* – the deadly approach of 'High Noon' – should be complemented and reinforced in the music.[7]

There can be little doubt that the film's *idée fixe* is the relentless progress of time towards inevitable confrontation. The remarkable tautness of the film is largely due to the close relationship between the time taken to unfold the action and the passing of real time. Yet the theme song patently belongs to another important dramatic thread; the concern of the central character that his new bride and other associates in the town should not desert him in his hour of greatest need. The simple, evocative quality of the theme tune when heard in its original form effectively evokes the sense of isolation he experiences. However, in order to fulfil the film's other dramatic requirements, the theme is subjected to almost tortuous treatment, as Christopher Palmer colourfully describes:

[5] Karlin (1994), 26.
[6] Prendergast (1992), 102.
[7] Palmer (1990), 142.

The full orchestra throws out a nerve-shattering development of the melodic phrase set in the ballad to the words 'Oh to be torn 'twixt love and duty', the climax being reached with an ear-splitting blast from the whistle of the arriving train. The showdown sequence takes the theme to pieces in an eight-minute *tour de force* of variation-cum-symphonic development, and puts it together again, momentously, only in the closing bars as the conflict is resolved.[8]

The repeated juxtaposition of a musical theme with a dramatic concept will naturally cause the two to become associated in the minds of the audience, for 'having absorbed the diegetic association of its first occurrence, its [a theme's] very repetition can subsequently recall that filmic context'.[9] If a theme is not well matched with its 'diegetic associations', it quickly becomes nothing but an irritant, and nothing can be more irritating than gratuitous reappearances of a theme song complete with lyrics. The use of lyrics in a film score immediately interferes with the delicate mechanism of illusion on which the whole success of filmic narrative depends. The ability of the audience to sustain the suspension of disbelief is strongly challenged by the introduction of a separate element demanding attention. In contrast, diegetic song with lyrics used in feature films other than musicals serves a completely different function. The most common purpose of diegetic music is to add authenticity to a location. An organ grinder plying his trade in an East-End street is intended to make the setting seem more genuinely 'cockney'. In this case, diegetic music is really just another sound effect supplying the necessary atmosphere to a scene. The very existence of the score to *High Noon* demonstrates the chasm that could and did exist between the aesthetics of British and American film scores. Vaughan Williams may have employed themes in his film scores, and he may have written his own foxtrot, but the notion of his ever using a theme song as the generative musical construct is altogether improbable.

Apart from the general unsuitability of theme songs for delineating dramatic threads in feature films, there is one simple fact about the application of music to drama by thematic means which needs to be borne in mind. Unless the character of a theme is strongly individual, owing to irregularity in either its rhythms or its intervals, it may serve for a range of different dramatic nuances. While opinions differ as to the ability of music to express specific ideas, it can be extremely versatile in its application to drama. A theme such as that written by William Alwyn for *The Winslow Boy* could be used effectively for a variety of narrative ideas, always provided that they were unfolded at the same leisurely pace. If a theme is not too strongly individual, it can have the uncanny knack of appearing to 'fit' an assortment of contexts. The more anonymity a theme has, the wider its dramatic application can be. The narrative threads of *The Winslow Boy* are not drawn in bold primary colours. In common with those of many British films, they are muted, complex and interwoven. By contrast, American films are commonly built on dramatic ideas that are vivid and distinct. British

---

[8] Palmer (1990), 143.
[9] Gorbman (1987), 26.

composers did not often employ themes that were easily recognizable, because such themes were seldom appropriate for the dramatic material to which they had to relate.

The principal themes and leitmotifs of a score could be heard outside their dramatic context in the music for the titles of a film. The practice of introducing a feature film by means of static title-cards (which seems almost unacceptably old-fashioned today), meant that the music was the sole indication of what kind of drama the audience was about to witness. Given this function, the onus on the composer to provide themes that tied in with the dramatic threads of the film was all the greater. It is significant that British films of the late 1930s and early 1940s were more experimental than American films in the presentation of main titles. Their comparative lack of strong musical themes, in keeping with the character of the dramatic elements of a film, encouraged the use of introductory footage to set up the atmosphere of the film without relying on the music. It was as if the more anonymous themes in British scores could not be trusted to perform the task on their own. In Hollywood, on the other hand, it was

> quite common within the industry to turn the main title over to an arranger who created an overture from the composer's own material, saving the composer for more important work.[10]

Yet it is hard to imagine anything more important than the creation of something which

> because it preceded the actual diegesis had increased power to set atmosphere and mood for the entire production.[11]

British and American composers alike considered the primary function of music cues for main titles to be that of foreshadowing the principal dramatic elements of the film and the presentation of the main musical themes to be heard during the course of the film, much as in many an operatic overture. While British composers did present the major musical themes in their title music, seeking to introduce the essential dramatic threads of the film, they did not generally regard title music as having formal conventions. In the classical Hollywood score things were different:

> Freed from the restraints of the diegesis, title music was structured more by the conventions of musical form than by the dictates of narrative development.[12]

Kathryn Kalinak's description of Korngold's title music to the film *Captain Blood*, arranged by Ray Heindorf, serves to convey, albeit in a somewhat confusing manner, the idea of what was considered the appropriate approach to the composition of music for main titles in Hollywood:

[10] Kalinak (1992), 98.
[11] Ibid.
[12] Ibid., 97.

Typically, the main title was conceived in terms of the structure of concert music, here a variation of the **sonata-allegro** which encapsulates exposition, development, and recapitulation of one or more themes. Following the exposition is a developmental section in which the musical material is developed through instrumental variation: woodwinds with **pizzicato** (or plucked) string accompaniment and later strings with a horn countermelody. A bridge passage which modulates upward in gradual *crescendo* builds to the climactic moment when the main theme returns for a final reprise in its original instrumentation. A brief musical coda concludes the main title.[13]

This is quite an achievement in the space of 1½ minutes. Another glance at the theme of the main titles for *The Winslow Boy* (Example 1) will serve to show the economy with which Alwyn extends a straightforward thematic idea in a single continuous sweep to encompass the same time-scale. There is no hint of a formal structure here, and even the modulations result merely from spontaneous harmonic shifts.

British composers did not attempt to make a formal structure out of the music for the main titles, but they generally did present the main themes of the score in order to introduce the elements of the film to the audience. In contrast to the single theme of the main titles to *The Winslow Boy*, a British score would more usually have around three main musical themes that related to varying dramatic ideas. A good example of this is found in the score by Bernard Stevens for the film *Once a Jolly Swagman* (1948). The first theme in the main titles cue is an energetic, rhythmic melody which is identified with the driving ambition and thirst for fame of the central character.

Example 2. 'Ambition' theme from the main titles to *Once a Jolly Swagman*

Bernard Stevens, *Once a Jolly Swagman*. Reproduced by the kind permission of the Bernard Stevens Trust.

Dirk Bogarde, in one of his early spiv roles, plays the obnoxious Bill Fox, who claws his way up to become a champion of speedway. Frequent scenes depicting speedway racing are not conducive to a leitmotivic treatment, or, indeed, to any kind of extended orchestral score. The bulk of the music is made up of diegetic cues coming from the Tannoy system of the racetrack, which gives this film a bleak air of harsh realism, in keeping with its depiction of the austerity of life in post-war London.

[13] Kalinak (1992), 98.

The first theme is heard again over a montage showing Bill's rise to fame and riches. Cut into this montage are stock shots of Hitler and Mussolini in the years leading up to the war. As the first theme is treated here only by extension, without the spotting of stock shots by the use of different material, the implication of the musical treatment is that Bill is to be equated with these dictators because of his blind ambition. This theme is heard for the last time at the end of the film as Bill wins a trial race to prove that he could still be a champion if he chose. The extended version of this theme works well, even in competition with the noise from cycle engines, because the theme is unusually vigorous for a British score not written for a comedy film. The reason that it can afford to be so uncharacteristically strong is that it is unequivocal in its intentions to convey Bill's striving for success, and also that it is never heard with dialogue, but is confined to the illustration of two main action sequences.

The second theme used in the main titles is in clear contrast, both musical and dramatic, to the first.

Example 3. Pat's theme from the main titles to *Once a Jolly Swagman*

Bernard Stevens, *Once a Jolly Swagman*. Reproduced by the kind permission of the Bernard Stevens Trust.

Pat provides the love interest of the film, and, as in many dramatic plots, this creates a conflict of interest for the central character. Pat cannot co-exist in marriage with Bill's self-interested ambition. The way Pat's theme is used in this film exposes a very great difference from the way it might have been handled in a Hollywood film. Although Pat has appeared in several scenes earlier in the film, it is not until she is on her first date with Bill that the theme is heard. American composers would already have conveyed to us that Pat was to be a significant person in the plot by plying us with her theme every time she appeared on screen. In this film, what the theme really portrays is not the character of Pat, but the relationship between Pat and Bill and, by implication, Bill's challenge to rise above his desire for fame. As they lean on the Thames embankment during their first date, the theme is subtly introduced by a new eight-bar phrase heard on the saxophone.

Example 4. Prefix to Pat's theme from *Once a Jolly Swagman*

This phrase acts both as a prefix to the main 'Pat' theme, and as an independent entity. Thanks to the use of the saxophone, the cue at first has the character of implied diegetic music drifting from a nearby café. After the first eight bars of the theme are heard, the remaining bars are taken up by the orchestra as Bill and Pat recognize their feelings for each other. While the theme serves reasonably well as a romantic culmination to a scene ending with a clinch, the character of the theme relates more to the challenge contained in the relationship. This is best observed in the 13th and 14th bars of the theme, with the dotted rhythm on the falling fourth, and the ascending quavers repeated in sequence. There is a definite feeling of the overcoming of all obstacles, as the highest point of the phrase is reached with the upward rush to the D natural in bar 17. When Bill and Pat embrace on the Embankment, the theme is played straight through from bar 9 to bar 19 on upper strings, a treatment which enhances the romantic and culminative aspects of the theme.

The use of this theme in other dramatic contexts demonstrates how much flexibility can be applied by different treatments. When, towards the end of the film, Pat goes to Bill's mother to tell her that she no longer wants to pursue her intention of divorcing him, she walks uncertainly along the Embankment. The saxophone again plays the prefix to the theme, this time reduced to seven bars. When the main theme enters, it is given not to the upper strings, but to the oboe. This change highlights the loneliness and hesitancy that Pat is expressing in her tone and body language. To emphasise the change in the relationship since the theme was first heard in context, it does not follow through to its conclusion, but avoids reaching its climax by tailing off in bar 16. It has also been transposed down a fourth, which puts it into a particularly plaintive register of the oboe. In the final scene, as Bill walks towards Pat, leaving the speedway track for good, Pat's theme is heard from bar 9 to the end, this time returned to the strings, symbolizing the restoration of the relationship.

The most interesting use of Pat's theme comes at the point in the film where Bill discovers his wife has left him. He wakes to find himself alone in bed.

Because Pat is absent, the audience are permitted to witness a rare early appearance of the double bed in British cinema, which does much to enhance the realism of the scene. As Bill lights a cigarette, rises from the bed and puts on a dressing gown, we are alerted by a sinister little ostinato figure on the clarinets, alternating between two harmonies, to the fact that this is the prelude to something more than a daily routine.

Examples 5a and **5b** from *Once a Jolly Swagman*

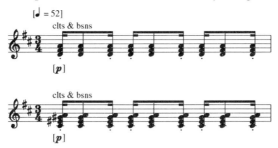

By its monotony, and by the alternation of these harmonies, the figure contrives to give exactly the right atmosphere of false security which Bill is soon to realize he has been experiencing. Under this figure, the first eight bars of Pat's theme, preceded by the prefix theme previously heard on saxophone, are played on bass clarinet and pizzicato cellos. The removal of this prefix theme into a low register, with subtle alterations to the intervals, transforms it from the innocence of its first appearance into something distinctly menacing.

Example 6. Transformation of Pat's theme from *Once a Jolly Swagman*

The 8th bar of Pat's theme is interrupted by a figure on the timpani as the camera pans to the newspaper headline on the hall floor, which reads 'Hitler's answer to Britain'.

Example 7. 'Headline' motif from *Once a Jolly Swagman*

Bernard Stevens takes elements from this figure and arranges them in such a way that the resulting resemblance to the timpani figure in 'Mars' from Holst's 'The Planets' makes its intended association with war inevitable.

Example 8. 'War' motif from *Once a Jolly Swagman*

This motif is used in the scene where Bill is carried off to war in a troop ship. Accompanied by a two-part arpeggiated figure on the horns, the softly sounding motif is made to suggest the ship's engines, while a further transformation of the prefix to Pat's theme, played on the cor anglais, is heard over it.

Example 9. Further transformation of the prefix theme from
Once a Jolly Swagman

The use of Pat's theme here, in combination with the 'war' motif, is one of the most subtle uses of themes for dramatic definition in the film. Pat is not present, and is not mentioned in the course of the conversation with Bill's comrade Duggie, but this scene is actually the turning point of the film, as Bill realizes that he is one of those who are 'never satisfied' and therefore 'cause trouble'. From the experience of going to war and of having his life saved by the sacrifice of Duggie, who exemplifies the moral values that Bill lacks, Bill is able to make the transformation in himself needed to rescue his relationship with Pat. All this is implied in the music by the manipulation of Pat's theme in combination with the 'war' motif. This treatment of themes in combination to herald a complex development in the plot is a very rare example of a British composer using the motivic techniques of the classical Hollywood score.

The third theme in the main titles of *Once a Jolly Swagman* is an arrangement of the tune to the popular song *Waltzing Matilda*, from which the title of the film is taken. While at first glance this may seem appropriate, if somewhat obvious, the truth is that the title of the film is completely misleading. Whatever the Australian connection may have been in the original novel from which the screenplay is extracted, in the film there is only one single reference to the country, and the American distributors for once came closer to the mark when they re-titled it, releasing it as *Maniacs on Wheels*. The film's tenuous connection with Australia would never have been identified at all if it were not for the use of this theme. The actor Bill Owen employs only a trace of an Australian accent in his portrayal of Lag, the leader of the speedway team, who is suffering from loss of nerve. The single reference to his origins comes when he returns 'back home to Australia' to recover from his nervous breakdown. Lag, however, is a significant character because he is symbolic of those who suffer the consequences of life as a speedway champion.

The use of such a well-known tune ensures that its association with Lag, however tentatively established, can conjure him up in his absence. When Bill sees on the mantelpiece a letter addressed to him, the audience knows before he does that it is from Lag, because of the accompanying music cue. Similarly, in a later scene, as Bill stares from his window, another snatch of the theme provides a clue as to who preoccupies his thoughts. This method of bringing Lag to mind in his absence having been established, there is a curious lapse of consistency towards the end of the film. When Pat is summoned to her superior's office during a dance, we know she is about to receive bad news. At precisely this point, the song *Waltzing Matilda* is sung diegetically from the dance hall. The musically literate in the audience immediately assume that it is Lag who is involved, because of his association with the theme. As the news concerns Bill, and not Lag, this seems to represent a serious breach of the thematic code. However, it should be remembered that, in many cases, diegetic music has the ability to stand apart from the twists of the drama. *Waltzing Matilda* was one of the most popular songs of the war, and it was more than likely to be played at a Forces' dance. To have used it as an encoder would have been an abuse of the true function of diegetic music, although composers on both sides of the Atlantic have been guilty of using material from their main themes in diegetic cues. Because this theme is such a well-known song, its use in this context must be regarded as realistic and not as a narrative hint. However, to have used that particular song at this juncture, when so many other war-time songs were available, is simply careless. The composer cannot be blamed for what would have been the choice of the director, the producer or the musical director.

The use of a pre-existing popular song in the main title music cue in order to connect with the actual title of the film is one of the less acceptable faces of musical signposting. It debases the currency of a theme's ability to convey, by its nature alone, information about the main narrative threads. If music has an automatic affiliation with an extra-musical idea, because of an already estab-lished association, then the composer who uses it has a short cut to his task. This is exactly the case in the music for the main titles of the film *The Holly and the Ivy*. This adaptation of a successful stage play has as its main narrative thread the effect on a family of years of emotional inhibition and suppression of the truth. The family are forced to confront the issues arising from this when they are brought together to celebrate Christmas. The use of the title for the original play has much more to do with the symbolic aspect of the contrasting natures of holly and ivy, and their correspondence with the characters of the two sisters, than with contemporary Christmas festivities. When Malcolm Arnold wrote a skilful orchestral arrangement of the traditional carol for the main title music for the film, it was for the purposes of its automatic association with its words, and hence with the title of the film, and he was probably complying with instructions from the director. This carol has become a part of the Christian celebrations of Christmas, and, through that association, the 'jolly' nature of its melody has obscured the esoteric meanings attached to the original. The deeper significance of the title and its relationship to the underlying narrative thread is further undermined by the inclusion of the tune of *The First Nowell* in his main titles arrangement. Nothing in the character of this arrangement of the two carols corresponds with the tensions and bitter undercurrents of the plot. The melody 'The Holly and the Ivy' is used throughout the film, but mainly in diegetic cues involving carol singing, and the theme itself is not treated in any meaningful way that mirrors the developments of the narrative. As a dramatic interpretation, the best that can be said for the use of the main theme of this score is that, by its anempathy with the real dramatic situation, it serves to highlight the hypocrisy of Christmas festivities.

There is one important motif in this score which does indicate the true state of affairs that exists beneath the surface. Margaret, the sister who is perceived as cold and selfish because of her hedonistic life-style in London, is suffering deeply from the death of her child, of whose brief existence the family are in complete ignorance. Margaret tries to control her private grief through the use of alcohol and the projection of a hard persona, and this attitude, described in the film dialogue as being 'askew with the world', is the subject for a slithery motif, first heard on the bassoon.

Example 10. Margaret's motif from *The Holly and the Ivy*

Malcolm Arnold, *The Holly and the Ivy*. Reproduced by the kind permission of Sir Malcolm Arnold, CBE.

The first hearing of this motif occurs before Margaret has actually appeared on screen. While the phone rings in her empty flat, the camera pans to the doormat and picks out her invitation to Christmas at the family home. The motif is heard on solo bassoon over a sustained chord on strings and horns, as her name is seen on the envelope. The nature of this motif is in such marked contrast to the main theme, and to the previous music cues, that the audience is alerted to the fact that Margaret is in some way out of step with those around her. This is emphasized, in the second appearance of her motif, by the contrast between the sleazy triplet and its bustling accompaniment in duple time. The motif appears in the middle of a travel sequence showing the relatives making their way to the family home in rural Wyndenham. The bustling duple rhythm continues through the sequence, which depicts various modes of transport. Margaret is again conspicuous by her absence as the motif accompanies a shot of the empty car seat in which she should have been sitting. Played this time on solo trumpet, and with the first three notes changed to falling semitones, the motif demonstrates even more strongly Margaret's alienation from the rest of the family.

Example 11. Margaret's motif in the travelling sequence from *The Holly and the Ivy*

Malcolm Arnold, *The Holly and the Ivy*. Reproduced by the kind permission of Sir Malcolm Arnold, CBE.

When Margaret finally does make her first appearance on screen, nearly halfway through the film, she is seen looking out of the train window on her way to Wyndenham. Arnold chooses to illustrate this anempathetically, by using a 'travel' variation of *The Holly and the Ivy* theme. Because of the quality of Margaret Leighton's acting, the audience is left in no doubt as to her dissociation from the jolliness and eager anticipation the music suggests. One shot of her expression as she looks from the train shows that she is totally out of sympathy with the music and, therefore, with the whole spirit of Christmas celebrations.

The high standard of acting in this film makes it worth viewing, but tends to draw attention to its theatrical origins, and emphasize its uncinematic aspects. It also inhibits the composer. With actors of the quality of Ralph Richardson, Celia Johnson, Margaret Leighton and Denholm Elliott, who all tended to act on the screen with an extraordinary degree of physical restraint, the use of music becomes almost an impertinence. Only two scenes involving direct dialogue are scored with nondiegetic music cues. Scenes taking place outside the family home are used as an opportunity for scoring, in an attempt to open the film out, but these occur early on. Once all the characters are established in the main setting, the use of music becomes less plausible, and as the drama unfolds towards the end, there are no music cues at all for 18 minutes.

Arnold uses Margaret's motif four more times in the film, confirming it as a major element in the score. One of its most interesting aspects is its functioning to represent Margaret in her absence. The first and second cues using the motif are heard in conjunction with two brief shots – the invitation addressed to her, and the empty car seat. As these were both of less than 10 seconds' duration, the motif needed to be capable of creating a vivid impression of a person who is not present and who has yet to appear on screen.

The use of motifs in the absence of the character to whom they are attached was a very popular ploy of Hollywood composers. There were three main ways in which the device could be employed, each serving a slightly different function. If a motif for an absent person is heard while a visible association with him or her is present on the screen, such as an empty place at the table, or some personal object, then its use may be considered gratuitous. Much depends upon the context, of course. There is all the difference in the world between the pointless repeated labelling of objects on the screen by musical codes that were prevalent in the classical Hollywood score, and the use Arnold makes of this motif in its first two appearances. When we see Margaret's name on the invitation, the motif suggests her dislocation from the rest of the family by its contrast with previous musical material, and its use serves a vital narrative function. If the envelope itself had made further appearances in the film, there would be no dramatic imperative to use the motif again, and we can be assured that Arnold would not have done so. The use of Margaret's motif in the second cue in the travelling sequence is, again, not the 'signposting' of the Hollywood composers, but the following of a narrative thread to hint at her anomalous situation.

The second main use of a motif for an absent person occurs when no symbol of that person is present on the screen, and there is no verbal reference to them. This most commonly happens when one or more characters are thinking of them, or when their influence is strongly felt. As the smoke drifts up from a devastated battlefield, for instance, it is almost a refreshing change from the habitual strains of the Last Post, to hear a funerary motif associated with Custer, or Davy Crockett or George Washington. This type of use, however, does border on the pictorial, as we can see the *results* of the character's actions clearly.

The use of motifs can be described as purely narrative in such instances as that already cited from *Once a Jolly Swagman*, when Bill is looking down from the window. The audience is informed by the music cue that he is thinking of Lag, rather that merely depressed by the weather, or stuck for something to do. This, more than anything, demonstrates how the use of themes that attach specifically to characters or situations can precisely interpret an otherwise ambiguous moment. Music certainly has the power to convey emotion in general terms, and the most obtuse and musically illiterate person can distinguish between anger and tenderness when properly portrayed by the composer. Much has been written about the numerous ways in which the shot of an actor's immobile face on screen can be interpreted. This is precisely the kind of cinematic situation where only music can communicate the underlying motivation, and in many such cases, nothing is as simple and effective as thematic association, especially when the theme is already familiar. The equation becomes elementary: if *Waltzing Matilda* equals Lag, then Bill staring pensively from the window plus *Waltzing Matilda* equals Bill thinking of Lag. In this type of equation, it goes without saying, the stronger and more memorable a theme is, the more quickly its associations can be absorbed. Thus we have returned full circle to Franz Waxman's thematic ideal.

The third most common use of themes for absent people is seen when they are discussed in the dialogue of those present on the screen. Again the theme or motif can function in two different ways, depending on the context. If the absent character is named in the conversation, then motivic use becomes dangerously close to redundancy, but if the subject of the discussion is not revealed in the dialogue, then the use of themes can be a useful narrative hint. Two villains may be planning their assault on an unnamed victim, but if this is underscored by a theme identified with a specific character, then the audience will have a shrewd idea who the intended victim is.

In *The Holly and the Ivy*, Margaret's motif is heard for the third time in her absence during a conversation between two other characters, concerning her drinking. As she is referred to by name, and the subject of the motif, that of being 'askew with the world', is discussed, the use of her motif here is gratuitous. There is, however, a kind of motivic development by means of the change of instrumentation. On all previous occasions, her motif was played on a solo wind or brass instrument: namely bassoon, trumpet or alto flute. Here, underscoring the voices of her sister and her sister's fiancé, the motif is heard on the violins and violas – the change from the 'cold' solo instrument to the 'warmth' of a body of strings reflecting the sympathetic attitude of Jenny and David to her plight.

Of the six cues featuring Margaret's motif, three are heard in her absence, two of them before she appears on screen. The way the music is used informs the audience how powerful her influence is. This is the only narrative thread to be singled out in this way, and so it would seem to be even more surprising that the motif does not feature in the main titles. However, Arnold had a very individual approach to the writing of main titles, preferring not to put all his goods on display at once. Other composers too came increasingly to feel that a quick preview of all the main dramatic ideas of a film was neither compulsory nor entirely desirable. As audiences became more sophisticated, or at least more practised, in film viewing the notion of giving too much advance information about the nature of the forthcoming drama began to seem old-hat, particularly if the drama had tense or unexpected undercurrents to it. In 1952, the year that *The Holly and the Ivy* was released, two other films, both scored by Arnold, and both with curious parallels to it, were also released.

Home at Seven was another direct translation to the screen of a successful stage play, and also starred Ralph Richardson and Margaret Leighton, this time as husband and wife. David and Janet are the ultimate representatives of respectable middle-class suburbia. David always returns home at seven in the evening from his banking job in the city, by train from Waterloo. The main titles appear over an introductory scene depicting his daily walk from the station, and are accompanied by a suitably bustling theme in the orchestra. The status quo of this diegesis is a parallel to the 'normality' of Christmas at Wyndenham, and the challenge to that status quo – a sudden attack of confusion and memory loss – is akin to the challenge posed by Margaret's 'askewness'. The motif associated with David's confusion is a peculiarly simple and eerie fragmented figure played on the cellos, under a 'mobile' of chromatic vibraphone clusters and clarinet trills.

Example 12. David's 'confusion' motif from *Home at Seven*

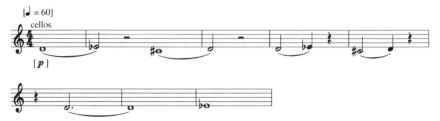

Malcolm Arnold, *Home at Seven*. Reproduced by the kind permission of Sir Malcolm Arnold, CBE.

Just as with Margaret's motif, this representation of disruption to the status quo does not appear in the 'jolly' main titles cue. In both films, it is the dramatic element that represents the undermining of normality, the cross-current of the narrative, that is not hinted at in the main titles. By reserving the musical motif until its appropriate place in the drama, the impact of the contrast is strengthened. The first appearance of David's 'confusion' motif is particularly effective. It comes after 2 minutes of dialogue that are without music. This is the first dialogue scene in the film, so the audience are not preconditioned to make value judgments as to the characters' relative mental states. The quality of the acting distracts the attention from the stage-bound nature of this scene, with its unimaginative camera work. The restrained hysteria of Janet, who claims that David has been missing for a whole day, and David's calm reasoning with her, are acted with astonishing physical control and vocal virtuosity. It is not until the moment when the motif is heard, as David stares, totally without expression, at the date on the newspaper which supports Janet's claim, that a true moment of cinema is experienced. The juxtaposition of the image, and the unusually impressionistic music cue, inform the audience at once that all the notions they had gathered from the dialogue – Janet's instability, David's rationality – are being challenged.

Ironically, this motif is, in its economy, akin to the three-note chromatic motif of *King Kong*. Its remarkably torpid pace, however, puts it into a category of its own. The ten notes of the theme, as heard on its first appearance, occupy almost 40 seconds. Of all the film scores from the period under discussion, no other theme corresponding to a specific narrative thread is quite as attenuated as this. Because its vague, colouristic, directionless nature so perfectly illustrates David's trance-like state of confusion over his lost memory, there is no need for it to be developed extensively, and because it always represents the same situation in much the same way, it is heard virtually unchanged on each of its six further appearances. Both its nature and its function make conspicuous treatment of it unnecessary. It may have few notes, but it is neither short nor memorable, and for that reason it operates as a narrative hint on an emotional rather than an intellectual level.

In the third film dating from 1952, Arnold demonstrates an altogether different method of 'withholding' a significant theme from the main titles music, by transforming it into something totally unrecognizable. The main titles to *The Sound Barrier* are themselves treated in an unusual way for the period, anticipating developments associated with the realism of the early 1960s. The first 2 minutes of the film are taken up with action sequences devoid of dialogue:

> The film starts with a clear sky above the cliffs of Dover, but as the camera turns we find ourselves beside the tail of a crashed aircraft on which appears a swastika. Soldiers are lounging on the cliff; we hear a mouth organ gently strumming; there is a Spitfire high in the sky. Then the music on soaring strings takes us up to the pilot who is full of the happiness of flight on a clear day, his machine racing across the sky. He goes into a dive – and suddenly the music changes into an ominous chattering sound. The plane is buffeting as it hits the sound barrier and the pilot tries frantically to pull it out of the dive. This is a fine piece of composition blended with the sound effects of the action.[14]

So there are two incidental music cues before the main titles, and the first cue is visibly diegetic, for the mouth organ is seen in the hands of one of the soldiers as he removes it from his lips. The use of a diegetic cue as the first piece of music in the film is both extremely unusual, and indicative of the changes that were to come in the use of music for film as the dramatic emphasis shifted towards naturalism. The main titles begin as the pilot succeeds in pulling out of the dive. The opening motif is an ominous figure played fortissimo on horns and trombones, warning of the dangers involved in the attempt to break the sound barrier.

Example 13. 'Danger' motif from *The Sound Barrier*

Malcolm Arnold, *Sound Barrier Rhapsody*. Reproduced by permission of Patersons Publications Ltd, 8/9 Frith Street, London.

This motif functions in expected ways to highlight the consequences and potential threats of supersonic flight. Much of the power of this film is derived from the chilling performance of Ralph Richardson as John Ridgefield, the

---

[14] Manvell and Huntley (2/1975), 135–6.

ruthless owner of the empire which is creating the first plane capable of breaking the sound barrier. The motif is used as a dirge at the burial of Ridgefield's son. The character of the theme is transformed by the change of instrumentation. Played legato on the cellos, it is softened into a lament. Directly after returning home from the funeral of his son, who has lost his life through fear of his father's disapproval, Ridgefield opens the package containing the model of the prototype, subsequently named Prometheus. When he holds the model up to the light, the theme is heard on muted horns, as his daughter realizes the potential threat to her husband, Tony, who will now assume the role of surrogate son to Ridgefield.

The unusual aspect of this motif is the way it is developed into something so unlike itself, that it qualifies as a separate motif altogether. Arnold effects this not by extreme measures, but by the usual methods of motivic alteration: changes to time signature, tempo and instrumentation. By transferring the motif to piccolo and celesta, and using the rhythm of a lullaby, Arnold enables it to create a completely different effect. It becomes hypnotic, as if from another world. Thematically, it is used to indicate how Tony's fascination with the challenge of breaking the sound barrier will lure him, like a siren, from his marriage to his death.

Example 14. 'Siren' motif from *The Sound Barrier*

Malcolm Arnold, *Sound Barrier Rhapsody*. Reproduced by permission of Patersons Publications Ltd, 8/9 Frith Street, London.

It is first heard when Tony is discussing the mysteries of the sound barrier with the aircraft designer, and he sees the plans of Prometheus on the drawing desk. Later, when Tony debates the future of Prometheus with his father-in-law after the death of the test pilot, the audience knows what is really behind his words as he tells Ridgefield that the decision must lie with him. Because the 'siren' motif is heard at this point, it suggests that Tony is willing to sacrifice his life if the decision is made to go ahead. The night before Tony tests Prometheus, his wife sees him silhouetted against the stars as he stares towards them from the window. The 'siren' motif is heard again as she has the premonition that Tony will die. Just as in *The Holly and the Ivy* and *Home at Seven*, the motif represents the unnatural element in a character's makeup which threatens the status quo, in this case the marriage of Tony and Sue. Arnold appears to demonstrate deliberately that the motifs are two separate entities by playing them one after the other. As Sue is about to give birth on the night following Tony's death, she looks at the stars representing the mystery that has lured her husband from her.

The 'siren' motif is heard, immediately followed by the 'danger' motif. They delineate independent, but inevitably connected, threads of the drama. This is a most unusual example of a theme assuming a separate identity from its original source, both by transformation, and the manner of its application to the narrative.

Malcolm Arnold demonstrates a very sound understanding of the dramatic requirements of a film score by his manipulation of themes. Both he and William Alwyn may have suffered by being so closely associated with film, but they were gifted musico-dramatists. The ability to respond effectively in musical terms to the exigencies of the drama is not, alas, something that comes of its own accord. The technique of film scoring may be learnt empirically, much as may any other musical technique, but the art of writing music that is truly in sympathy with the drama, and supports its development, is really dependent on the composer's natural affinity. An intuitive understanding of drama is a special gift, and is, unfortunately, not one of the talents granted to every composer.

British composers approached the task of film scoring from a variety of standpoints, and with a wide spectrum of attitudes ranging from contempt to great enthusiasm. Attitude, however, was sometimes at odds with ability, and perhaps nowhere more so than in the case of Arnold Bax, who gained the reputation of being less than sympathetic to the medium of film and the art of film scoring. A close examination of his use of themes in his single feature film will show how an innate gift for dramatic perception has been overlooked. Bax may have been temperamentally unsuited to the constraints of composing for film, but his score for *Oliver Twist* reveals how great a loss was his withdrawal from it.

5. Arnold Bax's musico-dramatic treatment of *Oliver Twist*

In many ways Arnold Bax was a curious choice as composer for the film *Oliver Twist*. He had not enjoyed the experience of composing for the documentary *Malta G.C.*, his single previous foray into the world of cinema. He felt that the constraints of writing for film interfered too much with a composer's natural style. He also appeared to have very little understanding of the way music should function in film, if his well-known diatribe against the medium is to be taken seriously:

> I do not think the medium is at present at all satisfactory as far as the composer is concerned, as his music is largely inaudible, toned down to make way for – in many cases – quite unnecessary talk. This is, in my opinion quite needless as it is possible to pay attention to two things at the same time if they appeal to different parts of the intelligence.[1]

Appealing to two different parts of the intelligence runs contrary to the primary function of music in film as perceived by the majority of film composers. The intention of Hollywood composers in particular was to assist in the suspension of critical judgment. A cinema audience whose intelligence is challenged in the way advocated by Bax cannot indulge in the customary state of narcosis necessary for absorption into the illusionary world of film.

Bax did not see the advantages that writing for film could offer to the composer, and he did not share the enthusiasm felt by many of his fellow composers for the stimulus to creativity engendered by the limitations imposed by film. He would certainly not have been in agreement with Vaughan Williams when the latter wrote

> Film composing is a splendid discipline, and I recommend a course of it to all composition teachers whose pupils are apt to be dawdling in their ideas, or whose every bar is sacred and must not be cut or altered.[2]

Bax found it hard to accept that a music cue should be modified to suit the needs of a particular film sequence. He is known to have queried why the footage could not be changed in order to fit his music.[3]

[1] Arnold Bax, quoted in Manvell and Huntley (2/1975), 219.
[2] Vaughan Williams, 'Film Music', in Huntley (1947), 177.
[3] Ronald Neame, in 'Lights, Camera, Action! A Century of Cinema', ITV broadcast, 4.2.1996.

Apart from these rather obvious indications that Bax might be an unsuitable composer to score a feature film, there were other, more subtle factors that might have given Muir Mathieson cause to hesitate before inviting him to score *Oliver Twist*. These factors relate directly to the nature of the original novel and, consequently, to the screenplay that was devised by David Lean and Stanley Hayes. Quite simply, Bax considered it to be ill-suited to his personal style of creativity:

> I am still plagued by the 'Oliver Twist' film for which I struggle in agonies to provide music – a very thankless task as there is no music in the subject. I cannot imagine any subject more unsuited to me.[4]

The problem was not that Bax was unable to respond to a literary text, for 'the importance of literature in spurring his creativity'[5] was one of his most widely recognized attributes. Under the assumed name of Dermot O'Byrne he had published his own novels in Dublin, and therefore had an inside knowledge of the workings of a novelist's mind. In Bax's own words, it was to the subject of *Oliver Twist* that he had so much difficulty in relating:

> It is the book of Dickens that I most dislike, and there is no music in the subject at all.[6]

Muir Mathieson could not have been expected to be familiar with the intricacies of Bax's literary tastes before he invited him to write the film score. Mathieson may well have assumed that because of Dickens's stature, the 'literary' Bax would be tempted by the offer. Unfortunately, Dickens's tendency to polarize his characters into extremes of vice and virtue was bound to be repugnant to a man of Bax's subtlety and sensitivity. In many respects Dickens's work has more than a resonance of the melodrama about it and *Oliver Twist* is certainly among those most clearly drawn in black and white. Little wonder that Bax had to be 'bullied'[7] into accepting the commission.

Just how far Bax felt himself to be out of sympathy with the subject of *Oliver Twist* can be judged from his description of the kind of film he would have preferred to score:

> I should like now to try my hand at a particular type of film which would really be in tune with the sort of thing I have tried to do in much of my music. A romantic subject, with beauty and poetry, with colour and gaiety, calm and green and pleasing, a subject that would be lyrical and full of the clean, country air.[8]

[4] Arnold Bax, quoted in Parlett (1999), 257.
[5] Anthony Payne, in Sadie (ed.) (1980), ii, 307, s.v. 'Bax'.
[6] Arnold Bax, quoted in Parlett (1999), 257.
[7] Bax wrote: 'I have been inveigled (not to say bullied) into writing music for the Oliver Twist film.' Parlett (1999), 257.
[8] Arnold Bax, quoted in Parlett (1999), 258.

While this imaginary scenario seemed to Bax to be more suited to his musical style, it is obviously lacking in any of the essentials of drama, and the question arises of Bax's ability to deal with the demands of dramatic interpretation. After all, as we have already seen, literature is not necessarily drama. Bax's 'creative dependence on the ideas of the moment and on visual and verbal images'[9] does not of itself testify to a strong dramatic sense. It is one thing to write 'dramatic' pictorial music inspired by some inner vision, such as the incomparable *Tintagel*, but quite another to have a true understanding of drama as enacted on the stage or unfolded on the screen. Bax did not produce any work based on a dramatic form, so there is little to suggest how innately attuned he was to the task of writing music for drama before he undertook the commission for *Oliver Twist*. Julian Herbage was confident that Bax showed the necessary potential:

> Only one field of music has Bax neglected – he has as yet written no opera. In his handling of a chorus in such works as *St Patrick's Breastplate* (1923–24) and *The Morning Watch* (1935) he displays a sure dramatic touch. . . . Turning to film music for the first time he has recently given us the vitally dramatic *Malta,G.C.* [sic] Dare we hope that the poetry of a Yeats or Synge may now fire his Celtic imagination to produce in operatic form a work such as Synge's *Riders to the Sea?*[10]

But it is pertinent that the suggestion here is that Bax should write an opera based on poetry. Such a suggestion only serves to emphasise the alienation Bax must have felt from a text as unpoetic as *Oliver Twist*. The screenplay itself is more or less confined to the bare bones of plot unfolding, and there is little Dickensian rhetoric except from the character of the Beadle. The generally down-to-earth nature of the dialogue discouraged its underscoring in this film – a distinct advantage to an inexperienced film composer.

Film directors vary enormously in the degree of their involvement with the production of music for film. Some are happy to leave the composer to get on with the job undisturbed, while others expect to have an input ranging from mild suggestion to near dictatorship. As with other specialist areas of film production, the more a director thinks he knows about music, the more damage he is likely to cause. Music holds a unique position in the arts, as it is universal in its appeal and application. Every man in the street 'knows' something about music in a way he would not presume to do with other arts. For this reason directors feel justified in meddling in an area that is nearly always better left to the experts. David Lean was a director who had strong ideas of how the scoring in his films should be approached. John Huntley gives a discreet comment on the effect that the director's input had on the score for *Oliver Twist* as he describes the circumstances in which Bax found himself before the composing process began:

---

[9] Anthony Payne, in Sadie (ed.) (1980), ii, 307, s.v. 'Bax'.
[10] Herbage, 'Bax', in Bacharach (ed.) (1946), 129.

[It] is very important to see how the director, David Lean, the musical director, Muir Mathieson, and the composer, Arnold Bax, visualised the music, conveyed their ideas, and collaborated in the final result after discussion on all the points involved. For example, here are David Lean's original notes for three sequences, showing how the working out of the music was effected in each case; the result on the screen you must judge for yourself.[11]

It is fascinating to imagine what the score would have been like if Bax had been allowed more freedom in its creation. It is altogether possible that, left to his own devices, Bax would not have used themes in the way into which he was coerced by Lean. John Huntley reveals how Lean pressured Bax into redundant thematic usage in a typical Hollywood manner. In this extract from Lean's notes we see the extent of his influence:

As daylight pours in, I should like the music to start again. Hopeful: a new day: new life. I should like the music to 'accent' the locket round the girl's neck, as it is a very important plot point.[12]

It is tempting to infer from this extract that the idea of using themes for the major elements of the story originated from Lean himself. The director was certainly responsible for the introduction to the score of an element that caused considerable controversy:

The use of a solo piano was suggested by David Lean, who felt that it 'emphasizes the isolation of the little boy in a world of bullying adults'.[13]

It is difficult to understand Lean's thinking on this point. Did he suppose that the timbre of the piano, which is heard on its own at its first entry in the score, was itself suggestive of isolation? In film scores of this period the piano was often used as a part of the orchestral sonority to bolster the bass notes,[14] but it was sparingly used as a solo instrument. Did Lean imagine that because of this it would stand in contrast to the other instruments which represent the 'world of bullying adults'? The timbre of the piano brings to the listener a jumble of diverse associations in a way that no other instrument is capable of doing. If a single note is heard softly played on a trumpet, the consensus of opinion as to the emotion it conveys would be 'heroism', on a bass clarinet 'menace', on a kettle drum 'suspense'. These associations have been built up unconsciously by composers, and predate their use in the cinematic context. The piano is an entirely different matter. Because of its enormous range of expression, and the almost unlimited ways it can be used, not to mention the inexhaustible repertoire at its disposal, the piano occupies a unique place in the European psyche. For this reason, the introduction of the piano tone in the score to *Oliver Twist* is both startling and confusing to the audience.

[11] Huntley (1949), 114.
[12] David Lean's working notes, quoted in Huntley (1949), 115.
[13] Parlett (1999), 258.
[14] See Appendix A, p. 195.

Plate 1. Muir Mathieson, Harriet Cohen and Arnold Bax during the recording of *Oliver Twist*.

David Lean may well have been influenced in this matter by the success of *Brief Encounter*, which in large part owed its popular appeal to the use of the Rachmaninoff concerto. There are many ways in which its use in the film can be criticized, but the fact remains that the intense emotional power of this music *exactly* conveys the painfully repressed emotions of the two central characters. It is no coincidence that the war years witnessed a rash of film scores featuring tabloid piano concertos. Richard Addinsell's score for *Dangerous Moonlight*, and Hubert Bath's for *Love Story* were both written in shameless imitation of Rachmaninoff's style. That both these films were released before *Brief Encounter*, in 1941 and 1944 respectively, only emphasizes the fact that something about the romantic piano concerto precisely echoed the spirit of the age. At a time when people in Britain were living on a precipice of emotional uncertainty, passionate sexual love had become an uncharacteristically powerful force. Nature's method of maintaining the birth-rate in times of war has always been to make the prospect of imminent death a potent aphrodisiac. Released at the end of 1945, *Brief Encounter* served as a deeply nostalgic reminder to all those who had suffered the pain of curtailed or unattainable love.

The ironic thing about the use of the Rachmaninoff concerto in this film is that it was not David Lean's idea, but Noel Coward's. He felt that it was exactly the kind of music that a woman like Laura Jesson would equate with her suffering,[15] and the enduring success of the film may owe more than a little to his idea.

Given these associations with the piano in film scores that the general public had come to expect, it is not unreasonable to assert that its use in the score to *Oliver Twist* was an error of judgment. This error was compounded by the way the piano is first introduced in the score. It is heard at the exact moment when Mrs Thingummy, the workhouse crone who has attended Oliver's birth, and whose theft of the locket leads to such ramifications of the plot, carries the new-born Oliver through the door into the main part of the workhouse. The solo piano abruptly takes over from the orchestra in the middle of the cue which contained the theme used to indicate the significance of the locket around the dead girl's neck as Lean had requested. John Huntley explains what the use of the piano was intended to convey:

> It was decided that Oliver himself was the primary factor in the scene that introduces the dingy, sordid surroundings of the workhouse. Therefore Bax wrote a part for the piano (played for the film by Harriet Cohen), and as Oliver is carried, crying, through the monstrously ugly and dimly lit hall, the tentative sounds of a piano are heard to emphasise Oliver and act as a contrast to his miserable surroundings.[16]

The main problem here, apart from the jolt to the system which this juxtaposition gives to the listener, is that the connection between Oliver and the piano is not really established. The fact that Oliver is considered by Lean to be the 'primary factor in the scene' is lost on the audience as the visual impact of the workhouse setting far outweighs the significance of what appears to be a small bundle of rags. To make matters worse, the theme played on the piano is not Oliver's theme in its original version, but a variant of it intended by Bax for another context.

Although Lean was responsible for instigating the use of the piano, it is only fair to point out that his notes reveal his original conception of a much more appropriate idea for the music in this scene. He had wanted the music for the walk through the workhouse to change to a 'more sombre note',[17] but had then come to his unfortunate conclusion that Oliver was the focal point of the scene. If he had stayed with his first intention, John Huntley would not have been compelled to write

> The piano music has been criticised as 'inappropriate', probably because the significance the director and composer were searching for has been missed; it may be therefore that Lean's original conception was the correct one.[18]

[15] John Huntley, 'The Train Now Showing', BBC Radio 4 broadcast, 11.1.1990.
[16] Huntley (1949), 115.
[17] Ibid.
[18] Ibid.

The whole attempt to highlight Oliver's isolation in a cruel world is far better illustrated in the score by Bax's use of other solo instruments and by his manipulation of Oliver's theme. Wherever the piano is involved, the cue almost invariably fails in its intended purpose. Lean, Bax and Mathieson would have done well to stop and consider why it was that so many British film composers had avoided using the piano except in those films where it was specifically featured.

Would Bax, left to his own devices, have used themes for the main narrative strands of the drama? His instinctive creative response to the subject of *Oliver Twist*, which was so repugnant to him, was to think in unexpectedly visual terms. Dickens's vivid portrayal of Victorian London low-life, and his extremes of characterization, most especially in the grotesque parody of the Jews in the person of Fagin, descends at times to the level of caricature. Because of this, Bax felt compelled to 'think up counterparts in sound of Gillray's and Rowlandson's savage cartoons'.[19] In other words, the lack of depth in Dickens's characterizations forced Bax to write his music for the film in a more illustrative way than was suitable for a man whose 'chief strength lay in the precision with which he characterized moods and soul states'.[20]

Muir Mathieson revealed something of the circumstances surrounding Bax's creation of the score when he wrote

> Sir Arnold wrote his score down in Sussex at the delightful country hotel where he lives, and I used to pay him regular visits during the ten weeks he was engaged in producing the music after he had seen the film twice in its entirety at Pinewood studios.[21]

The allocation of ten weeks to produce an original film score would have been considered a luxury by composers working in Hollywood. Such generous time-scales were rare in America. Bax was burdened by both the unfamiliarity and the uncongeniality of the task. Having seen the film twice, and 'collaborated' with Mathieson and Lean on the musical ideas, Bax would have been issued with a music cue sheet detailing the type of cues and the specific timings required. Mathieson's 'regular visits' betray a certain nervousness on the part of the musical director, who would not normally have a great deal of input at the creative stage. The real influence of the musical director was more generally seen at the later stages of production, when the composer's manuscript was prepared for recording, and at the recording sessions themselves. Bax's well-known commentary on his experience of writing the music for *Oliver Twist* has a curiously bland quality about it. It holds more than a hint of public-relations propaganda:

> Composing for the film was hard work, and I found I had to adapt my normal musical approach quite a bit; it was nevertheless an interesting experience, and I

---

[19] Arnold Bax, quoted in Parlett (1999), 257.
[20] Anthony Payne, in Sadie (ed.) (1980), ii, 309, s.v. 'Bax'.
[21] Mathieson (1948), 20.

Plate 2. Arnold Bax, centre, Muir Mathieson conducting, and Harriet Cohen at the piano in a recording session of *Oliver Twist*.

was particularly impressed by the ingenuity and skill of the musical director in the actual process of recording the music with the picture on the screen.[22]

In the light of Bax's literary accomplishments, his 'quite a bit' speaks volumes.

Despite the detailed collaboration over the music cues, and the visits paid by Mathieson during the composition of the score, many changes were made to Bax's manuscript during the recording process. Eleven of his music cues were omitted altogether from the soundtrack. Six were cut, one of them substantially, and others, as we have seen, were substituted for different cues, or repeated in different contexts. One cue was extended by repetition to synchronize with the picture.[23] The knowledge of such reconstruction does cause the observer to pause for thought before assessing the comparative musico-dramatic skills of the film composer. Once the manuscript has passed from the composer's hands, the use of his music in the film becomes the domain of the musical director and, generally to a lesser extent, the film

[22] Arnold Bax, quoted in Huntley (1949), 110.
[23] Parlett (1999), 256–63.

director. Only in exceptional cases does the composer have a controlling influence on the application of his music in the filmic context. Vaughan Williams gives a very humorous account of what can happen to a composer's best intentions for his music cues:

> You must not be horrified, if you find that a passage which you intended to portray the villain's mad revenge has been used by the musical director to illustrate the cats being driven out of the dairy. The truth is, that within limits, any music can be made to fit any situation. An ingenious and sympathetic musical director can skilfully manoeuvre a musical phrase so that it exactly synchronises with a situation which was never in the composer's mind.[24]

In the score for *Oliver Twist* we have the unusual felicity of being able to determine how Bax had intended to portray the dramatic elements of the film[25] and the extent to which his original intentions were diverted from their course.

David Lean's notes for the main titles indicate that he had no personal preconception of the nature of the music, only of how it should function in relation to the impact of the all-important transition from the end of the main titles into the first scene:

> I haven't the faintest idea what sort of music should accompany the titles, but I should like it gradually to fade away – a fade into an orchestration that suggests that something is about to happen, so that the last two titles of the screen will be in silence, and the first shot of the picture – that of dark clouds – will have a rumble of distant thunder.[26]

This suggests that Bax was allowed a free hand in the writing of the title music, but John Huntley's rather curiously worded sentence, 'The title music was eventually worked out with the two main musical ideas of the picture',[27] tends to endorse the theory that the use of themes was instigated by Lean. The two main musical ideas that Huntley refers to are distinctive themes, one associated with the locket, the other representing Oliver himself. Ten-year-old Oliver undergoes little character development during the course of the film. With the exception of two notable instances – the attack on Noah, and the defiance of Fagin – he conducts himself throughout with an astonishingly well-mannered innocence for one reared in a workhouse. His role is a reactive one, as he responds to the people and situations that impinge on him. This does not deny the possibility of developing his theme, and during the course of his adventures, the theme is rightly the one subjected to the most transformation.

By contrast, a theme which is intended to represent or interpret an inanimate object must of necessity suggest the circumstances surrounding the significance of that object. In the case of the locket, its significance is that it contains a

[24] Vaughan Williams, 'Film Music', in Huntley (1947), 179.
[25] Thanks to the work of Graham Parlett in Parlett (1999), 255–63.
[26] David Lean's working notes, quoted in Huntley (1949), 114.
[27] Huntley (1949), 114.

portrait of Oliver's mother, and hence, the clue to Oliver's true identity. The importance of this as the main plot element is indicated by its appearance at the beginning of the title music after a single bar of tremolo strings.

Example 1. The 'locket' theme, first appearance in main titles. *Oliver Twist*

The nature of this theme perfectly captures the essence of the enigmatic conditions of Oliver's birth. An unknown young woman has arrived at the workhouse at night, in the middle of a thunderstorm, and given birth to a boy before dying. In the words of the beadle, she had 'made her way here against difficulties and pain that would have killed any well-disposed woman weeks before'. The beadle has assumed that she was of lowly birth, but the expansive 'heroic' quality of the theme heard on the trumpet reveals to the audience that Oliver's lineage has more than a trace of nobility about it.

Immediately after the 'locket' theme is heard in the main titles, the theme representing Oliver makes its first appearance.

Example 2. Oliver's theme in the main titles. *Oliver Twist*

This is played on the upper strings only, which, combined with the rising and falling semitones of the first five notes, skilfully conveys Oliver's tentative and vulnerable character. The variation of the theme by extension, which starts at bar 5, looks at first sight to be a standard procedure for developing the material of an initial four-bar theme, but the triplet figure in bar 6 is one that becomes an important motivic fragment in the score. At this point the 'locket' theme takes over again, but with some subtle alterations to the intervals.

Example 3. 'Locket' theme variation in the main titles. *Oliver Twist*

This treatment of the theme by small adjustments to the intervals could be construed as a composer's whim. In fact this variant is the first indication of a parting of the ways in the use of the 'locket' theme. The original version, as heard in Example 1, stands for the enduring symbolism of the locket itself, the symbolism of Oliver's true identity. As it is not the locket which undergoes development during the course of the narrative, but the circumstances surrounding it, this variation of the theme is to become representative of the unfolding of events leading to the ultimate revelation of the secret contained in the locket. When Mrs Thingummy sees the locket round the girl's neck after her death, the music is an exact repetition of Example 1, transposed a tone higher. At this stage in the narrative, the locket is merely a static representation of Oliver's origins. There is no prospect or suggestion that the secret is to be unlocked, therefore the music represents the locket in its purely symbolic state.

After the variation of the 'locket' theme is heard in the main titles, the music is brought abruptly to a close by three string chords played pizzicato followed by a sustained string tremolo in octave unison:

> Lean's idea of 'something about to happen' and the 'last two titles on the screen in silence' eventually became incorporated in the form of a tremolo string sound that quivers through the last of the titles and acts as a bridge into the opening scenes of Oliver's mother in the storm, struggling on to the workhouse.[28]

Such simple and well-tested devices as the string tremolo are still the most effective way of solving problems of transition in dramatic terms, and of representing

---

[28] Huntley (1949), 114.

suspense, but Bax would have been justified in feeling that this was one of the occasions where he had been obliged to modify his style 'quite a bit'.

Having so effectively passed from orchestral sonority to the naturalistic sounds of a storm on the soundtrack, Lean appears to have changed his mind about the inclusion of a music cue to illustrate the storm. Bax had written seventeen pages of score for this sequence, but the cue was not used on the soundtrack. Even the most successful music depicting storms (and the orchestral repertoire has some fine examples) would sound hopelessly artificial when combined with the naturalistic sounds of a storm. Such pictorial or programmatic music can only work in the context of the imagination. It was decided, however, that one shot from this storm sequence should be high-lighted by a music cue. As the camera cuts from the shot of the young woman, revealed by a flash of lightening to be suffering the sudden intense pains of labour, to a close-up of bramble thorns against the skyline, the symbolism implied by the juxtaposition of the two shots is superbly illustrated by three chords, linked by glissandi, played on violin harmonics, extracted from the rejected storm music.

The use of this cue neatly demonstrates the aesthetic divide between British and American film scores. Although it is only 3 seconds long, the cue links the two shots, and because of that, the audience knows that it conveys the sharp pain the girl is experiencing. It is symbolic, not pictorial. Despite the fact that we see the thorns and hear the tearing glissandi simultaneously, we are aware that this is not a gratuitous musical illustration of an image on the screen. The way the music is employed here is at the opposite end of the spectrum to the 'roguish little arpeggio' used to illustrate the trickling of beer down the drinker's throat that so offended Maurice Jaubert in his condemnation of Max Steiner's music.[29]

This short cue is all that comes between the music for the main titles and the music that follows the death of Oliver's mother. The use of the 'locket' theme here and the introduction of the piano have already been discussed, but it is time to see how Oliver's theme differs from its original version:

Example 4. Variant of Oliver's theme. *Oliver Twist*

---

[29] See above, pp. 29–30.

It can be seen how confusing the use of the initial part of this theme is when taken out of its intended context. The first four bars heard on the piano bear only the most tenuous connection to the thematic outline of the original version of the main titles music. It is not until the triplet crotchets in the 7th bar that any exact intervallic correspondence occurs. Bax's own idea for this scene is far more appropriate. He had written a mournful, angular melody for the cor anglais, taken over by the flute, which bears no relation to Oliver's theme.

Example 5. Bax's original cue for Oliver carried through the workhouse.
Oliver Twist

The piano music which is used in its place is copied from the cue that Bax wrote for a later scene where Oliver decides to run away to London after his ordeal at Sowerberry's. The last four bars of Bax's original music for the workhouse scene are used for the end of the cue as Mrs Thingummy leaves the main area of the workhouse and, passing through another door, descends a bleak staircase. Here, the solo clarinet plays a variant of Oliver's theme, and it is in this version that Bax himself intended the theme to make its first appearance in the diegesis. The use of solo clarinet to carry the theme here demonstrates a far more effective way of expressing Oliver's isolation and vulnerability than was gained from using the piano. The intervals of the theme exactly follow those of its first appearance in the main titles, with the single exception of the whole-tone alternating step in the 3rd bar. At this point Mrs Thingummy and Oliver are briefly alone on the staircase, and, unlike their position in the earlier part of the scene, they are the central focus of the shot. The connection of Oliver with his theme is much easier to make.

Example 6. First variant of Oliver's theme as intended by Bax. *Oliver Twist*

Oliver's theme is not heard again until the first time Oliver as a boy is seen on the screen. It appears in a brief scene where a group of boys are scrubbing the workhouse floor. Oliver has his back to the camera, and the focus of attention is on his bare feet. This first impression of a defenceless child, at the mercy of the harsh conditions surrounding him, is perfectly conveyed by the music cue. Lasting only 12 seconds, this cue proves again how much more effectively Oliver's isolation can be expressed by the use of instruments other than the piano. Here, the plaintive quality of the solo oboe, supported by sustained upper strings, movingly portrays the abject misery of the small boy. Oliver's theme is simplified by the removal of the second and third bars. The upward semiquavers at the end of the phrase come to an abrupt stop as the music parallels the interruption to Oliver's work by the arrival of the Beadle.

Example 7. Oliver scrubbing. *Oliver Twist*

The simplicity of this cue shows that Bax had an innate understanding of one of film music's most important tenets. By the limited use of resources, the most effective dramatic interpretation can sometimes be achieved. Bax did not always keep this principle in mind during the process of composing for the film, and the occasions when he indulged in more complexity are nearly always detrimental to the cause of dramatic interpretation.

The next appearance of Oliver's theme is effective for the same reasons. A mere two bars in length, this snatch of the theme serves as an introduction to the funeral march that follows, and appears to have been added hastily to the score following a change to the sequence of cues. These two bars accompany Oliver as, dressed as a mute, he takes up his position behind the funeral cortège. The use of two solo flutes for Oliver's theme, sounding a major third apart, cleverly conveys the gentle irony behind the solemnity and pathos of the scene.

Example 8. Oliver as funeral mute. *Oliver Twist*

This same figure, again played on two solo flutes but transposed a fifth higher, is used to introduce a much longer version of Oliver's theme at its next appearance. Following his uncharacteristic attack on Noah, provoked by the latter's taunts about his mother, Oliver is thrashed and sent to bed. The two flutes accompanying his sobs serve not only to reflect the misery of the small boy, but to suggest that his time at the undertaker's has come to an end by recalling the context in which they were last heard. As Oliver resolves to leave Sowerberry's and escapes by night, the piano makes what Bax intended to be its first appearance on the soundtrack. Instead of entering with the rather misleading variant of Oliver's theme heard in Example 4, the first six notes of the piano are the same as those of the first flute part at the beginning of the cue. The piano is thus introduced quite naturally with a repetition of material, and accompanied by pizzicato strings. This is very different from the sudden 'dropping in' of the solo piano in the middle of an orchestral cue which Bax never intended.

Oliver's theme is not heard for some time at the start of his new life in London. Through Oliver's initial encounters with the Artful Dodger, Fagin and the other characters who have such a profound impact on his destiny, Bax introduces other themes relating to the alteration in his circumstances. It is not until Oliver faints in court after he has been wrongly accused of stealing from Mr Brownlow that the first two bars of his theme are used, this time played on solo bass clarinet. The tone-colour of this instrument, and the downward glissando of the cello which takes over from it, express in the most obvious terms the faintness and nausea experienced by Oliver. But the use of his theme at this point suggests that, as he temporarily escapes from his circumstances, he also escapes from the influences that have prevented him from being true to himself.

When Oliver recovers from his illness, he finds himself in a totally new environment. He has been cared for at the home of Mr Brownlow in luxurious surroundings. Whereas he has hitherto known only harshness and privation, now all about him is kindness and comfort. The opening music for the scene where the housekeeper Mrs Bedwin darns by the fire while Oliver sleeps is purely atmospheric, the strings being accompanied by rippling hypnotic figurations on the piano. Oliver is for the first time safe and at peace, as symbolized by the piano. As Mr Brownlow enters the room with his friend to look at Oliver, the piano takes up another variant of Oliver's theme.

Example 9. Variant of Oliver's theme. Oliver at Mr Brownlow's. *Oliver Twist*

The theme has been transformed by rhythmic variation to suggest the change from hesitancy to a sense of security in Oliver's life. The loss of the alternating semitones also implies the removal of anxiety. As Oliver wakes up to find Mrs Bedwin at his bedside he experiences the first gestures of physical affection he has received from any human being as she smoothes his hair and touches his cheek. Bax very cleverly takes the version of Oliver's theme used for the scrubbing of the workhouse floor, and by transferring it to the strings, and extending it, successfully shows how Oliver's experience of his life as a cruel and lonely existence had been transformed by his first exposure to love.

Example 10. Oliver and Mrs Bedwin. *Oliver Twist*

This time the semiquavers, instead of being interrupted, as they were in the scrubbing scene by the appearance of the Beadle, coincide with the moment on the screen when Oliver throws himself into Mrs Bedwin's arms. The semiquavers move on to the second half of the phrase, incorporating a further modification to Oliver's theme, which now reaches up, heightening the emotional intensity of the scene. The music breaks off as Mr Brownlow enters the room. Although he is deeply moved by what he has witnessed of the scene, Mr Brownlow hides his feelings by pretending to have a cold. This truly British reaction is most aptly highlighted by the sudden cessation of music on the soundtrack.

There is one instance in the score where Bax uses its two major musical themes in the same cue to carry information to the audience about the unfolding of the plot in a way that comes close to the combining of themes in a Hollywood score. In this scene, Mr Brownlow is in his library having an important discussion with Oliver about the future. This is the first and only time that Oliver's theme is used during a dialogue scene. All other occasions of its use, with the exception of the main titles, have shown Oliver as a helpless pawn in the hands of others. Whether the theme has been used to interpret Oliver's situation as he scrubs the floor, or acts as a funeral mute, or steals away from the Sowerberrys, or faints in court, all the music cues have tended to the same purpose. Even when Oliver hugs Mrs Bedwin, the use of the cue is serving that purpose because we are merely seeing him react to a more pleasant situation. In the library scene, Oliver is enjoying his first adult conversation in the film. As Mr Brownlow finishes uttering the words: 'I find myself more interested in your behalf than I can well account for, even to myself', Oliver's theme steals onto the soundtrack.

Example 11. Oliver's theme. Oliver and Mr Brownlow in the library.
Oliver Twist

The theme is only heard for one bar before the strings take up free material. but during that one bar, Oliver turns his head – almost as though compelled by the music – to look at the portrait of a young woman, hanging hitherto unnoticed on the wall. The free material continues as Mr Brownlow asks Oliver if he likes pictures, but as he goes on to say: 'Now that is a portrait, a likeness', on the word 'likeness' the 'locket' theme is introduced. This is a key moment in the film, when the audience realizes that Oliver has unwittingly found his way to his rightful home. Mr Brownlow does not yet understand why he is so drawn to Oliver, but the two themes, played for the only time in the diegesis in the same cue, have assisted the audience in coming to that understanding.

The next use of Oliver's theme in the context of the drama also escapes from the norm established by its previous appearances. Oliver himself is absent from the scene, having been sent on an errand from which, as the audience already knows, he cannot return. The Brownlow household is not yet expressing overt anxiety. As the scene opens, Mr Brownlow is playing chess with his friend. There is no music. It is not until Mrs Bedwin enters the room that the music cue begins with Oliver's theme played softly on the violins.

Example 12. Oliver's theme in Oliver's absence, part 1. *Oliver Twist*

The audience immediately knows that Mrs Bedwin is concerned for Oliver. Without the appearance of the theme here, this silent scene could be interpreted in several different ways. As Mrs Bedwin clears the cups from the table, leaving only Oliver's meal visible in the shot, the music cue is taken over by the sound of the piano.

Example 13. Oliver's theme in Oliver's absence, part 2. *Oliver Twist*

This variant of the theme is derived from the one heard when Mrs Bedwin was keeping watch over Oliver during his illness (Example 9). The transition from the original version of the theme to this variant mirrors the transition from the concern Mrs Bedwin feels for Oliver to the more practical care she demonstrates by leaving his food on the table for him. The juxtaposition of this version of Oliver's theme with the shot of his place at the table does not simply and gratuitously highlight the fact that Oliver is absent, it also speaks of the trust that Mrs Bedwin has in him, and the care she extends to him.

After Oliver's abduction, the emphasis of the drama shifts to the network of relationships that exist between Nancy, Fagin, Sikes and the Dodger. Oliver's role increasingly becomes that of an object over which infinitely stronger characters do battle. It is in this context that the final, and most uncharacteristic version of Oliver's theme makes its appearance in the diegesis, and we will examine it when the context is discussed.

The other major musical theme, that associated with the locket, has almost as much weight in the score as has Oliver's theme. After the scene in which Mrs Thingummy sees the locket on the dead girl's neck, where the music is an exact repetition, a tone higher, of its first appearance in the main titles, the following scenes relating to the locket are increasingly concerned with the revelation of the secret it carries. When Mrs Thingummy appears at Sowerberry's and enters the shop while Noah scrubs the floor, the music cue reveals that she has come on business relating to the locket.

Example 14. The 'locket' theme. Mrs Thingummy and Noah. *Oliver Twist*

Again, Bax uses the simplest means to convey a strong dramatic point. The change of the fourth interval from a minor third to a minor second, combined with the mournful timbre of the solo cor anglais in low register, instead of the upper register of the trumpet, is enough to transform the theme from its original version into something very different. Not until the 10th bar does Mrs Thingummy speak the words, 'I want to see the boy. I knew his mother', but the urgency of her mission, the overwhelming impression that there is a tale that must be told, even the burden of her guilt, are all implied by the music.

As she lies on her deathbed in the workhouse, Mrs Thingummy begins to tell the matron what happened on the night that Oliver's mother died. The truth about the secret contained in the locket is about to be revealed. Bax continues to use the transformed version of the 'locket' theme, as first heard when Mrs Thingummy began her quest to reveal the truth (Example 14). Bax intersperses two-bar sections of the theme with meandering tremolo string lines. The music has the effect of mirroring the state of the querulous old woman as she slips in and out of coherence. What transpires between Mrs Thingummy and the matron is withheld from the audience until much later in the film. In the scene where the matron recounts the episode of Mrs Thingummy's death to Monks, who has a personal interest in the outcome, a flashback to the deathbed scene shows what really took place between the two women. Not too unexpectedly, the music is the same as that used in the original deathbed scene. With cuts to the bars containing the string passages that were heard in the previous cue, the 'locket' theme is repeated more insistently. Ironically, Mrs Thingummy dies before she can release the secret she has been keeping for so long. It is the piece of paper clasped in her hand that provides the clue. As it falls from the dead woman's hand, a snatch of the 'locket' theme is heard.

Example 15. The 'locket' theme. Discovering the piece of paper. *Oliver Twist*

The theme has been transformed into something barely recognizable from the noble trumpet phrase of the main titles. The tiny scrap of paper is the pawn ticket needed to redeem the locket that was entrusted to Mrs Thingummy by Oliver's mother. At last the truth about Oliver's identity has begun to emerge. As Monks opens the locket, which the matron has passed to him following her account of the story, its theme is heard on solo muted trumpet. Using a theme at this point when the associated object is in close up on the screen might seem to smack of the worst type of Hollywood banality. This would be true if Bax had used the same cue as that for the moment when the locket is seen on the dead girl's neck. In fact the locket has not been seen since that occasion, and the four subsequent music cues incorporating the 'locket' theme have all been concerned with the symbolism of the locket. At the moment that Monks opens the locket, and the portrait of Oliver's mother is seen inside, the first piece of the puzzle falls into place, and it is the 'revelation' variant of the 'locket' theme that is played.

The final appearance of the 'locket' theme in the diegesis occurs in the scene between Oliver and Mr Brownlow in the library. The association has now been made between the 'locket/revelation' theme and the portrait of Oliver's mother inside the locket. When Oliver sees the original portrait on the library wall, and the theme is heard again, the last connection is made for the audience. Oliver's theme and the 'locket' theme have progressed separately through the score, only coming together at the moment of revelation. As if to signify their blending, both themes are played on two solo clarinets, a tone colour not previously associated with either of them.

Bax's handling of the two major themes in his score demonstrates a natural empathy with the dramatic intentions of the film. He never falls into the trap of gratuitous labelling or signposting, except in the one instance which we know is attributable to Lean. His instrumentation, when not hampered by the use of the piano, is most effective in its interpretation of the dramatic nuances. Curiously enough, for a composer who is renowned for his skilled orchestrations, Bax's music is far less effective in dramatic terms in those parts of the film where his natural style was less constrained. There are various scenes where the music cues required could almost be regarded as set pieces, because the plot calls for an action sequence which appears to stand apart from the drama itself. In the film, these action sequences have an unmistakably stagey quality about them. It is as if the whole cinematic imperative has been turned on its head. The opportunities for physical movement provided by such scenes as Oliver's fight with Noah, the chase, and, worst of all, the first pickpocketing lesson, all seem like embarrassingly contrived time out from the real 'action' of the film. Some of the blame may be laid at Bax's door. The orchestration of the music cues is all too elaborate, the music itself is too 'busy', and, most damagingly, the timing is wrong. To see the first pickpocketing lesson without the soundtrack is to see how Bax, electing to play up the comedy of the scene by writing a skittish frolic, has misjudged the pace entirely. Without the somewhat frenetic music cue, the scene is revealed to be measured, stealthy, menacing. Oliver may laugh uproariously at the charade, but the music denies the underlying darkness that motivates the scene. Mistiming has led to a false representation of dramatic intention. All these are, however, the miscalculations of a novice in the art of film scoring. Bax viewed the film only twice. He did not have the advantage enjoyed by present-day composers, who can watch a sequence repeatedly, until its internal rhythm is grasped.

In addition to the two major themes of the score, there are a number of other themes that serve to represent people or situations. The most easily identifiable of these was never intended by Bax to act as a leitmotif, and the way it is used in the film does him a great disservice. In the film, the Beadle is twice seen walking towards Sowerberry's. On the first occasion, he is taking Oliver there to start his apprenticeship. On the second, he has been summoned by Sowerberry following Oliver's fight with Noah. He is striding purposefully, swishing his cane in anticipation of Oliver's punishment. The music that Bax wrote for this cue perfectly matches the mood of a man roused to self-important indignation.

Example 16. The Beadle's purposeful walk to Sowerberry's. *Oliver Twist*

Arnold Bax, *Oliver Twist*. Music by Arnold Bax. © 1947 Chappell Music Ltd, London W6 8BS. Reproduced by permission of IMP Ltd. All rights reserved.

Bax was not trying to establish any connection between this music and the Beadle himself, merely with the mood he was experiencing at the time. Unfortunately for Bax, the music he wrote for the previous cue, where the Beadle is simply accompanying Oliver to his new employer, was rejected in favour of this same cue. This decision must have been taken at the recording sessions, for the music has been re-recorded at a slower tempo to synchronize with the first eight steps of the Beadle. For a number of different reasons, this is an unfair misuse of Bax's music. To synchronize music with the steps of a man who is merely walking from A to B is to fall into the trap of musical redundancy. Gerald Cockshott had written on this subject only a year before the production of *Oliver Twist*. In his example of the soldiers marching being synchronized by the music he goes on to explain:

> A mere march tune would be a useless addition to the visual image and the natural sound of tramping feet, whereas a piece of music in march time expressive of the mood of victory or defeat would heighten, perhaps determine, the spectator's reaction to the scene.[30]

Bax's music for the purposeful walk to Sowerberry's was justifiable because it was also interpretative. To use that same music for the first walk was a double offence. Because the music synchronizes with the Beadle's steps, he becomes the focus of attention. If this scene is viewed without the soundtrack, an extra-

[30] Cockshott (1947), 2.

ordinary thing happens. The whole scene takes on a different emphasis. Instead of the Beadle dominating the screen, it is the atmosphere of the setting, with its dark, deserted street, which takes precedence. Without the attention being brought to bear on the rhythm of the Beadle's walk, the pace of the scene becomes slower. It is particularly unfortunate for Bax that the cue itself, the only nondiegetic music associated with the Beadle, and so apt for its original use, should be one so easily recognized, and that it should be used in such ostensibly similar contexts. It leads the unsuspecting viewer to the conclusion the Bax is guilty of demonstrating a deplorable lack of subtlety.

On other occasions in the score, Bax does use thematic material to make associations in the plot. In the music for the sequences where the Dodger takes Oliver to Fagin's den, the opening bars are interrupted twice by rolls on the xylophone and bass drum.

Example 17. The Dodger takes Oliver to Fagin's den (first six bars).
Oliver Twist

This purely visual sequence is served by one of Bax's most successful music cues in the film. Here, Bax achieves a gradually increasing intensity which perfectly coincides with the pacing of the scene, as the two boys rush up flight after flight of stairs. Half way through the cue, a thematic fragment, which is used as a motif in its own right at the end of the film, makes its first appearance.

Example 18. Crime motif. *Oliver Twist*

Heard in this context, it is an integral part of the cue, and there is little indication that it will later play a more important role. The overall effect of this cue, as the boys climb to the top of the building, is extremely sinister. The alternation of bars dominated by the semitone with those based on the whole-tone scale, and the very dark orchestration, including muted brass, tremolo strings and solo percussion, give an overwhelming impression of menace. It is not until the boys reach the bridge across the buildings, and see the spectacular view of the roofs of London, that the music bursts into triumphal diatonic harmony scored for full orchestra. The audience has been warned by the earlier part of the cue that Oliver faces danger, although he has been willing to go with the Dodger. Later in the film, when Oliver is again brought to Fagin, the change in the circumstances is brilliantly conveyed in the score. This time Oliver is being forcibly dragged back to Fagin. The music for the ascent to Fagin's den is used again, without the triumphant ending, and with some repetitions to time the cue to the action, but Bax makes a subtle change to the original. In place of the solo percussion bars which interrupted the brass phrases (Example 17), Bax introduces tumultuous interjections on the piano, based on another variant of Oliver's theme.

Example 19. Oliver's theme as Oliver is dragged to Fagin. *Oliver Twist*

The theme is barely recognizable in this treatment, with its strong chords and furious semiquaver decorations. The juxtaposition of this version of Oliver's theme with the menacing theme associated with Fagin accentuates Oliver's angry resistance to the circumstances in which he previously acquiesced. Oliver displays a fair amount of spirit in this scene. He is no longer content to accept the treatment he receives from others without question, and the music cue reflects his defiance of Fagin. Although, much earlier in the film, Oliver had reacted angrily to Noah's taunts about his mother, the music for the ensuing fight scene does not contain his theme, because he has reacted automatically, as any small boy would. When Oliver defies Fagin, however, it is because he knows he can no longer simply trust without discrimination. This final treatment of Oliver's theme signifies the way in which his ingenuousness has been tempered by experience.

The thematic fragment that appears in the middle of these two cues (Example 18) becomes a motif associated with the criminal activities of Fagin and his companions. When it is used for the sequence depicting the posting of the 'wanted' notices after Mr Brownlow has revealed their names to the police, the 'crime' motif alternates with a three-part trumpet fanfare suggesting a summoning to justice.

Example 20. Posting the 'wanted' notices. *Oliver Twist*

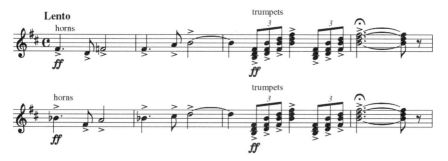

This suggestion is borne out when the fanfare is used to herald the finale. As the crowd throw their hats in the air in jubilation at the rescue of Oliver, the minor key of the fanfare takes on a more triumphant air, but Oliver's rescue has been effected through the death of Sikes, and it is the sense of justice which predominates.

Bax uses the same technique of taking a section from the middle of a substantial cue to create an associated motif. In the first pickpocketing lesson, which begins with a light orchestration of upper woodwind and strings, a more boisterous section is introduced by the horns, playing fortissimo in unison. This vigorous theme is connected with Fagin's boys, and with their cynical attitude to crime.

Example 21. Theme for Fagin's boys. *Oliver Twist*

Bax cleverly uses this theme to demonstrate Oliver's ignorance of the real meaning of the pickpocketing lesson. When Oliver is alone with Fagin, he is encouraged to take a handkerchief without being noticed. The ironic disparity between Oliver's innocent eagerness to succeed, and the Dodger's casual expertise, is humorously communicated by the use of a solo bassoon in place of the horn section. The last appearance of this theme is in the cue for the evacuation of Fagin's den. The boys act swiftly to remove evidence of their occupation of the den. The theme is separated from its pickpocketing context, dealing only with the plight of the boys themselves, who, through dint of circumstance, are old before their time. In complete contrast to its previous gentle instrumentation, the cue is played on horns, trumpets and strings, over repeated aggressive chords on the trombones. By this treatment, all trace of humour is removed from the theme.

The last theme of the score which has some identifiable association with a dramatic theme of the plot comes late in the film and makes only two appearances. By now Bax was running short of time, and he resorted to a time-honoured trick of film composers working under pressure. He lifted the melody from his orchestral work *In Memoriam* dating back to 1916[31] for the finale and for the 'Dawn' theme. This practice, while it may elicit some sympathy, can create problems. In this instance the time gap poses questions of stylistic consistency. Although many of the music cues in *Oliver Twist* are simple in the sense of being uncomplex, none of them have quite the same straight-forwardness of melodic progression as found in this one. There is an unmistakably Edwardian flavour to it, with a ghostly impression of the famous Elgar 'tread'.

Example 22. 'Dawn' (First twelve bars). *Oliver Twist*

This cue had the working title 'dawn', as it is heard as the first light appears on the morning following Nancy's murder at the hands of Sikes. In the beginning of the scene, various shots depicting the dawn coming up over London show how welcome the morning light is for those going about their everyday business. The musical theme is both serene and noble until the

---

moment in the action where the curtains blowing into Sikes's room alert him to the fact that morning has come, and with it the possibility of discovery. The music changes to a haunting figure on tremolo strings, taken over by the brass, as Sikes strides over to the curtains and closes them abruptly, on the last note of the cue.

Example 23. 'Dawn' (End of cue). *Oliver Twist*

The music in this single cue had conveyed the transition from the normal world to the madness of Sikes's world. In the cue that follows, Bax uses the string tremolo figure as a backdrop to illustrate Sikes's state of mind as he hallucinates that Nancy and Fagin come and speak to him. That the two cues both use this figure does not grant it the status of a theme, as both occur in the same scene and the same context, and the figure never recurs.

The music used for the dawn sequence *can* be regarded as a theme, as it has an association that connects the two different contexts in which it is found. Immediately following the beginning of the finale, with its extended version of the triumphant trumpet fanfare, the 'dawn' theme is heard again as Mr Brownlow walks hand-in-hand with Oliver back to their home. The symbolism of dawn as restoration after the darkness of night is paralleled by Oliver's restoration to his rightful place after the ordeals he has faced. As the end titles appear on the screen, Oliver's theme and the 'locket' theme are heard again, before the 'dawn' theme brings the finale to a triumphant conclusion.

Considering that it was his first venture into the hazards of composing for feature films, the score for *Oliver Twist* demonstrates that Bax had a natural feeling for drama, especially given his personal antipathy for the subject-matter of this particular story. Perhaps the main criticism to be levelled against him is that, in overwriting for some of the action sequences, he emphasized their separation from the main flow of the drama.

It is not without significance that these cues all appear in the concert suite concocted from the score by Mathieson. There is a case for arguing the opinion that a film score which always puts the dramatic needs of the picture first would be unlikely to make a viable concert suite. Certainly, where Bax is most effective in his musical interpretation of the drama, notably in his treatment of themes, the resulting cues could not be said to constitute music that justifies an existence outside its context.

This is the dilemma for the 'serious' composer. Writing music that success-fully interprets the sometimes fleeting nuances of filmic diegesis yields little in the way of intrinsically musical satisfaction. For a composer whose main concern is to serve the drama, the rewards are to be found in achieving that end.

6. Three other first attempts at feature-film scoring: *49th Parallel*, *The Halfway House* and *Blue Scar*

The extent to which Bax succeeded in composing a score which served the dramatic needs of the film *Oliver Twist* can be gauged by comparing the achievements of other British composers faced with the challenge of writing for their first feature film. A number of concert composers had been drawn into the world of film during the 1930s. Most of these had been introduced to the medium by writing for documentary film, which gave scope for a rather freer hand than feature film. Alwyn, Britten, Easdale, Frankel and Rawsthorne had all written for documentary before moving on to feature films, or in Britten's case the single feature film, *Love from a Stranger*, in 1937. Even Holst wrote a score in 1931 for *The Bells*, a film which is, regrettably, lost. The comments of the recording engineer for this film give some indication of the loss to British film music occasioned by Holst's death. The man who 'showed a remarkable and speedy insight into the requirements of music for the screen'[1] died just before the British film score came into its own.

Three established composers in Britain each began their film careers in the 1930s by writing a score for a feature film, without the benefit of first working in documentary film, and with varying degrees of satisfaction. When he wrote the score for *Things to Come*, Bliss had enjoyed the best conditions that could be offered to a composer – major artistic input at an early stage, true collaboration with the director, and seemingly unlimited funds. By contrast, Walton's first experience with the film *Escape Me Never* in 1935 was a far from happy one. Years later he described how this early attempt at film scoring 'nearly drove me into a lunatic asylum'.[2] Such a discouraging start did nothing to daunt the spirit of the man who was to become, in the opinion of many, the finest composer for film in Britain. The third composer who began writing for feature film at this time was the Australian-born Arthur Benjamin, who, although he himself had little inclination for film composition, is significant for the part he played in introducing Vaughan Williams to it. In the opening paragraph of his well-known article on film music, Vaughan Williams describes the sequence of events:

[1] Huntley (1947), 208.
[2] William Walton, in 'A Portrait of Sir William Walton', BBC Radio 3 broadcast, 4.6.1977, in Tierney (1984).

Some years ago I happened to say to Arthur Benjamin that I should like to have a shot at writing for the films. He seemed surprised and shocked that I should wish to attempt anything which required so much skill and gained so little artistic reward. However, he mentioned my curious wish to Muir Mathieson, whom, at that time, I hardly knew, though we have since become firm friends. The result was that one Saturday evening I had a telephone call asking me to write some film music. When I asked how long I could have, the answer was 'till Wednesday'.[3]

In this rather haphazard fashion, the leading British composer of the day entered the arena of film scoring. It is unclear whether Mathieson was referring to *49th Parallel*, the feature film which was to become Vaughan Williams's first attempt, or whether he had some documentary in mind. Either way, Vaughan Williams was the first of a handful of British composers in the 1940s who tackled a feature film without the experience of writing for documentary.

The nature and subject-matter of *49th Parallel* place it in a completely different category from *Oliver Twist*. By 1941, when the film was released, its creators, Michael Powell and Emeric Pressburger, were just emerging as the *enfants terribles* of the British film industry. Under the umbrella of the Rank

Plate 3. Michael Powell, Muir Mathieson conducting, and Ralph Vaughan Williams at a recording session of *49th Parallel*.

[3] Vaughan Williams, 'Film Music', in Huntley (1947), 177.

organization, they were nevertheless effectively independent film producers with a unique approach to the art. While it is unwise to make generalizations about their diverse output, their films share certain characteristics that distinguish them from the standard British product. They have a distinctively allegorical, other-worldly quality to them. There is often a deliberate attempt to avoid naturalism. The techniques of film production create endless possibilities for the use of symbolism, and to aspire to realism was considered by Powell and Pressburger to be a squandering of those resources. The standard of their films is far from even, but their two masterpieces, *Black Narcissus* and *The Red Shoes* are generally regarded as being among the finest films produced by any country.

49th Parallel, if not a cinematic masterpiece, is a powerful and unusual film, and was the biggest box-office success of 1941. Emeric Pressburger wrote the original story, which won an Academy Award. It tells of a group of German submariners, stranded on the shores of Hudson Bay when their U-boat is blown up, who try to make their way through Canada to escape back to Germany. During the course of the film, their numbers gradually dwindle until only one remains. The subject-matter of the film is the men's various encounters on their journey with groups or individuals, but the real *idée fixe* is that the people of a country like Canada could never be seduced by the Nazi dream of racial supremacy. This is peculiarly hard to illuminate in musical terms. Even the main dramatic tenets of *The Winslow Boy* and *The Fallen Idol* are easier to grasp and to convey. It is almost impossible to write a theme that adequately suggests the resistance of a free democracy to the fanatical delusions of Nazism. No wonder Vaughan Williams retreated into the adoption for the main titles of a broad extended melody that could have been used to cover any number of eventualities.

Example 1. Theme from the main titles music for *49th Parallel*

Ralph Vaughan Williams, *Prelude 49th Parallel* © Oxford University Press 1960. Extract reproduced by permission.

The story of *49th Parallel* has nothing like the tight construction and development found in *Oliver Twist*. The plot lines of Dickens's novel are skilfully unfolded in the film, never allowing it to sag. The difficulty with the screenplay was the plethora of dramatic material, and its shaping into something cohesive in cinematic terms. By contrast *49th Parallel* has very little continuing storyline. The Germans encounter different people on their journey, and leave them behind without a backward glance. In this respect the film has the same lack of integrated dramatic purpose as a six-part serial. For this reason, there is little dramatic shaping to the film and very little build-up of tension. These factors make the film intrinsically less suitable for musical treatment, and it is not surprising to find that whereas *Oliver Twist*, lasting 116 minutes, has a score totalling 44 minutes, *49th Parallel*, slightly longer at 123 minutes, has less than half that amount of music.

The main titles theme is not used at all during the film proper, and is not heard again until the end titles, so it does not serve the customary purpose of main titles music of advising the audience about the principal dramatic threads of the forthcoming diegesis. There is no hint in this music of the threat posed by the Nazis, or of their confrontations with a people possessing a very different ideology. As far as dramatic interpretation goes, this theme could be said to suggest the expansiveness of the landscape and people of Canada. Because the theme itself is so expansive, it would be extremely difficult to use motivically. It does not have the required brevity and simplicity needed to render it suitable for any kind of encoding.

Certain features of the main titles theme align it with the more lyrical themes of Hollywood main titles music, as exemplified by Max Steiner. With the exception of the C sharp in bar 6 it is entirely diatonic. Approximately half of the melodic progression is by step. Diatonic stepwise melodies were the fingerprint of a Steiner melody, and yet this extended theme is unmistakably English. The first eight notes, with the three reiterations of the opening B, the repeated major second below, and the hesitant return to the B via a quaver G, are in contrast to the generally wider-ranging themes that are associated with American films. As the melodic range opens out from the ninth note, Vaughan Williams introduces the triplet crotchet rhythm, a feature prominent in the development of Bax's theme for Oliver, and one which has haunted the broader themes of many English composers.

49th Parallel has frequently been described as a semi-documentary film. The transition from the main titles to the opening scene of a film is of crucial importance in establishing the intentions of its director. David Lean had been particularly concerned with this transition in *Oliver Twist*, and rightly so, as a miscalculation at this point can seriously undermine the picture. The main titles of *49th Parallel* are superimposed onto shots of the snow-covered mountains of Canada. The final chord of the main titles music is still fading as the octave unison string tremolo of the music for the opening scene introduces a close-up of a globe showing the map of Canada and the United States. The clue is thrown out immediately that the main concern is not with the dramatic imperatives of the film, but with its message. To reinforce this, the first words heard on the soundtrack are not those of one of the characters, but are delivered by an unseen narrator in the authoritative, paternalistic tones typical of a BBC broadcaster of the day: 'I see a long straight line athwart a continent . . . the 49th Parallel, the only undefended frontier in the world.' The audience have been warned that they are about to be educated as they witness a heavy piece of anti-Nazi propaganda disguised as a feature film.

The documentary nature of the film continues with a brief scenic tour of Canada, depicting mountains, wheat fields, a city, and lakes. Vaughan Williams illustrates these changing scenes in the score, portraying them by high glacial string chords, a calm rustic melody on the oboe, energetic chords in the brass, and a stately melody on upper strings. The first of these is the most interesting. Although the main titles music had coincided with shots of the mountains, it had obviously not been intended to illustrate them. This cue is, therefore, Vaughan Williams's first attempt at musically interpreting a screen image. The violin melody, with its slow-moving tremolo figure is a forerunner of his response to the image of the south pole in his score for *Scott of the Antarctic.*

Example 2. Theme for the mountains of Canada. *49th Parallel*

Ralph Vaughan Williams, *49th Parallel.* Reproduced by the kind permission of RVW Ltd.

The dramatic action of the film begins with the surfacing of the U-boat into the bay of St Lawrence after it has attacked a neutral ship. As the submarine is seen emerging from the water, Vaughan Williams uses the simplest motivic fragment, three repeated notes followed by a falling fourth. The following five bars of the cue reveal the source of this four-note motif. Vaughan Williams used Luther's *Ein feste Burg ist unser Gott* to represent the German characters in the film.

Example 3. The U-boat surfaces. *49th Parallel*

Ralph Vaughan Williams, *49th Parallel.* Reproduced by the kind permission of RVW Ltd.

After this initial cue, the four-note motif is used independently from the descending diatonic steps which form the secondary motif. The four-note motif, which represents the brutal Nazi regime, is heard twice more. To indicate the rapid spread of the news of the attack, a montage of Morse code signalling, operation rooms, telegrams and maps is shown, accompanied by urgent music dominated by the xylophone. In the middle of this cue, the 'Nazi' motif is played fortissimo on trumpets, indicating that it is the might of Germany which has caused all the agitated bustle.

In its last appearance, the motif is put to very subtle use. It is not radically transformed or developed in itself, but it is the context of its use which demonstrates a keen dramatic sense on the part of Vaughan Williams. The leader of the Germans, Hirth, is a fanatical Nazi, but it is the clever use of this motif that informs the audience of his doubts concerning other members of his group. He witnesses the previously blameless Vogel crossing himself at the death of a comrade. An innocuous horn melody suggesting the regret of the comrade's loss is interrupted by a strident rendering of the motif on trombones as Hirth stares at Vogel. The use of the motif communicates the suspicion aroused in Hirth that Vogel is not a true Nazi, and without its use, the audience would not have been made aware of the significance of Vogel's instinctive response.

The second motif associated with the Germans relates to their interaction with the environs of the country of Canada. After its use in the first cue where the U-boat emerges, the intervals are changed at subsequent appearances to reflect the changing circumstances. When the U-boat is under threat from icebergs, the motif still begins on E flat in the trombones, but moves down in whole tones to A natural. The rhythm also reflects increased urgency, being changed to triplet quavers followed by a minim. As the U-boat moves into calm waters and the passage into the bay is sighted, the transition from a situation of danger to one of safety is intimated by the changing instrumentation, to solo flute followed by solo clarinet, and the omission of the fourth note.

This shortened version of the motif, with the intervals as they were in its first appearance, is used twice more to form two very simple cues. As the U-boat approaches land and the Germans discuss strategy, the motif, transposed up a semitone, is repeatedly played on violins. In another short scene where the Germans are on a hill looking down at the trading station through binoculars, the motif is tellingly used to indicate their stealth and the threat they pose to the locality. The strings play alone without vibrato, producing a very unpleasant edgy sound that perfectly captures the atmosphere of the scene. This writing is particularly effective because the soundtrack offers no distracting natural sounds, and the strings are heard in isolation – a rarity in British film scores of the period.

Example 4. The Germans spy on the trading station. *49th Parallel*

Ralph Vaughan Williams, *49th Parallel*. Reproduced by the kind permission of RVW Ltd.

This three-note version of the motif is used in an extended form three times in the score as the Germans make their way across Canada. Changes to the instrumentation on each of these occasions shows the men's increasing desperation. As the four remaining men walk towards a Hutterite farm, the extended version of the motif is played pizzicato on violins.

Example 5. Walking towards the Hutterite farm. *49th Parallel*

Ralph Vaughan Williams, *49th Parallel*. Reproduced by the kind permission of RVW Ltd.

The last four notes are, of course, the whole-tone version of the original motif. Heard in this light instrumentation, there is still a faint suggestion of optimism. After the execution of Vogel, however, as the three set off on their journey to Winnipeg, the motif is played on pizzicato cello and with bassoon an octave lower, increasing the impression of heaviness. The last time the motif is heard in this form, the men have decided to walk the entire distance to Vancouver, 'Two thousand kilometres is plenty of kilometres.' This time the pizzicato cellos are doubled on muted trombone and tuba, suggesting the enormous physical drudgery of the journey.

The motif appears for the last time in its original four-note version as the last two men flee from Vancouver after the capture of their comrade. At the end of a perfectly adequate 'escape music' cue, which contains no related material, the four-note motif is played fortissimo on strings, woodwind and brass as the men fall exhausted to the ground. This is the only time the motif has been played by these three sections of the orchestra together, symbolizing the might of Germany brought under the most intense pressure.

One of the main dramatic ideas of the film is that on their journey the Germans encounter four different men who all express their opposition to Nazi ideology. For these parts Powell and Pressburger brought in four contemporary screen idols: Laurence Olivier, Anton Walbrook, Leslie Howard and Raymond Massey. This has the unfortunate effect of reducing their contributions to cameo interludes. Their characters are differentiated chiefly through their racial origins: Olivier plays an unconvincing French-Canadian trapper,

Walbrook a Hutterite settler of German extraction, Howard a visiting Englishman, and Massey a 'genuine' Canadian. All four, in their different ways, defend the personal freedom that can be enjoyed in a democracy. Three of them appear in what amounts to only a single extended scene, so there is very little opportunity or justification to attach a musical motif to them. Unfortunately, this does not prevent Vaughan Williams from using a most basic labelling device in the section featuring Olivier. The manager of the Hudson Bay trading station, returning in his canoe, notices that a visiting trapper has arrived in his absence. As he walks up the jetty to his cabin to discover who it is, Vaughan Williams very kindly gives the audience a clue to the trapper's identity in the music cue.

Example 6. Johnny's theme. *49th Parallel*

Ralph Vaughan Williams, *49th Parallel.* Reproduced by the kind permission of RVW Ltd.

The use of this French-Canadian traditional song for the cue probably results from the fact that it is used later as a diegetic music cue, when Johnny's singing from the bath informs the manager of his unexpected guest's identity. However, it seems unnecessary to prime the audience in this way.

The other three men encountered by the Germans have no theme directly attached to them. The episode with the Hutterites is the most involved, and dramatically the most important. Here, the Nazi ideology is challenged by the beliefs of a whole community. Their simple, hardworking way of life is symbolized by the wheatfields. Vaughan Williams uses a lilting, rustic theme on the oboe to accompany the first shot of the wheatfields.

Example 7. The wheatfields of the Hutterites. *49th Parallel*

Ralph Vaughan Williams, *49th Parallel.* Reproduced by the kind permission of RVW Ltd.

This same theme is used for a conversation between the leader of the Hutterites, Peter, played by Walbrook, and Andreas, another member of the community. They are standing in the wheatfields initially discussing the farm's produce, so the use of the theme is appropriate. However, as the conversation turns to darker things – the internment of their friends, and the attack of the Germans – no attempt is made to follow the changing tone of the conversation in the music. There is no question of interpreting the dialogue with the music, which would be the first objective of a composer such as Steiner. Vaughan Williams merely introduces a timpani roll just before the conversation turns to the impending storm – a far from subtle illustrative technique.

The Englishman and the Canadian have no music attached directly to them. The only music cue between the last nondiegetic cue and the end titles, a gap of nearly 32 minutes, is a rather curious diegetic cue which begins as the Germans approach the Englishman's camp. A solo piano is heard rippling softly. At first this seems to match the tranquil mood of the scene, as the Englishman fishes in the lake from his canoe and discusses with the Germans his detachment from the war. However, the cue continues for over 4 minutes through a number of dialogues until the implied source of the music – a radio in the tepee – is briefly shown on the screen. As a diegetic cue, this is a confusingly empathetic one.

Although the film is something of an oddity, *49th Parallel* was in certain respects a suitable choice for Vaughan Williams's introduction to film composing. Only a very small proportion of the dialogue scenes are scored, and none of them in anything but the most impressionistic terms. The subject-matter of the dialogue has much to do with it. Anton Walbrook's impeccably delivered 3-minute denunciation of Nazi ideology, one of the longest non-Shakespearean monologues in mainstream cinema of the time, simply could not be enhanced by any conceivable method of scoring. The majority of the important dialogues take place between people who do not share a first language, and consequently there is little actual conversation, merely exchange of information. At the same time, Vaughan Williams was offered the opportunity to portray something of Canada and its diverse people – a task well suited to a composer who preferred to score his films in a way which could 'intensify the spirit of the whole situation by a continuous stream of music'.[4]

Three years after Vaughan Williams first turned his hand to film scoring, another British composer of very different reputation and stature was introduced to the medium. Lord Berners is generally considered today to be an eccentric amateur composer of little consequence. Publishing his music in his original name, Gerald Tyrwhitt, before he inherited his title in 1919, Berners was roughly contemporary with Vaughan Williams. In 1925 he was considered important enough to have one of his best-known works, the *Fantaisie Espagnole* performed in a Royal Philharmonic Society concert alongside the music of Bax, Howells, Ireland and Vaughan Williams.[5] The *Fantaisie Espagnole* is a brilliant parody on 'all the Spanish capriccios that ever were',[6] in which 'every detail of

---

[4] Vaughan Williams, 'Film Music', in Huntley (1947), 178. See above, p. 28.
[5] Foreman (1987), 103–4.
[6] Westrup, 'Berners', in Bacharach (ed.) (1946), 163.

monotonous reiteration, every little conceit of orchestration is brought into the picture'.[7] It would take an amateur of considerable accomplishment to succeed in the art of writing musical parody so skilful that after listening to it one finds it 'impossible to hear most Spanish music without a certain satiric feeling breaking through'.[8]

Berners's reputation as an eccentric amateur has some justification. As a composer he was largely self-taught, and too much of his music was parodistic. He spent too much of his time being other things; a diplomat, a painter, a writer. He was vastly wealthy and enjoyed an ostentatious lifestyle on his estate where he 'had the doves dyed in assorted colors, put jewelled collars on the dogs, and kept birds-of-paradise on his lawns'.[9] None of this quite coincides with the image of a serious composer. And yet, according to Osbert Sitwell, 'in the years between the wars, he did more to civilise the wealthy than anyone in England'.[10] He is also considered as 'far from being a mere playboy in the world of sound',[11] for 'his art is disciplined, and even when it seems most novel pays its tribute to tradition'.[12]

In the British film industry composers were cast for a film in much the same way as were its leading players. It comes as no surprise, therefore, that the first film Berners scored was somewhat out of the ordinary. Released in early 1944, *The Halfway House* was a curious mixture of propaganda, moral message and ghost story. The producers at Ealing studios were particularly fond of the 'mini-stories' plot structure, in which a number of separate dramas are played out in the context of a certain locality. Ealing also took its responsibilities regarding its influence on an audience very seriously. All its films have a strong moral tone. The basic plotline of the film, taken from Denis Ogden's play *The Peaceful Inn*, is that various people, all with different problems in life, make their way to an inn at Cwm Bach, where they gain a fresh insight into their situation, and resolve to lead better lives thereafter. It is gradually revealed during the course of the drama that the inn was destroyed by an air-raid exactly one year before, and that the innkeeper and his daughter are both ghosts.

In contrast to *49th Parallel*, where each episode of the drama is completely separate, the characters in *The Halfway House* all congregate and interact in a single location. This type of plot structure lends itself readily to the use of musical themes to identify the specific characters. Berners selects three individual characters and two couples to be assigned a theme. None of these themes appear in the main titles music but are first heard in the context of the characters' initial appearances in the diegesis. The majority of the thematic material used in the film is derived from the main titles, which contain a number of motifs associated with the inn itself and with its influence on the

[7] Westrup, (1946), 163.
[8] Lambert (1948), 123.
[9] Greene (1986), 1020, s.v. 'Berners'.
[10] Osbert Sitwell, quoted in Ronald Crichton, in Sadie (ed.) (1980), ii, 623, s.v. 'Berners'.
[11] Westrup, 'Berners', in Bacharach (ed.) (1946), 161.
[12] Ibid.

people who come to it. Berners did not orchestrate the score himself, the task being undertaken by Ernest Irving, but it was not uncommon for Irving to orchestrate the film scores of composers hard-pressed with other commitments.[13] Roy Douglas, who orchestrated *Les Sirènes* for Berners, said of the composer: 'I have an idea, by the little bits that he did scratch out on paper, that he *could* orchestrate',[14] and there is no reason to suppose that Berners, like any other composer in the same situation, would not have indicated on his short score exactly what he wanted.

The thematic material of the opening four bars of the main titles music show a most striking contrast to the main titles theme for *49th Parallel* (Example 1).

Example 8. Main titles music for *The Halfway House* (opening four bars)

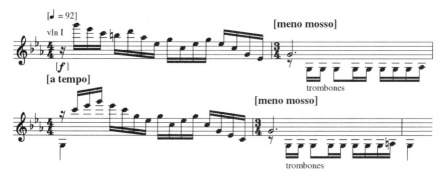

Lord Berners, *The Halfway House*. © the Berners Trust. Reproduced by the kind permission of the Berners Trust.

In the opening bar, Berners has covered a span of two octaves, and within the space of two bars has introduced two strongly contrasted thematic ideas. The first bar, in which there is only one stepwise interval, portrays the agitation of the inn's visitors, and their lack of control over their own lives. The trombone motif of the second bar symbolizes the steadying influence of the inn. However, it is also a warning that fate compels the guests to make a reckoning of their lives before disaster overtakes them. Hence this theme is both stabilizing and menacing, the repeated notes acting as an anchor after the precipitous first bar, and the instrumentation and rhythm suggesting a summons. The two ideas are presented again in bars 3 and 4. This time the first bar has been simplified to a purely arpeggiated minor chord, and the single intervallic movement of the second bar has been changed from a minor second to a major second. Both these changes suggest a lessening of tension, one of the chief effects the inn itself has upon its guests.

After another two bars of agitated semiquaver movement in which the opening bar is developed, the cellos and basses come to rest on a low F sharp. At this point an important new motif is introduced on the cor anglais

[13] Information supplied by Philip Lane in a private conversation with the author.
[14] Roy Douglas, in Appendix A, p. 205.

and strings. This motif consists of a pendulum major third, a figure which is a fingerprint of Welsh folk song. This may be a happy coincidence or an intentional device. Its significance lies in the way the mystery surrounding the Welsh inn is symbolically represented in the film by the striking of a pendulum clock at crucial moments.

The 'pendulum' motif is twice interrupted by a bar of agitated semi-quavers, once by the arpeggio figure, and once by a new motif of rising and falling semitones. These are underpinned by the 'warning' motif on the trombones.

Example 9. Four motifs from the main titles music to *The Halfway House*

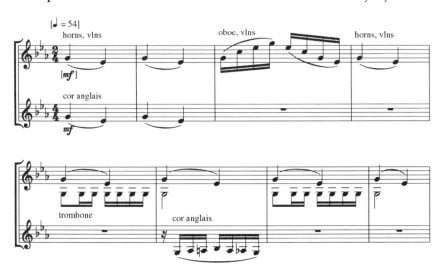

A fifth motif is introduced at the end of the main titles music. This fragment has an obvious affinity with the 'pendulum' motif, but being based on the interval of the tritone instead of the major third, it relates to the problems confronting the individuals in the drama, to the way in which they are at odds with themselves. The downward glissandi emphasise their weariness with the burdens they carry.

Example 10. Tritone motif from the main titles music. *The Halfway House*

These five motifs are all easily recognizable, and are all musically descriptive of the circumstances they represent. By their nature they are simple to manipulate, and can be used in combination while remaining individually identifiable. For those characters who have not been assigned a theme, the main titles motifs immediately identify them as people in need of help, whose situation is changed by contact with the inn.

As is the custom with this type of plot-line, the character or characters of each mini-story are introduced in turn. To make it clear to the audience that these scenes are unconnected, a title card indicating the location of each scene is superimposed on the establishing shot. Unfortunately, the practice renders the intention of the music cues far from clear to an audience, reared on American films, who expect to hear 'PARIS' accompanied by accordion music.

The first caption, 'CARDIFF', covering the establishing shot of the opening scene of the city, is accompanied by bustling 'city' music. This seems suitable enough, but the cue turns out to be a visibly diegetic one, with the first protagonist conducting a live orchestra in a concert. The music for this sequence, lasting only 40 seconds, is not thematic, and does not reappear, except as the end titles music, where its use is symbolic. The terminally ill conductor, David, must choose between continuing his career for the few months remaining to him, or resting in an attempt to prolong his life. His sojourn at the inn gives him the courage to go against his doctor's orders. The use of the diegetic concert music for the final statement of the film is an imaginative dramatic touch, and a highly unusual device, if not actually unique.

The second story involves three people, a divorcing couple wrangling in the solicitor's office, and their young daughter, who is determined to bring them together. The title card 'INNER TEMPLE, LONDON', with the establishing shot, is accompanied by a lively music cue, which, again, seems highly appropriate for a bustling city scene.

Example 11. 'Wrangling' theme. *The Halfway House*

Lord Berners, *The Halfway House*. © the Berners Trust. Reproduced by the kind permission of the Berners Trust.

The problem with this cue is that it is actually intended as a motif for the quarrel between the couple, Richard and Jill. This is difficult to grasp because the cue finishes as the camera cuts to the couple in the office, and is broken off as Richard says 'and that's my last word'. The cue would serve well enough to represent marital strife, but is first heard with the establishing shot and its title card, and it is not until much later in the film that the dramatic significance of the theme becomes clear.

The theme for the daughter is more easily recognized as belonging to her because it is introduced as she makes her first appearance.

Example 12. Joanna's theme. *The Halfway House*

This cannot be faulted as a characterization of an opinionated pre-adolescent. The problem is that Berners effects no transformation of these themes. They are repeated in their original version in different contexts. When Joanna is trying to manipulate her parents by faking a drowning, she is seen in a canoe on calm waters. Joanna's theme is preceded by an undulating figure on strings and celesta. The use of the theme may seem redundant, as the audience can clearly see Joanna on calm waters, but Berners actually intended this theme to represent Joanna's impish scheming to reunite her parents. This is made clear when the two themes are brought together as Richard and Jill resolve their differences. The 'wrangling' theme is immediately followed by Joanna's theme as the couple gaze into each other's eyes and then kiss. This is an elaborate way to tell the audience what they already know – that it was Joanna's machinations that reunited them – and because Berners has done nothing to transform the themes from their original versions, they seem somewhat inappropriate for such a tender moment.

The establishing shot with its title 'PARKMOOR PRISON' causes further confusion at the start of the next story. The cue certainly suggests the grim exterior of the prison.

Example 13. Cue accompanying shot of the prison. *The Halfway House*

However, the significance of the cue lies in the timpani and trombone figure. Fortesque is an army officer convicted of embezzling mess funds. The perfect fourth deviating to the tritone is a succinct method of suggesting the corruption of a military man. This cue is not used as a motif, as Fortesque becomes identified, musically and literally, with another character in the film who has a strong motif of his own. Oakley is the only evil character in the drama. A profiteer who makes his fortune from the misery of others, he is unrepentant as he arrives at the inn. When his theme is heard with the establishing shot of his first scene, the music is obviously intended to illustrate something other than the London buses helpfully identified by the title card 'WEST END, LONDON'.

Example 14. Oakley's theme. *The Halfway House*

Lord Berners, *The Halfway House*. © the Berners Trust. Reproduced by the kind permission of the Berners Trust.

At last the music cue has been able to dissociate itself from the establishing shot.

The tritone motif from the main titles music is used to introduce the story of a couple who have become estranged following the death of their son. As none of their dialogue scenes are scored, this is a simple way to indicate their burden of suffering.

Example 15. Tritone motif used interpretatively for an establishing shot. *The Halfway House*

Lord Berners, *The Halfway House*. © the Berners Trust. Reproduced by the kind permission of the Berners Trust.

The music cue for the introduction to the last story is deliberately intended to illustrate the establishing shot. 'TEMPLE MEADS STATION, BRISTOL' is most aptly accompanied by a jostling figure on the clarinets.

Example 16. Illustrative cue for an establishing shot. *The Halfway House*

This is because the couple involved in this story have not yet confronted the issue that will cause conflict between them. Terence considers that, as an Irishman, he is justified in taking a neutral stance over the war. He has yet to tell his English girlfriend, Margaret, that he intends to take up a post in Berlin. The dialogue scenes revolving around this conflict are not scored, and there is no intimation from this cue of the impending problems.

Berners intensifies the use of motifs as the various characters converge on the inn. Richard, Sally, Terence and Margaret, having met at the village station, and discovered that they have a common destination, set out together on foot to the accompaniment of the 'pendulum' motif in the strings and horns. Downward glissandi evoke the 'weariness' of the tritone motif. The camera pans across the valley to a shot of Fortesque searching for the inn through his binoculars. The semitone motif (Example 9, bar 6), heard this time on the oboe, has been transformed by inversion and extension to match the direction and range of the tritone motif. The associations of two motifs have again been incorporated. Oakley is seen approaching Fortesque, but it is not until the camera cuts back to Fortesque that Oakley's theme is heard in the cue. By this means the connection between the two men, and the corrupting influence of the more dominant Oakley, are indicated. As the inn mysteriously materializes in the spot where Fortesque has previously failed to find it, the 'pendulum' motif is played in the horns, this time without the glissandi, and the 'warning' motif is gently played on the cor anglais. By these means, the two motifs are more strongly connected to the beneficial aspects of the inn's influence. As the two men enter the inn, and the interior is seen for the first time, the 'pendulum' motif, played tremolando in the violins, is interrupted by the chiming of the clock. The symbolism of the motif is clarified at this moment, just as the landlord and his daughter emerge.

It is not the outward appearance of Rhys and Gwyneth but the trance-like quality of their delivery which suggests that they may be ghosts. A lyrical melody on the flute accompanies this first appearance of Gwyneth. As befits her tranquillity, this theme is more expansive than any of the motifs previously employed.

Example 17. Gwyneth's theme. *The Halfway House*

Of all the visitors, it is David who benefits most directly from his contact with Gwyneth. As he drives his car towards the inn, the burden of his choice is evident from the tritone motif in the violins, but when he turns into the driveway of the inn, the motif is immediately changed to Gwyneth's theme. Because the theme has reached its 4th bar before she becomes visible in the shot, the use of her cue is not merely superfluous labelling, but indicates that her influence already extends to David. This theme is also used to suggest that there is something supernatural about Gwyneth. It is heard in its original form during the discussion between Oakley and Fortesque as, observing her walking across the lawn in the sunshine, they realize that she is casting no shadow.

A variant of her theme, again heard on the 'ethereal' flute, accompanies the scene where she gives David the courage to defy death by continuing to work. This cue does not represent any significant development of the theme, as its essential character remains the same. But its use in this scene provides the context for a dramatic comparison in the final scene of the film, as Rhys and Gwyneth stand alone in the burning inn to face their own death once again. The 1st bar of the theme, played on upper strings, woodwind and trumpets, is played three times fortissimo, in the key of B minor. The gentle melodic theme is transformed into a motif of heroic defiance.

All four scenes showing the arrival of different guests at the inn are treated musically. Three of these cues begin with a motif from the main titles music. The four who set out from the station on foot are seen approaching the inn to the strains of the opening semiquaver arpeggiated figure of the main titles. The same figure was used in the cue for the approach of Fortesque and Oakley. Both these cues end with the pendulum motif. We have seen that the cue for David's arrival consisted of the tritone motif followed by Gwyneth's theme. The fourth cue, however, introduces fresh material. This seems at first glance to be merely illustrative, in much the same way as the cue for the establishing shot of Temple Meads station (Example 16). The cue in this scene accompanies the arrival in a pony trap of the estranged couple, Alice and Harry. This theme also suggests repetitive movement, and if its use were an isolated one, it would be easy to mistake it for a simple representation of travel.

Example 18. Arriving in the pony trap. *The Halfway House*

However, this theme reappears at the climax of the film as the guests prepare to escape from the blazing inn. Each character reflects on the resolution of his problem with a brief 'inner voice' monologue. As Alice says 'Later, my son – not yet', indicating that she will give up the attempt to make contact with her dead son, the cause of her marital strife, the theme is heard in a different guise.

Example 19. The resolution of Alice and Harry's problem. *The Halfway House*

The first use of the theme can now be seen as an evocation of the rancour between the couple. The transformation of the theme to one of lyrical reflection has been achieved by the simplest of means. Merely by relaxing the tempo, changing the articulation from staccato to legato, and transferring the theme from the bassoon, dark and sinister, to the oboe, piercing and sweet, Berners has effected a masterstroke of dramatic interpretation.

Another new theme, introduced late in the film, makes its second appearance in the resolution scene. Although this places it in the same context as the previous theme, its use serves a different dramatic purpose. This beautiful extended melody accompanies the scene where Rhys persuades Terence to question the intransigence of his patriotism.

Example 20. Theme for the 'compromise' dialogue. *The Halfway House*

As the theme reaches the end of the 4th bar, Rhys suggests 'perhaps compromise is the answer, sir'. The dialogue in this key scene is delivered in a measured pace, and is greatly enhanced by the music. The leisurely theme is supported by a repeated quaver pattern in the violas which increases the hypnotic effect of the ghostly landlord's delivery. Terence is won over by Rhys's final words: 'I'm proud to be a Welshman, sir, but I wouldn't put the betterment of Wales before the betterment of humanity.' In the resolution scene, as we hear Margaret thinking the words 'He's not going to Berlin', a modified fragment of the theme, taken from the 8th and 9th bars, is heard in the violins.

Example 21. 'Compromise' theme in the resolution scene. *The Halfway House*

The use of the theme in this context makes it clear that it was the conversation between Rhys and Terence, during which Margaret was not present, that led to the resolution of the conflict between the young couple.

In a very different kind of dialogue scene, Rhys is also the catalyst for Oakley's change of heart. Here Rhys is obliged to confront the profiteer in the strongest terms, so that he may be compelled to see the destruction to which his path will lead him if he continues his activities. In a scene that provides a startling contrast to his customary demeanour, Rhys builds to a climax his rhetoric concerning the fear that Oakley faces. It is not until this tour de force from the actor Mervyn Johns culminates with the words 'Fear that is gradually turning your world into a living hell' that the music cue begins. As the truth of Rhys's words strikes home, and Oakley registers the fear that will haunt him, the first two bars of Oakley's theme, played furiously on trumpets and strings, are taken over by a variant of the tritone motif.

Example 22. Variant of the tritone motif in Oakley's confrontation with Rhys. *The Halfway House*

The rising semiquavers that join the two notes of the tritone are a reference to Gwyneth's theme. Inverted and in the minor key, this theme, heard in juxtaposition with Oakley's, denotes the struggle between the forces of good and evil that are the key element of this scene. The 'pendulum' motif is played in the full orchestra as Rhys says; 'Look into your own heart', indicating that the relentless pressure of time has caught up with Oakley.

A new theme is introduced almost at the very end of the film. As David finally looks with calm acceptance on his approaching death, he begins an inner recitation of Psalm 23. The accompanying theme, played on solo horn, is one of noble resignation.

Example 23. David's 'resolution' theme. *The Halfway House*

David is the last to take his leave of Gwyneth and Rhys as they remain in the burning inn. After the defiant version of Gwyneth's theme is heard while they stand alone in the conflagration, a wordless female chorus takes up David's new theme as an aerial shot pulls away from the inn. The camera pans to the skyline of the valley as the theme soars. This is not simply David's theme, but one representing acceptance of time's inexorable power over the human condition.

In his first film score Berners reveals an astonishingly deft touch in handling the dramatic nuances of the film. He almost always uses his motifs and themes with a purpose dictated by the necessities of dramatic interpretation. There is no gratuitous deployment of themes as a substitute for fresh musical ideas. The appearance of every motif and theme is carefully calculated with regard to its symbolic implications. This first attempt at a difficult and demanding art discloses the hand of a dedicated craftsman.

Plate 4. Doreen Carwithen with an unidentified editor in the cutting room at Denham.

If Berners was an amateur composer by circumstance rather than by accomplishment, a third composer drawn into the world of film scoring in the 1940s was fully professional. This initiate, however, was that rarest of creatures – a Welsh female composer. Women composers were not altogether absent from the scene in the early days of sound films in Britain, but they had previously played a subsidiary role. Some had acted as assistant composers, their contributions to the score mostly unacknowledged. Doreen Carwithen worked with Mathieson at Denham, beginning with a Rank apprenticeship scheme in 1947. She describes how the job ranged from copying and making last-minute alterations to orchestral parts to ghost writing for composers and being subcontracted by them to write sections of their scores.[15] Some had written isolated songs appearing in films scored by another composer, such as Anna Marley's 'Hullalooba' in *Dead of Night*, and Mabel Buchanan's 'Throughout the Years' in *Give Me the Stars*. Others had been allowed to compose for documentary films: Ursula Grenville for *The Key to Scotland*, as early as 1935, and Molly Berkeley, a year later for *Out to Play*.

Elisabeth Lutyens was the first recognized woman composer to work in films, but her first contributions were again for documentaries. In the mid-1940s she worked for the Crown film unit, composing for *Jungle Mariner* in 1944, and *The Way from Germany* in 1946. It was not until the 1960s that Lutyens began composing a number of scores for feature films. *Never Take Sweets from a Stranger* from 1960 was followed by such films as *Paranoic*, *The Skull* and *Dr. Terror's House of Horrors*. Lutyens was a rare example of a British concert composer who was generally recognized as having modified their natural style when composing for feature film, but it is significant that, even with this compromise, she tended to specialise in horror films.

Suitability of natural musical style for the subject-matter was the reason that Grace Williams became the first woman composer in Britain to score a full-length feature film. (She led the field by only a few months. Her film *Blue Scar* was released in May 1949, and in December of the same year Doreen Carwithen followed with the score to *Boys in Brown*. However, Carwithen had scored the 44-minute second feature *To the Public Danger* in 1947, so perhaps honours are even.) The subject-matter of the film for which Grace Williams's style was considered suitable is alluded to in the rather curious title. 'Blue scar' is the name given to the discoloration to the skin caused by coal dust entering an open wound. Although *Blue Scar* deals with the working conditions of coal miners in an almost documentary fashion, the film embraces a wider issue: the individual's choice between remaining in the community and culture in which he was raised, or moving on to an alien culture in the hope of betterment. The film is, for once, an honest attempt to portray a Welsh community, and to deal with the complex issue of *eisiau bod y Sais* ('the desire to be English' claimed by some to reside in the heart of every Welshman).

In 1949 Grace Williams's musical style was still under the influence of her

---

[15] See Appendix C, p. 219.

illustrious teacher Vaughan Williams. Her style, throughout its development, remained predominantly lyrical, and never lost its connection with the roots of traditional Welsh music. She had used Welsh folk songs for some of her vocal works, and for the orchestral *Fantasia on Welsh Nursery Themes* of 1940. The opening theme of the main titles music for *Blue Scar* is based on the Welsh folk love song *Mae Nghariad i'n Fenws* (My Love is like Venus).

Example 24. Main titles music for *Blue Scar* (first ten bars)

Grace Williams, *Blue Scar*. Reproduced by the kind permission of Marian Glyn Evans.

The choice of this particular folk song is a clever one. The upward fifth at the opening makes it so distinctive that its subsequent appearances ensure that it will be recognized. This interval is rare in Welsh folk song, which generally favours the much gentler contours of stepwise movement or pendulum thirds. It gives this Welsh folk melody a most atypical atmosphere of striving or aspiration, entirely apt for the film's dramatic purposes. It is the ambition of Olwen – to escape from the restrictions of her upbringing and become a famous singer – that destroys the relationship between her and Tom, her childhood sweetheart. The theme suggests both separation, in the upward fifth, and, in the rocking repeat of the A to B stepwise movement, reconciliation.

The main titles are superimposed over a panning shot of the mining village, and the main titles music shadows this. The opening shot is of the mountains against the skyline accompanied by the first ten bars, with the melody in the violins. As the shot pans down to the valley and the village streets, the theme is transferred to the cellos and violas an octave below, while the violins play a countermelody. As the shot lingers on the narrow streets, a small melodic figure is introduced by the oboe.

Example 25. 'Narrow streets' motif from the main titles music. *Blue Scar*

Grace Williams, *Blue Scar*. Reproduced by the kind permission of Marian Glyn Evans.

This motif, which is taken from the opening phrase of the traditional Welsh folk song *Y Gwŷdd* (The Loom), is to become an important theme later in the film.

As the shot pans from the streets towards the mine, the main theme is played on the trumpet with the introductory fourth from the second phrase.

Example 26. Trumpet cue from main titles music. *Blue Scar*

Grace Williams, *Blue Scar*. Reproduced by the kind permission of Marian Glyn Evans.

Taken out of the context of the folk song, this cue sounds similar to many another rallying trumpet call, and further demonstrates the unusual shape of this folk melody. The main titles music continues to reflect the accompanying footage. An overhead cable car is seen descending the valley. The music cue is purely descriptive at this point, but the descending figure is introduced by an upward melodic fragment which is adapted from the second phrase of *Y Gwŷdd*.

Example 27. Melodic fragment introducing descending motif in main titles music. *Blue Scar*

Grace Williams, *Blue Scar*. Reproduced by the kind permission of Marian Glyn Evans.

The descending motif is taken over by a simple alternating figure in the violins, suggesting both the mechanical action of the pit wheel and the monotony and drudgery of the work.

Example 28. 'Monotony' motif from the main titles. *Blue Scar*

Grace Williams, *Blue Scar*. Reproduced by the kind permission of Marian Glyn Evans.

This is yet another fragment from the main titles music that will appear, significantly developed, later in the score. This method of introducing thematic material in the main titles music for later development is very similar to the one employed by Berners in *The Halfway House*. Grace Williams also uses these ideas in conjunction to suggest the connection between extra-musical dramatic elements. As we have seen, this method of dramatic interpretation by thematic use was employed by Vaughan Williams in *49th Parallel*, but not with material introduced in the main titles music. The fragment from Example 27, introduced as the first shot of the pit appears on screen, is cleverly developed to represent Tom's attachment to his job as a miner, and, by association, to his culture. From Olwen's point of view, it is Tom's reluctance to leave the mine and make something of his life that is causing the problem between them.

The first four music cues heard in the film after the main titles are all diegetic, and all help to create an impression of the close-knit community. The miners sing hymns as they scrub down after their shift. The family all sing round the piano, and choir practice is heard in the background as Tom and Olwen walk through the streets of the village at night. The strains of the choir are heard as the couple express their differences, encapsulated in two brief sentences. In response to Olwen's insistence that 'Everyone leaves who can better themselves', Tom replies 'Perhaps all the more reason to stay'. As the debate becomes more personal, the melodic fragment associated with Tom's attachment to his culture is introduced on the oboe. This time the intervals are exactly as they are heard in *Y Gwŷdd*.

Example 29. Tom's 'attachment' motif. *Blue Scar*

Grace Williams, *Blue Scar*. Reproduced by the kind permission of Marian Glyn Evans.

In Grace Williams's arrangement of this traditional Welsh folk song, she uses her own translation into English with some additional material which is peculiarly apt for the dramatic threads of the film. The weaver, wearied with his task, finds respite from his labours by walking out into the star-filled night. The beauty of his surroundings eases his heart before he returns to his loom. Variants of the 'attachment' motif are used in different dramatic contexts to suggest the underlying motivation that will eventually persuade Tom to stay in the valley. There is a subtle twist to the end of the cue that contains the first appearance of this motif during Tom and Olwen's altercation. Their friend Glenis, who carries a torch for Tom, is an unseen witness to the end of their scene, where they patch up their quarrel with a kiss. As she is seen sadly but resolutely walking away from them, the motif makes a sudden tonal shift to F major. Glenis is a true daughter of the valleys, and this common bond with Tom is indicated in the cue.

Grace Williams makes use of another Welsh folk song in the score. In a series of shots showing the crowd from the village making their way up the mountain to attend the football match, the camera cuts to a group of older men struggling up the slopes. The folk song that has come to be associated with rugby matches is played by solo oboe accompanied by pizzicato strings.

Example 30. First appearance of *Sosban Fach. Blue Scar*

Grace Williams, *Blue Scar*. Reproduced by the kind permission of Marian Glyn Evans.

Although the common association of this folk song with a sporting event might make its use for this cue seem rather obvious, its characterization by the use of instrumental colour renders it into a dramatic interpretative device. Not only is the physical frailty of the old men emphasized, but also the threat of change to the tradition that they embody. Less happy, in musico-dramatic terms, is the composer's second cue involving this folk song. As the camera follows the football bouncing down the slope, the music cue is graphically descriptive of the shot. This is coming uncomfortably close to the less agreeable habits of Hollywood composers.

Example 31. *Sosban Fach* used as an illustrative cue. *Blue Scar*

Grace Williams, *Blue Scar*. Reproduced by the kind permission of Marian Glyn Evans.

This is Grace Williams's only lapse of taste in the score, and the only occasion when she fails to use her themes or motifs in a dramatically interpretative or symbolic way. She makes up for it by the beauty and subtlety of the final cue based on traditional Welsh music. As Olwen's father is brought home in an ambulance following his accident at the pit, a solo viola, doubled by flutes, heard above an accompaniment consisting only of string trills, plays as a lament a theme taken from the Welsh hymn commonly known as *Hen Dderby* or *Hen Ddarby* (Old Derby)

Example 32. *Hen Dderby* as a lament

Grace Williams, *Blue Scar*. Reproduced by the kind permission of Marian Glyn Evans.

In this cue a snatch of the main theme precedes the lament, its interval of the fifth transformed from a symbol of aspiration to an echo of the Last Post.

Example 33. Transformation of main theme fragment. *Blue Scar*

Grace Williams, *Blue Scar*. Reproduced by the kind permission of Marian Glyn Evans.

The main theme, far from being liberally scattered throughout the score, is used for only three more cues before the end titles. On each occasion, the context and nature of its use are very different. The first of these cues is heard as Tom is trying to concentrate on the socialist tract he is reading when he knows Olwen is out dancing with Alfred. As an image of Olwen, floating in the arms of his rival, is superimposed on the text of the book, the main theme is played on alto saxophone. Although this suggests a diegetic dance cue, the use of this instrument is really symbolic of Tom's fear that Olwen will be seduced, literally or metaphorically, by the well-to-do Englishman. The second cue uses solo horn and strings, mournfully repeating the main theme in rising semitone modulations as Olwen reads the letter from her mother telling her that her father is back on the dole. The chromatic shifts underline Olwen's agitation at the news, and this use of the folk song suggests her frustration at the old way of life that she has left behind. The final cue exploits the versatility of the rising fifth to demonstrate the achievement of aspiration, as a montage depicting the improving conditions of the miners is shown.

Example 34. Further transformation of the main theme fragment. *Blue Scar*

Grace Williams, *Blue Scar*. Reproduced by the kind permission of Marian Glyn Evans.

One of the film's longest and most important music cues accompanies Tom as he walks to the railway station, angry at Olwen's decision to abandon a date with him in order to go dancing with Alfred. Over repeated pizzicato pedal crotchets on the cellos, the clarinets play an agitated figure.

Example 35. Start of Tom's walk. *Blue Scar*

Grace Williams, *Blue Scar*. Reproduced by the kind permission of Marian Glyn Evans.

Olwen has rejected him in favour of Alfred because he will not give up his job as a miner, and the whole cue is an expression of Tom's sudden frustration with his way of life which is indicated by this development of the 'monotony' motif. Later in the cue the upper strings, in close harmony, play an extended melody.

Example 36. Extended melody from Tom's walk. *Blue Scar*

Grace Williams, *Blue Scar*. Reproduced by the kind permission of Marian Glyn Evans.

This melody not only contains the figuration connected with the variant of the 'monotony' motif, but is in itself derived from the main theme. Under the sustained notes of this melody, the oboe plays Tom's 'attachment' motif as it first appears in the main titles, this time in the minor key. His attachment to his culture is being questioned. As Tom strides onto the station platform, his agitation, and the frustration he feels with everything around him is summed up in a tonally ambivalent theme played on alto saxophone.

Example 37. Saxophone theme from Tom's walk. *Blue Scar*

Grace Williams, *Blue Scar*. Reproduced by the kind permission of Marian Glyn Evans.

The variant to Tom's 'attachment' theme in bars 4 and 5 is preceded by a variant of the motif, heard in the main titles music, associated with the narrow streets of the mining village. For the first time Tom is experiencing the restriction of his environment. It is another tonally ambivalent variation of this theme that is played on the cor anglais just before Olwen breaks the news to Tom that she is going to marry Alfred.

Example 38. Variation of the 'narrow streets' motif. *Blue Scar*

Grace Williams, *Blue Scar*. Reproduced by the kind permission of Marian Glyn Evans.

Her motivation for marrying a man she does not love is revealed by the use of the cue associated with the narrow streets of her home town. Earlier in the scene, a variant of Tom's 'attachment' motif is played on upper strings as Olwen says 'It's mining. I must get away from it all.' The use of the motif implies that Olwen is rejecting Tom's values as well as his work.

One of the most deft uses of musical symbolism occurs in the final dialogue scene between Glenis and Tom before he goes to London to visit Olwen. As they walk together in the gardens, the 'narrow streets' motif and Tom's 'attachment' motif are transformed from their previous tonal ambivalence into a simple diatonic statement which is played by the violins.

Example 39. Theme for Tom and Glenis. *Blue Scar*

Grace Williams, *Blue Scar*. Reproduced by the kind permission of Marian Glyn Evans.

The shift to diatonic major, which Grace Williams clearly wanted emphasized, indicates Glenis's complete sympathy with Tom's values and way of life, and suggests the possibility of a happy outcome for the couple.

When Tom is seen arriving in London to visit Olwen in her new house, the first four bars from the music for Tom's walk, heard in the brass, is alternated with a motif based on the Westminster chimes, on woodwind and glockenspiel. Far from being a superfluous location signifier accompanying shots of London buses, the juxtaposition of these two motifs symbolically hints that the significance of clock-time for those living in the centre of London is very different from its significance for those who inhabit the valleys of South Wales. In a final scene accompanied only by a diegetic radio broadcast of Olwen's singing, Tom realizes that their two worlds are irreconcilable. The end titles music uses juxtapositions of three motifs. Snatches of the main theme are interspersed with triumphant repetitions of Tom's 'attachment' motif and the 'narrow streets' motif, as Tom and Glenis are seen standing on the mountain together, looking down on their valley. This juxtaposition of these three themes indicates that it is the bond of their shared values that has overcome Tom's temptation.

Because of the episodic nature of its scenario, *49th Parallel* could not provide Vaughan Williams with a framework for complex thematic development in his score. Lord Berners and Grace Williams both took advantage of the dramatic structure of their films to employ a system of tightly knit thematic or motivic symbolism. In accordance with the contrasting subject-matter of their respective films, the themes and motifs used by Grace Williams were generally more lyrical and less fragmented than those of Berners. All three composers responded to the challenge of scoring their first feature film with a willingness to put the dramatic needs of the picture before purely musical considerations, and in this respect the achievements of all three compare favourably with that of Bax. Their natural musical styles were, however, far better suited than his to the nature of the films they were scoring, and were, therefore, less vulnerable to compromise.

7. Dialogue scoring of British films of the 1930s

In the earliest days of cinema, it did not take the experimenting film makers long to realise that they had discovered a new vehicle for the age-old art of story-telling. Those who had laboured to bring the new medium into existence had not originally envisaged such a role for it. In their early efforts they were content to reproduce in moving pictures scenes merely of natural or mechanical motion. It was sufficiently enthralling for contemporary audiences to witness these snatches of reality – a train coming into a station, a horse put through its paces. Very quickly, however, the true genius of cinema for conveying fictional narrative began to be exploited. Since then, through its many periods of transition, mainstream cinema has been preoccupied with the task of story-telling.

Silent films were a means of story-telling without the use of words. Inter-titles, of course, were used to assist in the unfolding of narrative, but the success of a silent film can be judged by the extent of their use. The more a narrative can be conveyed by the images and by the skill of the actors, the smaller the number of inter-titles needed. The absence of speech and naturalistic sounds relating to the diegesis facilitated the audience's absorption into the realm of fantasy. Music had various important functions in the silent film. These are clearly explained by Maurice Jaubert:

> It was natural that music should have been required to accentuate still further this flight from the actual, which seemed for so long to be the true goal of cinematography, as well as to 'explain' certain intentions of the director, who had not yet at his disposal the powerful instruments of speech and sound for elucidating the story. At the moment when the sound film was about to come into being, music constituted for the film a kind of running commentary designed sometimes to plunge the spectator into the atmosphere desired by the director, sometimes to prolong in him a rhythmic impression, sometimes to make still clearer the story that was being told to him.[1]

The role of music as a narrative and emotional interpreter was absolutely crucial to the silent film, but the various methods of applying live performances to the unrelenting progress of the film projector often produced haphazard results. Some indication of the wide differences in standard that obtained in

[1] Jaubert, 'Music', in Davy (ed.) (1938), 102.

these performances, and in the attention paid to the details of this specialized art, emerge from William Alwyn's account of his own experiences of playing for silent films, first as a schoolboy novice and then as a professional musician:

> I was just beginning to get underway when another signal from the violinist left me stranded in mid-air (or mid-blow!) as my teacher expertly and rapidly whipped over the pages into the next piece in order on the desk and off we went again at a different tempo and so on till the next signal. It was a game of hare and hounds with one small terrier puffing well in the rear. The essential link in the performance was the pianist who bound this hotch-potch of music together with his rapid modulations and improvised chords. It was some years before I repeated this breathless performance and then I was a young professional musician in London. By that time the art of fitting music to a picture had been brought to a high pitch of efficiency and in the big London cinemas, which employed expert orchestras of symphonic dimensions, more often than not, considerable time and taste had been spent in selecting appropriate music and the signalling for a change of piece was done by ingenious coloured lights on the music desk.[2]

It was just as this art was reaching a pinnacle of sophistication that the introduction of sound heralded its demise. Quite apart from the catastrophic effect this had on the livelihood of musicians in the larger cities of Britain and America, the impact on the very nature of narrative film was of such magnitude that it has sometimes been imperfectly apprehended. Hanns Eisler revealed an extraordinary degree of insensitivity to the significance of this impact when he claimed that 'a talking picture without music is not very different from a silent picture'.[3] Nothing could be more different than the stilted, visually static early talking pictures from the fluid, expressive, wordless poetry of the silents. Maurice Jaubert gives us one of the most perceptive and illuminating descriptions of the effect the introduction of sound had on the evolution of narrative film:

> With the introduction of word and sound, cinematographic style has undergone a profound change, a change which too few directors and scenario writers have perceived and understood. Driven by the absence of speech to a lengthy method of visual paraphrase in order to make the story clear, the silent film built up for itself, little by little, a special idiom designed chiefly to compensate for the silence of the actors. This convention became familiar to all habitués of the cinema, who believed, legitimately in those days, that it gave occasion for a special art of the screen – an art which in its finest development would be essentially allusive, and so poetic. But as soon as speech came to destroy this early convention, the cinema – although hardly anyone recognised it at first – changed its character. It became, it is, and it remains *realistic*. We must understand by this that while it no longer needs the visual syntax which it had built up with so much trouble, it is now impelled to borrow even the elements of its language (images) from immediate reality.[4]

[2] William Alwyn, quoted in Manvell and Huntley (2/1975), 23.
[3] Adorno and Eisler (2/1994), 77.
[4] Jaubert, 'Music', in Davy (ed.) (1938), 106.

The effect of this intrusion of reality on a medium that had seemed almost magical can be illustrated by a comparison with an everyday experience common to many. If we repeatedly catch sight of the same attractive and mysterious stranger, a fantasy can be built around that person. If the eagerly awaited day comes when that stranger chances to speak to us, the spell can be broken in an instant. Reality, in the form of an unsympathetic accent or vocal timbre, shatters the illusion. If a number of great silent-movie actors found themselves out of a job with the advent of sound, it was only partly because they were discovered to have 'unsuitable' voices. The fact that they spoke at all was enough to destroy their mystique. Rudolph Valentino has become immortalized not so much because of his early death, but because he has for ever remained in the twilight world of silent films.

When the principal focus of an actor shifts suddenly from the expressive gestures of his face and body to the words emerging from his mouth, his function in the narrative changes from archetype to informant. If Hanns Eisler's comment that 'speech in motion pictures is the legitimate heir to the captions'[5] had been accurate, then the problem would not have been so severe. Motion pictures experienced a large hiatus simply because everything became sub-servient to the new invention. For several years after the coming of sound, film took an enormous backward step by abandoning its unique abilities as a narrative vehicle in favour of a sterile replication of theatrical productions. One of the main reasons why *King Kong* was such a successful film was that its dialogue *could* be equated with captions, for it is incidental to the action. This is a silent movie with spoken inter-titles, and hence a suitable vehicle for the extensive use of dramatic music.

In the late 1920s and early 1930s, films like *King Kong*, where the dialogue was mainly incidental, were the rare exception. The sudden jolt into 'reality' occasioned by the addition of a soundtrack, posed a dilemma for directors. Was there a place for music in the talking picture? Gerald Cockshott considered that

> since the sound film is fundamentally a visual art it is not unreasonable that incidental music should be commissioned for it; but the presence of such music as a matter of course is explicable less by necessity than convention.[6]

Convention dictated that music was an indispensable ingredient. It had become so much a part of cinema that its continued use in the sound film was assured. The problem was to determine the way in which it was to be used. Maurice Jaubert describes the approach taken by film directors to the use of music in the early days of sound:

> But if we now voluntarily leave aside all that can be called the 'real' music of a film (jazz in a night club, organ in a church) whose function is obvious, what is it that

---

[5] Adorno and Eisler (2/1994), 77.
[6] Cockshott (1947), 1.

most of our directors demand of music? First of all to fill up the 'gaps' in the sound, because some scene is considered too silent, or because the director has been unable to find in real life a convincing natural sound – above all, if no such sound is suggested by the image. We need not stress this elementary conception. More commonly, music is called upon to annotate the action. Is the scene tragic? A few notes of the horn or trombone will accentuate the gloom.[7]

It was the musical accompaniment of dialogue that posed the most problems. Directors felt that as the narrative was now being explicitly unfolded through naturalistic speech, there was little justification for its interpretation through the 'unreal' medium of music. Maurice Jaubert adds a valid point to this argument:

> In any case they fail to notice that, simply from an acoustic standpoint, the superposition of music on a voice or a sound tends to destroy the emotional values of the one and the authenticity of the other.[8]

It was this aesthetic consideration that contributed to the general policy of British film makers regarding the scoring of dialogue. Authenticity was considered by them to be a more worthy goal than the purveying of dreams. This fundamental divergence in the objectives of British and American film makers is one of the main causes of the differences between their films. The dialogue of a film that is designed to transport its audience into another realm will be different in every respect from that which is intended to be true to life. Britain's strong documentary tradition left a lasting legacy to its feature films thanks to its basic tenet that the medium of film could be a vehicle for the conveying of factual information. As a consequence, dialogue in British films is constructed, delivered and scored in very different ways from its counterpart in American films.

The expectations of the audience have sometimes been held responsible for decisions regarding the use of music in films. The Russian commentator Leonid Sabaneev writing in 1935, at the time when music for the sound film was establishing its parameters, has this to say about the influence of the audience:

> a film of a psychological nature, with love episodes, would find it difficult to dispense with music, not merely from an aesthetic point of view, but also because the audience, accustomed to the musical tradition of the silent film, expects it. The cinema has a public of its own . . . its aesthetic psychology is infantile, its tastes undeveloped, its comprehension of, and ability to distinguish, musical details and texture limited. All this must be borne in mind. The cinema audience regards as vital those forms which, in the eyes of advanced art, bear the impress of banality, and on the whole its tastes are more antiquated than those characterizing the main tendencies in art. Effects long since relegated to the museum still bring tears to the eyes of the cinema-goer, and sentimentality and naïve methods of exciting him have not yet lost their sway. Hence melodeclamation, to which any dialogue to music is reduced in cinema, offers a wide field for development.[9]

---

[7] Jaubert, 'Music', in Davy (ed.) (1938), 107.
[8] Ibid.
[9] Sabaneev (1935), 30.

Sabaneev's experience of cinema audiences extended to those in France, Germany, Britain and America, so it is not possible to point the finger of blame in any specific direction. He might have been surprised, however, to hear the comments of a British cinema-goer from 1947 which cast a rather different light on the aesthetic tastes of cinema audiences in this country:

> We hate the music, or most of it. Not only is it painfully loud, but equally painfully obvious . . . surely, after all these years, we can grow up just a bit . . . or do most audiences really like having the traditional tunes for each emotion? Maybe they do, but lots of us don't . . . And isn't it maddening to everyone to have suitable soft music braying out just when the hero and heroine are murmuring sweet nothings? After all, some people would like to hear what the pair of them are saying.[10]

This voice from the British cinema audience exemplifies one of the nation's most characteristic traits; that of restraint. There were many technical differences that separated British and American films, and that led to a very different treatment of the spoken word in their respective scores, but at the root of it all there existed an unequivocal discrepancy of taste between the two nations which extended even as far as their 'infantile' and 'limited' cinema audiences.

The coming of sound had irrevocably introduced a naturalistic element into filmic narrative that ruptured the illusionary quality of silent films. At first the sound of the human voice and everyday noises on the soundtrack seemed only to distract attention from the diegetic flow. Few realized that this was the painful birth of a completely new medium. Because the moving picture had existed for thirty years before the introduction of sound, it was easy to assume that this was merely an exciting addition to an established medium. As Jaubert points out, the full implications of sound for the narrative film were simply not grasped at the time. The intrusion of 'reality' met with a different response from British and American film makers after the initial novelty had worn off. Hollywood retreated from the disruption of reality by evolving its dream package. In order to lull its audience back into the suspension of disbelief necessary for total absorption into the narrative flow of the film, music became an essential part of the package:

> The classical narrative model developed certain conventions to assist expressive acting in portraying the presence of emotion, primarily selective use of the close-up, diffuse lighting and focus, symmetrical mise-en-scène, and heightened vocal intonation. The focal point of this process became the music which externalized these codes through the collective resonance of musical associations.[11]

Kathryn Kalinak goes on to demonstrate how music was specifically used in the Hollywood film to draw the audience into the world of the filmic narrative, thus keeping both reality and critical faculties at bay:

---

[10] Elizabeth Croft, quoted in Huntley (1947), 163.
[11] Kalinak (1992), 87.

Music's dual function as both articulator of screen expression and initiator of spectator response binds the spectator to the screen by resonating affect between them. The lush, stringed passages accompanying a love scene are representations not only of the emotions of the diegetic characters but also of the spectator's own response which music prompts and reflects.[12]

In accordance with its intention to avoid the intrusiveness of naturalism, the delivery of dialogue in films of Hollywood's golden age developed a style that was anything but realistic. In the dramatic picture, especially in films directed towards female audiences, dialogue delivery verged on the melodramatic. Typically, the actor's voice employed a wider range than was characteristic of the average American. There was a tendency towards a lilting, rhythmic, deliberate way of speaking that still contained an intensification of emotion. The more emotionalism there is in the voice, the more easily can the presence of music can be justified. Hollywood actors were aware of the significance of the music accompanying their dialogue scenes. In certain circumstances, the conception of the composer dictated the rhythm and pacing of their delivery. Korngold was known to use operatic techniques to shape dialogue scenes for the actors:

> For his next film, *Anthony Adverse* (1936), Korngold would develop this technique, composing music just under the pitch of the voices and 'rushing' into pauses left open by the dialogue. As Korngold explained the process: 'I wrote the music in advance, conducted – without orchestra – the actor on the stage in order to make him speak his lines in the required rhythm, and then sometimes weeks later, guided by earphones, I recorded the orchestral part.'[13]

Korngold was exceptionally fortunate to have been allowed such a degree of control over an area normally closed to composers. It was rare for composers on either side of the Atlantic to have that degree of input in the creative phase of film production. Ironically, Vaughan Williams, in the section of his article on film music which outlines his proposed plans for the increased autonomy of the composer, suggests the technique which, unbeknown to him, had already been instigated by Korngold:

> When music is to accompany dialogue or action, surely the actors should hear the music before they start rehearsing, and at rehearsal act to the music, both from the point of view of timing and of emotional reaction.[14]

Vaughan Williams's concern with a technique such as this seems surprising considering that his scoring of dialogue scenes is atmospheric rather than illustrative. However, he is airing the general frustrations of the film composer whose contribution is normally limited to the adding-on of music after all other artistic decisions have already been made. That was the standard practice in

[12] Kalinak (1992), 87.
[13] Ibid., 95–6.
[14] Vaughan Williams, 'Film Music', in Huntley (1947), 180.

British films of the period, and Vaughan Williams is attempting to challenge the accepted state of affairs:

> I believe that this and many other problems could be solved by those who have had much experience, if the composer insisted. As long as music is content to be the maid-of-all-work, until the musicians rise to their responsibilities, we shall achieve nothing.[15]

Although Korngold's prior fulfilment of Vaughan Williams's ambition had been an unusual example of a composer's influence on film actors, there is no doubt that Hollywood actors were far more conscious than their British counterparts of the role of music in their films. Bette Davis, although reputed to be resentful of Max Steiner's part in the success of the films in which they were both involved, admitted that 'Max understood more about drama than any of us'.[16] Although Christopher Palmer asserts that *Now Voyager* is not the best film to substantiate this accolade, it is none the less an interesting example of an American film whose score is used almost exclusively to accompany dialogue scenes. This is a classic example of the 'woman's picture'. During its course Bette Davis is miraculously transformed by psychotherapy from a neurotic ugly duckling into a sophisticated, wise and caring woman. Steiner enjoyed scoring this genre of film, but Palmer had reservations about its suitability as a vehicle for a good score:

> Yet eminently suited as Steiner's style undoubtedly was to this women's-magazine-type escapist entertainment, I question whether it ever really brought out the best in him. The characters in these films are mostly stock and two-dimensional, and the music generally moves on the same level of cliché and stereotype, emotionalism and sentimentality doing duty for genuine emotion, and rhetoric for eloquence.[17]

In other words, a formula had been established by custom for the scoring of such pictures. While this type of cloying dialogue had elicited a particular style of scoring, familiarity with this music had led the actors to develop, consciously or unconsciously, a more leisurely, almost lyrical style of delivery. Hollywood's policy of steering the sound picture away from naturalism into the realm of fantasy can be clearly observed in the way that dialogue delivery had evolved during its golden age. The score of *Now Voyager* is remarkable for the fact that it contains only two short cues without dialogue, compared to thirty-five nondiegetic cues with dialogue. No British film score of the period comes anywhere near this ratio, or compares with the distribution of music cues throughout the film – the longest unscored section of *Now Voyager* has a duration of less than 3 minutes.

The scoring of the dialogue in the film is predominantly for strings, although

---

[15] Vaughan Williams, 'Film Music', in Huntley (1947), 181.
[16] Bette Davis, quoted in Palmer (1990), 45.
[17] Palmer (1990), 38.

certain words or phrases are punctuated with additional chords from the woodwind and brass. The use of these punctuation marks, or 'stingers', was a common practice in the American film score to give further impact to certain words and images. In the scene where Charlotte shows the psychiatrist round her room, the lyrical theme accompanying their conversation about the ornamental boxes that Charlotte has carved is interrupted by a stinger placed between the phrases 'my mother sent for me' and 'the chisel slipped'. The placing of an accented minor chord at that moment highlights the significance of the synchronicity of the two events – the music conveys the message that Charlotte's mother is the cause of her daughter's problems. The same chord is used again a few moments later when the psychiatrist sees some cigarette ends in Charlotte's waste bin: the connection between Charlotte's 'deviant' behaviour and her mother is reinforced.

This technique of using an interrupting chord to draw attention to the significance of certain words in the dialogue was established in the Hollywood score during the period that saw the formulation of dialogue scoring techniques. Steiner's use of strings for the scoring of dialogue in *Now Voyager* was not purely a question of sympathy with the romantic nature of the film. Hollywood composers had their reasons for the type of scoring they generally employed:

> The thirties also saw the development of guidelines for composing and orchestrating music to be placed behind dialogue. Musicians and soundmen felt that woodwinds create unnecessary conflict with human voices, and they stated a preference for strings. They concurred on questions of range, too: even in the seventies Laurence Rosenthal advised 'keeping the orchestra well away from the pitch-range of the speaker – low instruments against high voices, and vice versa', although other composers note that combining voice and orchestra in the same register can sometimes be a creative move, if a sort of indistinguishable tone color is desirable.[18]

Kathryn Kalinak makes clear the extent to which this type of formula in the classical Hollywood score, particularly in relation to dialogue, had become standard practice:

> Conventions for underscoring developed to bring the expressive possibilities of music to the human voice. These included relying on the strings; avoiding the woodwinds, whose timbre tends to obscure the dialogue; avoiding extremes in register; using melody and avoiding counterpoint; and relying on simple rhythms, slow tempi, and low volume. All of these conventions, however, could be violated for a specific thematic purpose. Nonetheless, conventions for underscoring were tacitly assumed throughout the industry.[19]

Such a recipe for bland, inconspicuous music confirms the deliberate policy of Hollywood film makers to steer their products away from any taint of realism. Although their actors' style of delivery had evolved to the point where a

---

[18] Gorbman (1987), 78.
[19] Kalinak (1992), 94.

continual background of strings did not seem totally incongruous, the persistent wash of music tended to blur the edges of the actors' performances. The projection of true emotion was pre-empted by the sentimentality of the music. By this means, the Hollywood package included an insurance for its audiences that they would not actually suffer the discomfort of genuinely painful empathy with the characters on screen. By being drawn into this world of pseudo emotions, they escaped from the more poignant feelings that can be experienced when watching a British film. In these moments the quality of the acting, often demonstrating the suppression of visible emotion, is left to stand on its own. A fine example of this is to be found in Michael Redgrave's performance in *The Browning Version*, a film totally devoid of nondiegetic music, which is so emotionally harrowing that it is almost too painful to watch.

Dialogue scoring in the Hollywood film was not always unobtrusive. According to Roy Prendergast,

> There are times when music accompanying dialogue can take on a definite foreground character . . . Generally, such music is treated musically in a recitative style reminiscent of the opera: blank spots in the dialogue are filled with fragments of music, which come to the foreground momentarily to comment on the dialogue and then drop back into the background when the next line is said. All of this has to be done, of course, by the way the composer writes his music, not by the simple turning of knobs in the dubbing room.[20]

Techniques of this sort are almost entirely absent from British film scores, and they are nowhere to be found in scores from the 1930s. There is one very notable use of recitative style in the score to *Oliver Twist*. After Oliver has asked for more gruel, there are three successive close-up shots of the reaction of three characters to the event. This is a clever cinematic device to suggest the rapid spreading of the news. After each character exclaims 'What!', a single sharp chord in upper strings, upper woodwind and snare drum echoes the cry. This 'comment' had its ancestry in the recitative of comic opera, but it is also a simple imitation in sound of the single word. It is an illustrative device, not an interpretative one, although it does convey the shock experienced by the characters.

A similar operatic technique is used in the score of *The Ladykillers*, in the scene where the professor tells Louis that they will never be rid of the old lady. His exaggerated despair is mocked by skittering fragments on solo woodwind and xylophone, interjected between the lines of the dialogue. The scoring of comedy films, however, has a different function altogether from that of mainstream drama. The dialogue does not need interpretation, or a setting of emotional tone. Verbal gags are more likely to elicit a cue after, rather than during, their execution. The score to *The Ladykillers* has only a handful of cues involving dialogue, as most of its cues are used to illustrate visual gags or to highlight the reactions of the characters. The scoring of such films is a

---

[20] Prendergast (1992), 219–20.

specialized art, but it is one that has its origins in the music hall and the circus, and need not concern us here.

Hollywood composers did not always choose to interpret the content of dialogue directly. In certain circumstances they chose to hint at a situation that the words themselves belied. Kathryn Kalinak describes how Korngold scored some of the dialogue in *Captain Blood* to suggest that the characters' words were not in accordance with their true feelings:

> Thus Korngold's music responds not to what is explicitly stated in the dialogue (they are either coy or insulting to each other), but to what is implicit in their demeanor and reinforced by conventional expectations of classical narrative (that two attractive stars of the opposite sex belong together). When Blood, for instance, responds to the inquiries of Miss Bishop with a cavalier attitude and high-handed remarks, the music reassures us that he is hardly as indifferent as his demeanour suggests. Similarly, when Arabella Bishop tells Blood that she hates and despises him, the soaring violins of the love theme soften, even negate, her rejection, pointing to her true feelings, thinly disguised beneath the surface. Music draws out the emotional content of the scene, hidden from the characters but not from the spectators.[21]

The writer seems a little confused as to whether the characters' demeanour reinforces their words or their underlying emotion, but the issue is with the music's anempathetic treatment of the dialogue. One of the finest examples of this kind of treatment is found in the score to *A Place in the Sun* – a film which still causes controversy among critics regarding its intrinsic merit. In one of the key scenes of the film, the central character, George, is seen rowing on a deserted lake with the woman who is pressurizing him into marriage. As she prattles on about how happy they would be if they were the only two people left on earth, the music does not reinforce the contentment of her words, but conveys the emotions that they are arousing in George. Bassoons, clarinets and low strings repeat a two-note motif of a downward semitone, gradually increasing in tempo to suggest George's rising frustration and anger. The cue culminates in a fortissimo chord from the strings, woodwind and horns, as the camera cuts to a close-up of George's face, showing his fury and resentment at the words 'Only there's going to be more than two of us, isn't there?' As George tries to recover his composure, excusing himself by saying, 'I'm out of breath – it's just the rowing', a simple clarinet trill reveals the agitation behind the lightly spoken words. Although Franz Waxman won an Academy Award for the score, he did not write the music for this sequence. Fred Karlin gives a full account of how parts of Waxman's score failed to satisfy the director George Stevens, and provides details of the uncredited contributions by other composers. According to Karlin, Daniele Amfitheatrof wrote the music for the scene in question.[22]

This type of anempathetic scoring of dialogue is very rare in British films, where such anempathetic treatment of words is usually confined to the use of

---

[21] Kalinak (1992), 88.
[22] Karlin (1994), 64.

diegetic music. It is dramatically effective to accompany scenes of high emotional intensity with an incongruously cheerful musical cue emanating from a realistic source such as a dance band. This treatment is particularly suited to British films because it accords with the automatic reflex of the British character to put a brave face on things when confronted with tragedy. In keeping with the restrained expression of emotion by British actors, this naturalistic treatment of tragic moments in film is far more affecting than the manipulative heart-rending string passages characteristic of American scores.

There is one important consideration to bear in mind when comparing the scoring of dialogue in British and American films. As this is the element of composing for film that requires the most skill, experience and dramatic flair, it is self-evident that those composers who regularly perform the task as part of their employment will have a different approach from those who are trying their hand at a new medium. Roy Prendergast describes how, despite the care taken by composers in Hollywood over dialogue scoring, their efforts can sometimes go unrewarded:

> Dialogue rules supreme on a film soundtrack. Composers are very much aware of this fact and write their music accordingly, making sure that they don't overpower the dialogue with their music but, rather, 'write around' the lines. Music cues will occasionally be dropped after they have been heard against all of the other sound elements, or it will be decided that the music is a secondary element on the soundtrack and will be mixed very low in relation to the other tracks.[23]

If this could happen to the cues of composers who specialized in film writing, it can be imagined what problems confronted the novice composers of the British film industry who had nothing but a set of guidelines from the musical director and a music cue-sheet to work from. Some of them would have benefited from the experience of Miklós Rózsa:

> The lighter the orchestration and the texture of the music for a dialogue scene, the more one would hear of it after the dubbing. It is absolutely no use to write involved counterpoint, fast figurations, heavy brass orchestrations of highly pitched sounds for such scenes. The dialogue is always considered sacrosanct and is naturally featured. The more involved the accompanying music is, the lower it will go in the dubbing, and therefore the more one loses of it.[24]

While the superiority of the acting and the more naturalistic approach of film makers contributed to the restraint of dialogue scoring in British films, it is nonetheless salutary to bear in mind the comparative inexperience of British composers, and the effect that this had on the actual *amount* of cues involving dialogue that they were given to score.

After the initial confusion of film makers caused by the coming of the sound film, Hollywood had swiftly re-established the escapist quality of their

---

[23] Prendergast (1992), 273.
[24] Miklós Rózsa, quoted in Manvell and Huntley (2/1975), 229–30.

films, largely by the development of the classical Hollywood score with its codes of practice for the treatment of dialogue. By the mid 1930s, this type of scoring had evolved to a high level of complexity. In contrast, the British film makers in this same period were still struggling with the problems posed by the introduction of sound. The British film industry had been eclipsed by Hollywood in the making of silent classics. *The Lodger* from 1926 and *Moulin Rouge* from 1928 are two rare examples of British silents that are worthy of comparison with the great American silents. The coming of sound gave British films a chance to establish a genre that was uniquely their own. Because a large part of that individuality resulted from a more naturalistic approach, it took far longer to integrate the 'unreal' element of music. Maurice Jaubert, who as a European was more in sympathy with this approach than with that of Hollywood, explains how this affected the attitude to dialogue scoring:

> To-day when the talking film, abandoning the metaphorical and allusive style of the silent film, is beginning to substitute an elliptical narrative style, music ought to forgo – except at particular points of the drama – its own essentially lyrical quality, which is bound to bring an alien element into the film.[25]

It was exactly this perception of the lyrical quality of music as an alien element in film which distinguished the British attitude to film itself. American composers had rapidly evolved a system of dialogue scoring which was based on lyrical themes in the strings. Directors and composers in Britain, with some important exceptions, fought shy of this style of dialogue scoring. Gerald Cockshott, writing in 1947, expresses the British point of view with regard to scoring a sound film:

> Where a director considers it necessary for music, natural sounds and dialogue to run simultaneously he should call for the merest musical suggestions. Anything more complex is suited only to the accompaniment of sequences without dialogue or commentary, when, if the music is appropriate, it will assist the impact of the visual images and be apprehended by us consciously without taking us outside the world of the film.[26]

The opinion that 'only the merest musical suggestions' were suitable for the scoring of dialogue, especially dialogue with natural sounds, was one that was generally held by directors of British films throughout the 1930s. Visual sequences, especially those involving strenuous physical action, such as a chase or a fight, could be scored freely. Such action scenes positively demand the presence of music. The human race has nearly always felt the instinctive need to accompany co-ordinated action with some rhythmically based form of music. Perhaps it is for this reason that filmed action sequences shown without music appear incomplete. At such moments in a film, narrative development is

---

[25] Jaubert, 'Music', in Davy (ed.) (1938), 114–15.
[26] Cockshott (1947), 6–7.

almost suspended, because the outcome of the fight or chase is limited to a handful of possibilities, all of which are visually explicit.

The score for the 1935 version of *The 39 Steps*, composed by the uncredited Hubert Bath and Jack Beaver, contains only two nondiegetic cues. The first is used for the police chase across the Scottish moors, and the second supports the 'business' where Pamela first covers the sleeping Hannay with a blanket, and then decides to keep it for herself. The one and only cue involving dialogue is, therefore, a diegetic one. In the final scene where Mr Memory reveals the secret of the thirty-nine steps while dying from a gunshot wound, the orchestra has struck up a lively number to distract the music-hall audience from the shooting. This is a rare example of the deliberate, narrative-based use of anempathetic music. It has a different impact from the irony created by chance juxtaposition of cheerful music and a tragic event.

It is not surprising that Arthur Benjamin found composing for films unrewarding. All the cues in his score for *The Scarlet Pimpernel*, released in the same year as *The 39 Steps*, are diegetic. The use of music is entirely realistic, whether it is a drum roll for the guillotine, an army band, or an ensemble playing for the ball. Four of these cues are used during scenes containing extensive dialogue, but the music is intended only to provide a naturally occurring background. It has no interpretative role, and acts merely as a provider of rather spurious historical authenticity, containing uncredited contributions from Mozart. The film had plenty of dramatic action and opportunities for free scoring which are ignored. It is fascinating to compare the scoring of these two films with that of their respective remakes. The 1959 version of *The 39 Steps*, and *The Elusive Pimpernel* from 1950 demonstrate that there is nothing in the nature of these films to discourage the use of nondiegetic music in either their dialogue or their action scenes. It was simply that in the mid-1930s British film makers were finding their feet with the new medium, and the use of music for the sound film was still in its infancy.

It might be supposed that, with all the attention that was paid to the score of *Things to Come*, some innovations or developments in the scoring of dialogue in the film might be expected. But there were none. The subject-matter of the film is largely responsible for this. It is an allegorical epic which would have been more effective as a silent film. The opening sequences are strongly reminiscent of the Russian epic silents, and promise a quality of film which is simply not sustained. Because the characters in the film are allegorical figures, and because of the artistic control exercised by Wells, the dialogue is delivered in a style that is more suited to Speaker's Corner than to the film studio. Even such skilled actors as Raymond Massey, Ralph Richardson and Edward Chapman could not make this style of acting work for the screen. In the 1930s and 1940s, many great British stage actors made the transition to screen acting. This naturally required an extensive revision of technique. According to the British actress Jean Anderson,

It's a matter of learning not to project to an audience, and of being more relaxed, with less facial expression. You learn that in close-up your *eyes* can tell it.[27]

Even actors who had spent a lifetime in the theatre could be convinced of the necessity for a radical change in acting style. In his amusing account of his direction, during the filming of *Pastor Hall*, of the veteran actor Seymour Hicks, Roy Boulting reveals how stage techniques simply do not work in film:

> He wanted to know why I employed him since I wouldn't allow him to act! A moment's thought and then I suggested that he play the scene exactly as he wished. He brightened up at that but I went on to ask if he would indulge me, and film it again, playing it this time in the way I thought more effective. His doubts returned. 'Look, Sir Seymour', I said, 'we'll see both takes in tomorrow morning's "rushes". Whichever one you judge to be the best, I promise to use in the finished film.' At 8.30 the next morning, Seymour came and sat himself down in a theatre packed with the film crew. We ran the 'rushes'. Eventually, the disputed scene came up. As Seymour, looking magnificent, hammed it up, first there came titters and then outright laughter. The *second* take restored the situation. Seymour – doing nothing, as he thought – held the unit in pin-drop silence, so moving did they find his performance, and they gave him a round of applause.[28]

The dialogue delivery in *Things to Come* is rhetorical, exaggerated and consequently unreal. This style, dictated by the subject-matter of the film, is therefore capable of sustaining a more vigorous type of scoring than would be suitable for a more naturalistic dialogue delivery, and most of the Hollywood 'rules' do not apply to it. Despite this potential free hand, there are very few music cues involving dialogue. Two of these nondiegetic cues occur in the section of the film dealing with the wandering sickness. In these scenes the dialogue is almost incidental to the music, as it begins some way into the scene, after the music has been established in response to the images of the robotic victims of the disease. The dialogue merely endorses what the music already reveals. In another scene, the music of the well-known march, accompanying the arrival of the Chief, continues at reduced volume through the ensuing discussion of aeroplanes. In filmic convention this would imply that the whole cue is a diegetic one. However, as it is played by a full symphony orchestra, this makes no sense in diegetic terms.

The final scene of the film centres on an exchange between two characters who represent the forces of progress and conservatism. As they stand by a giant telescope against the background of the night sky, their delivery reaches new heights of rhetorical declamation. This is interpreted by a noble extended melody from the brass, woodwind and strings – a texture and volume that normal dialogue scenes could not tolerate. Even at this extreme of vocal projection, the music is overwhelming. The final words spoken in the film, 'Which shall it be?', are taken up by a large mixed chorus, accompanied by full

---

[27] Jean Anderson, quoted in McFarlane (ed.) (1992), 1.
[28] Roy Boulting, quoted in McFarlane (ed.) (1992), 35.

orchestra. The score of *Things to Come* may have broken new ground by the quality of its music and in the superb blending of music and image in the big visual sequences, but it did nothing for the development of dialogue scoring in British films. Bliss had simply fulfilled the requirement of writing music that was fitting for the nature of the film, and which had been written before the film was shot.

The film historian Rachel Low's description of *Things to Come* and of Wells's approach to fiction writing clearly indicates the impersonal aspect of the film:

> The film was very much a designer's film, outstanding for stagecraft and spectacle rather than for emotional involvement. Wells in his sixties was a polemicist rather than a story-teller and the several generations of people he invented were types rather than individuals, vehicles for the great issues which he wished to discuss.[29]

This 'designer's film', with its extended visual sequences, had provided Bliss with the opportunity to write music that satisfied its own formal and developmental requirements. The concert suite of *Things to Come* was the first major British film music to be put on disc; a practice deplored by purists, who maintain that the components of a film should be so well-integrated that their separate existence is impossible. *Things to Come* provides an exception because the visual sequences were made to fit the pre-recorded music. Bliss was given a rare opportunity to provide music that could earn the right to stand alone. There is also an obvious distinction between scoring intended to 'assist the impact of visual images' and suitable dialogue scoring: after all, there would be very few takers for a recording of 'the merest musical suggestions' recommended by Cockshott.

British film scores in the late 1930s did not develop much further in their treatment of dialogue. There was still a dependence on diegetic cues behind dialogue to provide a general atmosphere. In a later Korda spectacular, *The Drum*, released in 1938, the score relies very heavily on diegetic music in its dialogue scenes. A paean to the glorious days of the British Empire, the film is a vehicle for the child star Sabu, who plays an Indian prince. The score was composed by John Greenwood, unaided by Miklós Rózsa it seems, despite claims to the contrary.[30] There are two dialogue cues in the score which continue the music of the previous scene. This is very similar to the continued use of the march in *Things to Come* for the ensuing dialogue. Ironically, it is again a march, accompanying scenes depicting the massing of troops, which is used in *The Drum*. In the latter case, however, the scenes concerned are not continuations of those involving the march, but are separate dialogue scenes set in different locations. The only justification for this continued use of an unrelated 'visual' music cue is that in both instances Carruthers, the British army captain, is discussing strategical moves against

---

[29] Low (1985), 172.
[30] Both Halliwell and Low give a shared credit to Greenwood and Rózsa, but there is no
      reference to it by Rózsa in his autobiography *Double Life*.

the enemy, and the music can be supposed to reflect the tone of the conversation.

This type of 'blanket' scoring of dialogue is used for the scenes involving Prince Azim and his countrymen. Here, music of a generalized 'eastern' nature, reminiscent of Rimsky-Korsakof's *Sheherazade*, with a liberal use of melodic augmented seconds, is employed. No attempt is made to follow the twists of the dialogue, or to interpret it in any more specific way. This type of dialogue scoring is only a very small step away from empathetic diegetic scoring, which is intended merely to provide an atmosphere appropriate to the setting rather than to the dialogue itself.

However sincerely Korda desired to represent in his films the true quality of the British nation, his efforts could be no more successful than the English film makers attempts to create a faithful representation of the Hungarian nation. The theory that an outsider can perceive a nation more acutely than the nation can itself is simply not borne out by the results of Korda's films. In addition, Korda's infatuation with the British extended only as far as its upper classes. He had no interest in portraying the lives and conditions of its lower orders. In contrast, Ealing studios had promoted George Formby and Gracie Fields as working-class heroes. The unlikely vehicle of their musicals had brought the lives of ordinary people to the screen in a more human way than the earnest accounts of housing conditions produced by documentary film makers. In 1939 Ealing released *There Ain't No Justice*, a film which hints at the realism of the 'new wave' cinema of the late 1950s. Rachel Low describes the film:

> Moderately priced but not cheap and shoddy, it was a fairly realistic, if slightly cosy, treatment of ordinary British people. The advertisement ran: 'Real people – Real problems – a human document'. It was about the attraction the crooked fight game had for underprivileged youngsters, and starred young Jimmy Hanley. Unusual at the time both for its degree of realism and for the serious theme, it was a critical success.[31]

British films, after the time of the introduction of sound, may have been more naturalistic than the typical Hollywood product, but in the 1930s they seldom had more than a nodding acquaintance with realism. Stringent censorship had hamstrung the British film industry throughout the decade, politics being considered an even more sensitive issue than that of sex. The realism of *There Ain't No Justice* did not extend to its nondiegetic treatment of dialogue scoring. The diegetic cues, involving dance bands and music from the radio, all have a naturalistic function within the drama, and are not principally intended to provide an atmosphere for the dialogue scenes. Ernest Irving displays dubious taste and dramatic judgment in the scoring of the only two dialogue scenes in the film to be treated nondiegetically. Instead of allowing the awkwardness of the young hero and his girl-next-door in their more tender moments together to be expressed, Irving accompanies their stilted conversa-

---

[31] Low (1985), 254.

tions with a rendering of 'Just a Song at Twilight' on solo violin and piano. The use of this sentimental music-hall song undermines the film's attempt to portray the lives of the working-class youngsters realistically, and the fact that it acts as a theme for the young couple has the effect of trivializing the depiction of their relationship.

If the scoring of the spoken word in British feature films of the 1930s was a somewhat lacklustre affair, there is one example from a documentary film of 1936 which is worthy of mention because it introduced a new conception of the fusing of music with both word and image. In the famous sequence from *Night Mail*, the commentary suddenly changes from factual information about the Edinburgh mail train to a poetic fantasy of its journey. Naturalistic sounds are dropped from the soundtrack as the narration of Auden's poem and the recording of Britten's economically orchestrated score are synchronized with the motion of the engine's wheels and coupling rods. The fusion of these three elements of music, image and voice provided the most imaginative scoring of the spoken word to emerge from British film in the 1930s, and the example was taken up in the following decade for use in feature films. As British films began, with the advent of war, to establish their own identity, British composers grew away from the primitive methods of dialogue scoring characteristic of the 1930s. A new era in the development of the British film score was about to begin.

8. The impact of the Second World War on British films, and developments in dialogue scoring in the 1940s

The Second World War had a far greater direct impact on the lives of British people than had the First World War. For those remaining on the home front, the severest consequence of the 1914–18 war was the enormous loss of life of their kinsfolk on active duty. There were far fewer civilian casualties than in the Second World War; rationing was not as severe; and invasion was only a remote possibility. The Second World War touched the lives of every British person in a way that the Great War had not. Increased mobility, and advances in communications, brought the effects of war home to everyone, and made avoidance of them impossible.

The two wars, moreover, had very different consequences for British cinema. According to Alan Wood, in his biography of Arthur Rank,

> The First World War took the heart out of British production; while Hollywood, discovering such geniuses as D. W. Griffith and the London cockney Charles Chaplin, established unchallengeable supremacy. The audiences of the world, seeing nothing but Hollywood, soon acquired a taste for nothing but Hollywood; while no would-be rival, fighting for the same world market, could hope to rival the lavishness of Hollywood productions.[1]

So crippling was the effect of the Hollywood stranglehold on British production, that '[b]y 1923, only 10 per cent. of the films shown in Britain were made in Britain. By 1926 the figure was 5 per cent., or even lower.'[2]

If the First World War had been the cause of serious problems for the British film industry, the Second World War was to be its salvation. With rare exceptions, British films of the 1930s had been little more than diversions of the most superficial kind. War provided a compelling focus for the industry:

> British films of the 30s may have been conspicuous by their failure to address the social issues of the day or to reflect the 'agony of the times', but a world war was too monstrous a phenomenon to pass over in favour of West End farce, Edgar Wallace spy thrillers and cheap and cheerful seaside comedies. The war was

---

[1] Wood (1952), 48.
[2] Ibid., 49.

universal, affecting everybody: as a subject for movies, it could easily overcome the class and regional barriers which had previously split British audiences.[3]

While the subject of war provided material that was both cinematic and universal in its appeal, it was the changing circumstances within the British film industry, occasioned by the outbreak of war, that were to have the most far-reaching effects. Korda had been unable to finish shooting *The Thief of Baghdad* in Egypt and Arabia because of the hostilities, and had decided to transfer the production team to the Grand Canyon in Arizona. Karol Kulik gives a detailed account of Korda's subsequent sojourn in America, and puts forward some interesting theories as to why Korda did not return to Britain until 1943.[4] Whatever the truth about Korda's activities during the war, and the reasons for his being granted a knighthood, the fact is that, through a succession of remarkable circumstances, his supremacy in the British film industry passed to a man of altogether different character.[5]

Korda's position in the history of British film is somewhat anomalous. He dominated the industry for virtually the whole of the 1930s. His prestige productions – *The Private Life of Henry VIII, Rembrandt, The Four Feathers* – had saved British cinema from total obscurity. Without his productions, the output of the industry in the 1930s is a sorry affair. However, in the final analysis, his films were simply not British, but international. One of the foreign directors that Korda had employed, Jacques Feyder, saw the implications for British film resulting from Korda's methods and spoke out against them:

> Feyder himself struck a blow for the 'national' British film in a tirade against the sort of film that he was directing and Korda was continually promoting. It concluded: 'In short, English films about England made by English people. That is the ideal. No more foreign styles, no more foreign technicians, no more foreign film-craftsmen, no more foreign film directors . . .'[6]

There was one British producer who managed to create an oasis of Britishness in the desert of Korda's 'international' output. The producer Victor Saville was responsible for three of Korda's films: *Storm in a Teacup, Action for Slander,* and *South Riding,* which Karol Kulik felt stood out from the rest of Korda's output:

> These three films represented the 'English film about England made by English people' of which Feyder had spoken. They were all critically praised for 'digging down' into just those 'British roots' which Korda had always avoided as box-office poison.[7]

---

[3] Macnab (1994), 37–8.
[4] Kulik (1990), 240–60.
[5] For a detailed account of how Rank assumed the mantle of power in the British film industry, see Wood (1952), 106–9.
[6] Kulik (1990), 205.
[7] Ibid., 208.

Victor Saville's handling of these three films demonstrates what could be achieved by a British producer with all the facilities of Denham studios, and with the minimum of interference from Korda himself. These films also serve to highlight the inadequacies of Korda's more typical efforts because

> the underplayed acting, a trait of all three films, gave . . . a naturalness which Korda himself never really achieved. In fact, the simplicity and lack of pretension of Saville's Denham films show up the majority of Korda's own films for what they often are – vulgar and overblown attempts to make up for an emptiness of plot or idea or a shallowness of human characterization by an emphasis on superficial production values.[8]

Korda's chief offence had been to render his actors 'secondary to everything else'.[9] British film, from the 1940s onwards, came to be distinguished by the dominating position of its actors. Only in exceptional cases where the film's main protagonist is an element of nature, as in *Scott of the Antarctic* or *The Cruel Sea*, do the human characters become reduced in stature. Even in these cases, the characters are subservient to the forces of nature rather than to the film's special effects. Ultimately, Korda fought shy of attempting to portray the English and England honestly. If it is true that to understand a culture you must thoroughly understand the language, then perhaps the Korda brothers' relation to our culture can be best summed up by the famous, though possibly apocryphal, retort of Zoltan's: 'You think I know f*** nothing about pictures! I tell you I know f*** all!'[10]

Alexander Korda differed in almost every respect from the man who came to supersede him as the central figure in the British film industry:

> Korda has always been everything that Rank was not. Korda was a Cavalier where Rank was a Puritan; Korda was Bohemian where Rank was a Methodist; Korda had an artistic conscience where Rank had a Sunday School conscience. Korda was divorced and Rank was happily married; Korda had the gift of tongues and every social charm; Korda had perfect taste in food and drink; Korda was steeped in cultural and intellectual interests: Korda – though this is often forgotten since he became a financier – was a film director in the first rank before he put on too much glamour.[11]

J. Arthur Rank may have been 'almost completely devoid of any cultural interests whatever',[12] but he was an Englishman, and he was extremely rich. It might be wondered how a flour merchant came to be involved in the film industry at all, but the answer lies in the single most important thing in his life – his religion. In his own words, Rank, a Methodist lay-preacher, reveals how his interest in promoting religious films led him into the world of film production:

---

[8] Kulik (1990), 209.
[9] Ibid., 243.
[10] Ibid., 211.
[11] Wood (1952), 60.
[12] Ibid., 121.

> I saw that religious films could be a great power for good. I also saw that it was no
> use giving people in churches cheap, badly made films when they could see up-to-
> date well-made films at cinemas during the week. I saw that the thing to do was to
> have a hand in their making myself.[13]

That this simple intention resulted in Rank's ultimate position at the top of the
British film industry was also due to his religious beliefs:

> If I could relate to you some of my various adventures and experiences in the
> larger film world, you would not only be astounded, but it would, I think, be as
> plain to you as it is to me that I was being led by God.[14]

Rank certainly seems to have been engineered into a position where he
became the only possible candidate for the task of saving the British film
industry from extinction. At the initial outbreak of war, the British government
had not immediately seen the enormous potential of cinema as an agent to
inform and influence the population. It had hardly considered cinema at all:

> Among many other things, it had no policy ready for films. In expectation of
> immediate mass air-raids, all cinemas were promptly closed; when no raids came
> for the time being, they were gingerly re-opened. But the Government seemed to
> be going on the assumption that, as in the First World War, there would be little
> time or place for anyone to make British films. It was true that Michael Balcon
> and others had seen the importance of films in a total war, and had presented their
> views to the Government, but nobody in the Government paid any attention.[15]

The government's initial failure to realize the importance of an indigenous film
industry, and other conditions arising as a direct result of the war, almost led to
the collapse of the industry:

> Studios were rapidly requisitioned by the armed forces, and filled with sugar and
> other vital provisions. For a brief period, there was a very real danger that British
> feature film production might be abandoned altogether: shortages, rationing,
> which affected every part of filmmaking from set construction to costumes and
> make-up, the lack of studio space, the enforced absence of up to two-thirds of the
> technicians, who had been 'called up', and the voluntary absence of those select
> few who had hot-footed it to Hollywood as soon as hostilities were announced,
> threatened to destroy the industry, or, even worse, expose it to Hollywood
> takeover.[16]

Despite these daunting conditions, a few British film makers continued to turn
out a trickle of films in the early days of the war. However, with the threat of
worse things to come, they were hardly enough to safeguard the industry:

[13] J. Arthur Rank, quoted in Wood (1952), 69.
[14] Ibid., 68.
[15] Wood (1952), 103.
[16] Macnab (1994), 36.

Ahead lay the 1940/1 winter of continued blitz, emptying the cinemas and filling the tube stations and air-raid shelters. What lay even farther ahead nobody knew; as late as the spring of 1941 there were still recurrent rumours of impending German invasion. Only a rich man, with plenty of money to lose, could possibly save British films from a repetition of what happened in 1914–18.[17]

Realistically, there was only one likely saviour for the British film industry, and Rank did not shirk his responsibility, because he 'felt called to this work'.[18] In addition to his money and his commitment, Rank had one other attribute that was to serve the industry well:

His greatest virtue of all was undoubtedly the fact that *he knew nothing whatever about making films.* This, of course, by no means made him unique among British film magnates; but he *was* unique in realising that he knew nothing.[19]

It was this humility of Rank with regard to his position in the whole business of film production that led to the resurgence of film making in Britain, and to the flowering of a national art. His policy of non-interference in the creative process led to a new freedom of opportunity for artists of the cinema such as Powell and Pressburger and David Lean. Lean himself describes how this policy of Rank's affected the progress of the British film industry:

We of Independent Producers can make any subject we wish, with as much money as we think that subject should have spent upon it. We can cast whatever actors we choose, and we have no interference at all in the way the film is made. No one sees the films until they are finished, and no cuts are made without the consent of the director or the producer . . . Such is the enviable position of British film makers today, and such are the conditions which have at last given our films a style and nationality of their own.[20]

Rank's willingness to give this amount of artistic freedom and financial support to his producers was inevitably a target for both misuse and abuse at the hands of some less scrupulous individuals. The fiasco of *Caesar and Cleopatra* is universally held up as an example by those who condemned Rank's too liberal attitudes. The cynical exploitation of Rank's ingenuousness by producers such as Pascal should not detract from the enormous benefits to British cinema that were the result of his policy of trust.

Although Rank left the subject-matter of his films to the discretion of his film makers, it is important to remember that, during the war years, the subject-matter of all films was vetted by the Films Division of the Ministry of Information. After the initial failure of the government to grasp the significance of a national film industry, it did not take it long to realize how potent was the weapon for propaganda at its disposal:

[17]   Wood (1952), 106.
[18]   J. Arthur Rank, quoted in Wood (1952), 83.
[19]   Wood (1952), 121.
[20]   David Lean, quoted in Wood (1952), 125.

Plate 5. Alan Rawsthorne, Muir Mathieson and William Alwyn at the recording of an unknown wartime documentary.

> Clearly the cinema was always going to be of considerable use in furthering the national cause generally and, on the home front especially, it was ideally suited to help in sustaining civilian morale.[21]

The Ministry of Information realized that the feature film was an equally, if not more effective means of getting a message across to the audience. But the real significance of its contribution to the development of British films was in the policy it adopted in relation to their quality. The Ministry did not simply exploit the medium for its own purposes without considering the interests of British cinema:

> The public's desire for 'entertainment' should be indulged and film producers helped accordingly. But as far as the MoI was concerned, the 'entertainment' so provided could still be utilized for propaganda purposes, it should also be uplifting, and it should be invested with 'quality' and thereby further increase the overall standard of British film production. The MoI was especially keen on enhancing the 'quality' of British cinema and providing what Beddington referred to as 'good' films, and it claimed some credit on this front.[22]

---

[21] Aldgate and Richards (1986), 4.
[22] Ibid., 11.

While these factors contributed to the rise of a national cinema in Britain, it was, ultimately, the reality of war itself which was the major catalyst for change in the attitudes of the nation's cinema-goers. In the first two years of the war, when the British people were suffering severe hardship, the Hollywood package, produced by a nation which now had even less in common with them, seemed an irrelevance to their lives. Whilst these films still provided a sometimes welcome form of escapism, the British public had grown to expect more from their entertainment:

> Before the war, in the troubled 1930s, Hollywood had held almost uncontested dominion over the cinemas of the UK. Now, at last, British filmmakers had found a theme, a genre – the war picture – which was all their own.[23]

War provided both British film and the British people with a purpose. The film industry had floundered in the 1930s when the nation was increasingly polarized between extreme poverty on the one hand and hedonistic affluence on the other. War brought common concerns and shared tribulations to a divided nation, and although distinctions of class were never significantly altered, unprecedented closeness of contact between the classes, and a sense of a united purpose did result in an increase of understanding and sympathy. Britain's role in the war was not that of aggressor but that of defender, and the whole style of propaganda reflected this fact. Writing of one of the earliest documentary films produced in the war, Robert Murphy describes how the British approach to film making in the early days of the war created

> that stoical, underplayed, poetic spirit which was to prove so potent a force in British propaganda. In contrast to aggressive German militarism, the British, it was argued, were fighting because they had to, more in sorrow than in anger.[24]

British motivation to fight was skilfully called forth by the manipulation of patriotic sentiment regarding Britain's glorious heritage. Winston Churchill, who was without doubt a genius in the field of propaganda, knew how to draw from his people a fervour of nationalist pride and devotion:

> It was Churchill who was the official voice of Britain, speaking with a deep consciousness of the weight of history, his language deliberately archaic and therefore timeless. When he said after Alamein 'a bright gleam has caught the helmets of our soldiers' he might have been talking of Caesar's army or that of Richard the Lionheart. The golden rhetoric, delivered in those distinctive rolling cadences, drew on the majestic imagery and language of a heroic past, of Shakespeare and Milton, of Tennyson and Kipling.[25]

Churchill's 'golden rhetoric' and 'distinctive rolling cadences' were to provide the key to one of the paradoxes of British films from the war years.

---

[23]   Macnab (1994), 37.
[24]   Murphy (1992), 12.
[25]   Aldgate and Richards (1986), 46.

The effects of the war, and the British people's reaction to it, had resulted in a cinema that was establishing a strong identity. John Huntley describes the emergence of this new identity succinctly:

> 1940 saw the end of the slump, the end of quota quickies and Hollywood imitation. The film industry in this country was at last forced to stand on its own feet or disappear for good. It was in 1940 that we turned the corner into an avenue of a new type of national cinema – real, intense, intelligent cinema.[26]

The realism of British feature films had been encouraged by several factors during the war years. Apart from the treatment of serious subject-matter occasioned by the national crisis, there was the incorporation of documentary film-making techniques into mainstream cinema, to such a large extent that 'documentary realism became one of the critical tests of the successful entertainment feature'.[27] Additionally, censorship laws were relaxed sufficiently for 'subjects [to be] broached in the cinema that had barely been touched upon before'.[28] British films in the second half of the 1930s had, despite crippling censorship and a tendency towards incipient triviality, nevertheless been more realistic in their treatment than their Hollywood counterparts. The increased emphasis on realism brought about by conditions resulting from the war was the main factor in the growing alienation of the British audience from the Hollywood film:

> However elusive as a concept, 'realism' did serve as a means of distinguishing British pictures from their American counterparts, thus helping carve out a new, discrete identity for British film makers: the 'realistic' British film sets itself squarely in opposition to Hollywood, which Rank always called 'Fairyland'.[29]

The increased realism of feature films by the incorporation of documentary techniques applied not so much to the actors and their methods as to other factors in film making. Charles Barr thought that 'perhaps the main influence was in the areas of location shooting, editing techniques, *sober* narratives'.[30] The delivery of the dialogue in feature films would hardly have been rendered more realistic if actors had aped the typically bracing enthusiasm of the style of narration in documentary, or the self-conscious mumblings of its 'real-life' participants. The paradox in the nature of feature film from the war years lies in relation to acting style, because although physical restraint and a self-deprecating manner were still the order of the day, the 'golden rhetoric' and 'distinctive rolling cadences' of the 'official voice of Britain' had unconsciously coloured the vocal timbres of film actors. British patriotism, in keeping with

---

[26] Huntley (1947), 70.
[27] Aldgate and Richards (1986), 219.
[28] Ibid., 14.
[29] Macnab (1994), 38–9.
[30] Charles Barr, 'Projecting Britain and the British Character', *Screen* (Spring 1974), quoted in Aldgate and Richards (1986), 9.

the generally perceived national character, may have been discreetly under-
played, both by the people at large and by the film industry, but the intensity of
feeling was very real:

> The war brought into sharp focus the meaning of England and Englishness. There
> is in wartime a heightening of emotions, a quickening of the pulse. It is a time for
> poetry and brave words. Sentiments can be uttered and felt and believed which in
> prosaic peace time seem inflated, exaggerated, unreal.[31]

It was exactly the 'inflated, exaggerated, unreal' style of dialogue delivery in
Hollywood films that had resulted in such an elaborate code of practice for its
musical scoring. British films did not succumb to cheap emotionalism during
the war, but the heightened emotion of the nation as a whole, and of the content
of film dialogue, led to the increased acceptability of more complex dialogue
scoring.

The rise of patriotic sentiment encouraged a greater awareness of certain of
the nation's less tangible qualities which are sometimes reflected in the works of
its creative artists. Jeffrey Richards reveals how the actor Leslie Howard brought
these qualities to the attention of British audiences:

> What he represented to British audiences was that visionary aspect of Englishness,
> that fey, mystical quality, that striving after the secrets of the eternal that crops out
> periodically in English writing and English thought. It is there in the music of
> Elgar and Vaughan Williams, in the writings of Kipling and Haggard, in the
> poetry of Henry Newbolt and Rupert Brooke. It has a peculiarly potent linkage
> with war.[32]

Of course, Richards is not speaking here of the jingoism that unfortunately
came to be associated with certain of Elgar's works. It was not the rousing of
nationalist feeling by the use of martial music, so beloved of the Germans, that
summoned up the mystical connection to their country in British souls. It was
the music that evoked the spirit of the land itself which was most effective as
propaganda. Lewis Foreman describes the kind of music that was broadcast by
the BBC during the war:

> The new British music that tended to be projected to the overseas listener often
> had overtones of a rural England that may well have appealed more to expatriate
> Britons abroad in wartime that to more intellectual music lovers in Europe. A
> typical example is the treatment accorded Julius Harrison's soaring pastoral
> evocation *Bredon Hill* – very much in the mould of Vaughan Williams's *The
> Lark Ascending* of a quarter-century earlier.[33]

The strong nationalist influence of such music as *Bredon Hill* was certainly
not lost on the composer himself. In an interview broadcast to North America a

---

[31] Aldgate and Richards (1986), 46.
[32] Ibid., 53–4.
[33] Foreman (1987), 240.

few months before Pearl Harbor, he explained the connection between the work and his strong feeling for his country:

> [The work] grew out of itself in my mind from all those scenes I have known all my life. After all, we mustn't forget that this part of Worcestershire speaks of England at its oldest. It is the heart of Mercia, the country of Piers Plowman, and it is the spirit of Elgar's music too. If I've been able to catch something of all this then I'm indeed glad.[34]

The BBC were not slow to exploit the propaganda value of this work, and its attitude indicates how vital was the contribution of music to the war effort:

> It is a fact remarkable in itself that such music as this comes out of the present time. That it does, is perhaps the *best witness to the eternal spirit of England*. [my italics][35]

The exemption of British composers from active service was a complex problem. E. J. Moeran, writing to the *Musical Times* in 1941, was refreshingly frank on the subject:

> Are all composers to be exempt from service? Heaven forbid! There is far more contemporary music than can get itself performed, and always has been . . . Their services are essential to the cultural life of the country, but there is always a plentiful supply.[36]

Moeran was obviously not thinking of the work for documentary and feature film which was occupying so many British composers – released, if only temporarily, from active service for the purpose. A BBC memo dating from November 1941 indicates how all-consuming was the commitment to such work:

> I am sorry I did not mention that Addinsell was in the forefront of our minds too; but we did not include him in this present list, because we found, on asking for his collaboration in our 'Composer at the Piano' series, that he is so busy on Ministry of Information films he cannot spare the time ever to run up to Evesham (or even London) for a broadcast or recording.[37]

There was general recognition of the valuable part played by music in film, both for the promotion of patriotism and for its service to British films themselves. The critic C. A. Lejeune, writing of Muir Mathieson in 1944 affirms that:

---

[34] Julius Harrison, interview with Elizabeth Poston, Broadcast in BBC North American Transmission, 29.9.1941, in Foreman (1987), 240–1.

[35] BBC Overseas Service Pacific Transmission, 3.10.1941; African Transmission, 2.10.1941; North American Transmission, 29.9.1941, in Foreman (1987), 241.

[36] E. J. Moeran, letter to the *Musical Times* (October 1941), in Foreman (1987), 242.

[37] Kenneth Wright to R. S. Thatcher, BBC Internal Circulating Memo, 25.11.1941, in Foreman (1987), 245.

Of all the people who have served the British cinema brilliantly in wartime, I should put this young, ardent little Scotsman very near the top of the list.[38]

At a time when 'any good British production could be regarded as propaganda',[39] it was not a difficult matter to convince an English composer that writing for film was a contribution to his country as valuable as any other form of service, if not more so. Mathieson gives us a touching account of how his proposal that Vaughan Williams should provide a score for *49th Parallel* led the composer to appreciate the importance of such work:

> When I went to see Vaughan Williams at his country home in the spring of 1940, I found him strangely depressed at his inability to play a fuller part in the war. He felt that the musician had done little to express the spirit and resolve of the British people. At that time he was 'doing his bit' by driving a cart round the village and countryside, collecting scrap metal and salvage. (Vaughan Williams was then over 70 years of age). I told him the story of *49th Parallel* and tried to show how the cinema could help to achieve those very objectives for which he was striving. His enthusiasm was wonderful. He set to work right away – and remember this was the first time he had ever consented to write for the screen.[40]

We have previously observed the reasons why *49th Parallel* did not lend itself to extensive dialogue scoring. An examination of the dialogue scenes that are scored nondiegetically demonstrates that in none of these scenes is the dialogue itself the focus of musical interpretation. The first three cues containing dialogue are heard as the German submariners approach land in their U-boat, and all employ the theme associated with them. The sparse dialogue is mostly centred on the task at hand – the manoeuvring of the U-boat into safe waters. The characters are therefore engaged in a visible activity to which their exchanges of information are secondary. Similarly, in the scene where Hirth's suspicions are aroused by Fogel crossing himself, the words spoken, 'Herr Leutnant, he's dead' and 'So that's Kuhnecke!', are merely incidental to the visual images, and are subservient to the action. The two dialogue cues that occur in the Hutterite section of the film are both treated as impressionistic backdrops signifying the rural idyll of the community's lifestyle, no attention being paid to the darker content of the dialogue. The final nondiegetic scoring of dialogue again takes the setting as the principal focus. As Lohrman and Jahner, standing on a Winnipeg street in the pouring rain, discuss selling Hirth's binoculars to buy food, the music provides the atmosphere of the crowded city at night. The waltz reflects the affluence of the city, with its neon lights advertising food and its restaurant windows taunting the hungry, penniless Germans.

These dialogue scenes all have features in common which encourage a particular type of musical treatment. Without exception, the spoken words

[38]   C. A. Lejeune, in Huntley (1947), 34.
[39]   Jack Beddington, quoted in Aldgate and Richards (1986), 9.
[40]   Muir Mathieson, quoted in Huntley (1947), 56–7.

are a straightforward exchange of information or opinion – almost a trans-action. They carry very little emotional content, and require no sort of narrative interpretation from the music. The dialogues are all subordinate to the setting in which the scene takes place, and this is chiefly because, with one exception, they are all exterior scenes. Apart from the scene set inside the U-boat, all the others are set out-of-doors, whether on the deck of the boat, in the wheatfields, or on the streets of Winnipeg.

The placing of a film's characters in an exterior location has a profound effect on the impact of the dialogue. The most emotionally intense dialogue scenes – the ones that attract the most attention from Hollywood composers – usually take place between two characters in an interior setting. For one human being to engage fully in verbal communication with another human being, several requirements must be met. The participants should be in reasonably close proximity, with full visual contact, they should preferably be alone, and they should not be distracted by physical activity. In film, such scenes are generally shot in close-up or medium close shot. This focuses the audience's attention on the emotions and responses of the characters, and prevents the intrusion of the outside world. In these circumstances, dialogue can transcend the role of a 'transaction' and become a complex transmitter of emotional nuance and of plot development. This primary form of dialogue, where the meaning of the exchange between two characters takes precedence over every other element of the scene, is the one that lends itself most readily to interpretative thematic treatment in the score. It is also the one that needs the most careful use of orchestration to enhance rather than hinder vocal inflection.

With each transgression of the rules for primary dialogue, the supremacy of its position in a scene is progressively eroded. The nature of 'dialogue' takes on a different hue when there are more than two people involved. Any two people will modify their conversation in the presence of a third party, and words spoken to a group of people are automatically more constrained. Engaging in physical activity diffuses the intensity of a conversation by distracting the focus of attention – a tactic frequently employed by those who wish to avoid intimacy. The more vigorous the activity, the more the conversation is manoeuvred into a position of secondary importance. It is, for instance, difficult to negotiate a divorce settlement while playing a game of badminton; and where physical activity predominates, the dialogue tends to become merely incidental to the action.

When a conversation is conducted out-of-doors, attention is distracted by stimuli from the natural world. Similarly, a film's characters can become lost in the scene's setting. Exterior dialogue scenes are commonly filmed in long shot or medium long shot. The further away the character, the less, generally speaking, the audience can empathize with him or her, and the less the narrative complexities can be communicated. Dialogue between two stationary characters shot in close-up is a very different matter from the snatched exchanges of soldiers running along a beach, and it warrants a suitably different musical treatment. The dialogue in the latter case is basically a commentary on what is already being visually communicated to the audience, and its function is little more than that of any other naturalistic sound of the scene.

Exterior dialogue scenes shot in close-up usually indicate a studio mock-up. The conversation between Peter and Andreas in the wheatfield in *49th Parallel* is one that was obviously shot in the studio. An establishing shot of Peter standing in a large wheatfield lends an impression of space to the ensuing dialogue scene, and permits Vaughan Williams to assist the illusion by using the pastoral theme associated with the Hutterite wheatfields.

In scenes of primary and secondary dialogue, the audience is not addressed directly by the characters, and is an unacknowledged witness of events on the screen. There are, however, two other types of 'dialogue' which are direct communications from the speaker to the audience, and which are not addressed to the other characters in the film. These techniques involving voice-overs, whether or not the speakers are visible on the screen, change the audience's status from that of unacknowledged observer to passive participant because information is revealed to it which is withheld from the other characters in the film. This shift of position is a breach of the cinematic code which demands that the audience be allowed to lose itself in the narrative flow. By being directly addressed, as in voice-over narration where the speaker is not visible, the audience is made aware of itself – a situation which Hollywood film makers generally took pains to avoid.

The practice of having the thoughts of a character who is visible on the screen conveyed to the audience by voice-over is equally invasive. A considerable proportion of *Scott of the Antarctic* is given over to the reading by John Mills of extracts from the diaries of Scott, translated into the 'thoughts' of the screen character as he is seen wearily making his way through the landscape. Vaughan Williams referred to these readings as the 'inner voice'. This type of dialogue must be considered as something completely separate from primary dialogue because its function in the narrative is different. The other characters are not privy to Scott's thoughts and can therefore show no reaction to them. The majority of the actual dialogue in the film is incidental, not so much to the action, as to the film's chief protagonist – the landscape. The main theme of the film is the grandeur and the treachery of the Antarctic terrain, and the characters, often seen in extreme long shot, are accordingly reduced in significance. In that context, their vocal exchanges are all but irrelevant, and the score quite rightly focuses on the main thematic element of the film.

The technique of the 'inner voice' was much less frequently used in British films than was voice-over narration. But its use in films was encouraged by the incorporation of documentary techniques and ethos into feature film, and the use of footage from newsreel. Because narration introduces an 'unnatural' element into the diegesis, the scoring of it is exempt from the usual expectations regarding dialogue scoring. The most disturbing use of the technique is when a character on screen speaks directly and visibly to the audience. This violation of the cinematic code is very uncomfortable for the audience, whose status of invisible voyeur is challenged. Actors are occasionally filmed while staring directly at the camera, but the audience know this is a device to reveal something about the character, and never imagine that they themselves are exposed to his gaze. In the opening scene of *Went the Day Well?*, the audience is directly addressed by the church sexton, who is recounting the events of the narrative from some future moment in time. This is nothing less than a prologue, an antiquated contrivance abandoned by the theatre as being too antithetic to realism.

The scoring of primary dialogue in British films in the 1930s had generally been side-stepped by composers. There was much use of diegetic music, and a kind of general-purpose local-colour scoring such as that used by John Greenwood in *The Drum*. In neither of these methods are the emotional contours of the dialogue interpreted or highlighted by the music cues. The development of dialogue scoring during the war years was gradual, as British films began to discover their own identity. Three films released within a six-month period following the release of *49th Parallel* in October 1941, which all, in their different ways, deal with the subject of patriotism, demonstrate this slow evolution.

All three films make extensive use of diegetic music for scoring dialogue scenes. The old 'justification' for the presence of music, stemming from the early days of the sound film, continued into films of this period. In the first of these, *Dangerous Moonlight*, the diegetic music is absolutely central to the main storyline, and serves a different function from the more usual attempts to introduce music realistically into the scene. There is nothing very realistic about a Polish concert-pianist-cum-pilot conducting a conversation with a stranger while playing a grand piano during an air-raid. Despite impressions to the contrary, the unlikely plot was not devised as a vehicle for the tabloid concerto that came to be the most memorable feature of the film. As John Huntley points out,

> No one had foreseen the amazing popularity that the 'Warsaw Concerto' would enjoy. Thus when the film first appeared, the gramophone record had not been issued nor had the sheet music, but on discovering what a hit this elusive, haunting melody had become, the error was quickly rectified . . .[41]

The film was an honest if somewhat saccharine attempt to bring the plight of the Polish people to the attention of British audiences, but the use of so much plot-related diegetic music has an inhibiting effect on the use of nondiegetic music. There are, in fact, only a handful of nondiegetic cues in the film, and only two of these are used for scenes involving primary dialogue. Both of these cues make use of the main theme from the 'concerto', but Richard Addinsell had some justification for its use. Both dialogues take place between the two main characters, Stefan and Carole, and are shot mainly in close-up. The inspiration for the main theme came to Stefan as he watched Carole in the moonlight on the night they met in Warsaw, so it is quite reasonable, on dramatic grounds, to evoke their romance by these means. (This scenario is

[41] Huntley (1947), 54.

copied almost exactly in the 1944 film *Love Story*, where Kit provides the inspiration for the main theme of Lissa's piano concerto – Hubert Bath's *Cornish Rhapsody*.) Both scenes are directly concerned with their relationship, and neither of the music cues feature the piano – the theme being carried by solo clarinet or violins.

In *They Flew Alone*, a biographical film about the aviator Amy Johnson, with music by William Alwyn, dialogues scored with diegetic music still outnumber those treated nondiegetically. The diegetic cues are not merely incidental: they contain a deeper significance, as they represent the conflict in values that exists between Amy and her husband Jim Mollison. Amy's background is suggested by the use of the piano, either at her school (as in an early scene), or at her home where her mother regularly practises the popular classics. Jim's values are represented by dance-band music, played either by a live band or on the radio. In the scene where Amy and Jim realise that their marriage is over, dance music is heard coming from the radio, symbolizing that the responsibility for the break-up is Jim's.

William Alwyn already had experience of working in documentary film before he began scoring feature films in 1941. His music for the main titles music of the film is similar to that for *The Winslow Boy* in that he uses one extended theme for the whole cue, but he does not resort to this theme repeatedly for the dialogue cues. The first nondiegetic cue for dialogue is very unusual in its orchestration. In Amy's confrontation with her headmistress over the wearing of a straw hat, which is symbolic of Amy's rebellion against convention, their exchange – 'Straw hats are old-fashioned and useless', 'But it's the right thing. How can you succeed in anything if you flout convention?' – is accompanied only by rising phrases on solo cello and a timpani roll. This innovative scoring suggests the unusual character of Amy Johnson's achievements and determination in an age when women were expected to conform to rigid codes of behaviour. The end of the cue is a crescendo which leads into a triumphal passage accompanying the following scene, where Amy receives her university degree, thus disproving her headmistress's theories.

Alwyn resorts to another unusual method of dialogue scoring in order to suggest the inner feelings of the characters. In the exterior scene where Amy is about to take off on her first solo flight, she is seen seated in the open cockpit talking to her father and a crewman about the weather. The general anxiety, although not directly expressed, is conveyed by short phrases in the strings, followed by rests through which only a pedal in the bass is sustained. This subtle projection of underlying emotion in dialogue scenes demonstrates a major development from the typical scoring of the 1930s. It is all the more remarkable in that it is used for an 'exterior' scene that is dominated by the presence of an aeroplane. It contrasts with a superficially similar scene where Jim has just landed from a solo flight and jumps down from the cockpit. Here, Jim's snatches of conversation with a member of the ground staff are incidental to the action of the scene, and the music cue uses the triumphal theme associated with flight, which is heard in the film's flying scenes.

In the scene from Amy and Jim's honeymoon where the couple are shown relaxing in a country cottage, Alwyn uses a device which is effectively a stinger in reverse. The music for the dialogue is gently romantic, but as Amy, in response to Jim's statement that he wishes he didn't have to get ready, asks 'Get ready for what?' and Jim replies guardedly 'America', the sustained string chord makes a dramatic crescendo before being abruptly cut off. The shock effect indicates the intrusion of reality into a dream world, and the following discussion of Jim's forthcoming flight is conducted without music.

The final dialogue scene of the film to be scored gives a rare example of nondiegetic anempathy in a British film. Amy and Jim accidentally meet some years after their divorce. The light-toned restraint of their polite exchange is belied by the music cue which reveals the hidden emotions of regret and nostalgia experienced by the couple. This degree of sophistication was quite unheard-of in British films of the 1930s, but was almost a commonplace in the classical Hollywood score.

In *Pimpernel Smith*, the film that came second to *49 Parallel* as 1941's most successful film at the box office, John Greenwood introduces stingers and reverse stingers into the dialogue scoring. In the opening scene, where Dr Beckendorf is discussing the details of his work with both his colleague and his assistant, the music cue delivers a stinger played by the strings as the doctor raises his head at an imagined sound. The audience knows that he is fearful of the arrival of the Gestapo, and when the music cue ends with a reverse stinger a fraction of a second before the doorbell rings, the effect of shock is intensified. The film can be classified as a comedy thriller because of the exaggerated persona of the absent-minded professor adopted by Smith to avert suspicion. However, there is a difference between ironic humour and pure comedy. The dialogue scene between Smith and the French female shop assistant when Smith tries to buy some face powder, is humorous because of the incongruity of the situation, not because of any verbal gags. The whole scene is accompanied by a scherzo orchestrated in the style of light music including glockenspiel, which suggests the amusement of the shop assistant. This is in contrast to a typical scene from a comic film where the characters do not generally acknowledge the effect they are at pains to create – as in a Laurel and Hardy film – and where the musical treatment of the dialogue is on a completely different basis.

One of the main narrative threads of the film is the German commander's inability to understand the English sense of humour and its significance. As Jeffrey Richards observes,

> The film demonstrates unequivocally that a sense of humour is the English secret weapon: it is the essential quality which separates a civilized society from an uncivilized one. It is also one of the best means of transmitting propaganda and maintaining morale, something the Germans in reality never understood.[42]

---

[42] Aldgate and Richards (1986), 59.

The importance of humour was not so much its role as an emotional bastion in times of trouble, but its vital contribution to the art of lateral thinking – the real secret weapon of the English. The main titles music has two themes. The first is based on the song 'There is a tavern in the town', which is the signature tune that Smith uses to identify himself to those he is about to rescue. The second is a noble but restrained theme beginning with a rising and falling major second. These are the same intervals as the opening of the 'Dawn' theme from *Oliver Twist*, and like that theme this one is underpinned by the 'Elgar tread', and is unmistakably English. In the final scored dialogue scene, Smith and Ludmilla are leaving Germany by train. As Smith talks of England, the theme from the main titles is heard in full. This is the one point in the film where there is a direct appeal to the patriotism of the audience. As Smith quotes from Rupert Brooke, ending with 'For England's the one land I know/ Where men with splendid hearts may go', his 'rolling cadences' are supported by the noble character of the music.

Greenwood uses this theme in another context to convey the importance of humour to the British cause. In the scene where Smith has just outwitted the pursuing Germans by leaving a window open while hiding behind a curtain ('Well, I'm almost ashamed to have used that old trick'), he steals from the room with Ludmilla while quoting Lewis Carroll's famous lines – ''Twas brillig, and the slithy toves/ Did gyre and gimble in the wabe.' It was the absurdity of this poem that had earlier convinced the German commander that the secret weapon of the English was just a myth. As Smith delivers the words with irony, the first phrase of the theme is heard. The connection between humour, lateral thinking and the English spirit was clearly not lost on Greenwood.

The two Ealing films from 1942 that were both scored by William Walton have many features of their dialogues in common. *The Foreman Went to France* and *Went the Day Well?* have very different storylines, but both are propaganda films with a strong emphasis on action. The first of these is based on a real incident from the days of the fall of France. A foreman of a British engineering firm is sent to France to retrieve three pieces of machinery that are vital for defence. The main action of the film centres on the efforts of the foreman, Fred, an American secretary from the company, Anne, and two stray British soldiers, to convey the machinery in an old army lorry to a safe port, and thence by boat to England. The majority of the scored dialogue exchanges take place either on the open-fronted lorry, or during the course of an action sequence. They are, therefore, secondary dialogues, and Walton scores them accordingly, with music cues that highlight the setting or the nature of the action, rather than the tenor of the dialogue.

In the scenes where the four main characters are caught up among the streams of French refugees who have been forced to evacuate their homes by the advance of the German troops, their conversation is concerned with the terrible plight of the French people. The mournful theme that began with the first shot of the slowly retreating refugees – played initially on the cor anglais over a weary four-note ostinato on bass clarinet and cellos – is continued through the ensuing dialogues. In a similar vein, in the scene where the four come to a town that is ablaze following a massive German air-raid, the dialogue concerning the search for Anne's sister is accompanied by the theme that was previously heard as the fire was first sighted on the horizon. In both cases the dialogue is subservient to the setting, as the effective 'pictorial' music demonstrates.

There is only one scored primary dialogue scene in the film, and it contains features which challenge the usual conventions. As Anne recounts the details of her sister's death to Fred, the two are seen in medium-close shot against a background of people moving about the prefecture. At one point a nurse crosses in front of the camera obscuring the two characters. The soundtrack carries the naturalistic sounds of creaking, rustling and subdued conversation. In contrast to this realistic setting, and the flat, expressionless delivery of the account, Walton's scoring reveals the pathos behind the words. Using strings alone for the first time in the score, he suggests the pain of the speaker more by harmonic movement than by the contours of the melody in the first violins. As the couple move outside away from the people, the camera goes into close-up, and the natural effects are dropped from the soundtrack. As the audience are drawn closer to the private world of the two characters, the film's main message is delivered. In response to Anne's bitter words: 'Killing, destroying, they'll go on, the Germans, until there's nothing left', Fred promises: 'No they won't. It's our fault what's happened. Everything that's happened. We've been half-asleep – you, me, all of us. Well, we're waking up at last. It's not too late. By God, it's not going to be too late.' At the words: 'It's our fault', Walton doubles the first violin melody at the upper octave, employing the top octave of the register. Although Hollywood composers made frequent use of this high register in their dialogue scoring, its use on tutti violins was almost unheard-of in British films of the period.

The dialogue scoring of *Went the Day Well?* is dictated by the action of the scenes. After the film's prologue, which is accompanied by diegetic singing from an unseen church choir, the main action of the film begins with the arrival of the 'British' troops in the unsuspecting village. The sexton's prologue retreats into voice-over as the army vehicles approach, and there then follows a sequence of dialogue scenes as the two groups – the soldiers and the villagers – begin to make contact. Walton uses two contrasting musical ideas to suggest the impact of the new arrivals on the life of the village. The soldiers are represented by a brisk march on trumpets and military drums, while the peaceful life of the village is characterized by a rustic theme heard first on the oboe, with harp accompaniment, and later on strings and horn. The various dialogue scenes are accompanied by one or other of the two ideas until they become integrated in the final scene. Walton makes use of the associations of the two themes to make a subtle narrative hint. In the scene where two Germans, posing as British officers, are observed marching down the street by Oliver Winsford's maid, the conversation between her and her employer, unlike the other conversations among the villagers which are accompanied by the rustic theme, is highlighted with the march. This implies that Winsford is a quisling – a fact not revealed until later in the film.

In the final scene of this sequence, the two officers arrive at the village policeman's door to the strains of the march, but as they begin a conversation with him, it dissolves into the rustic theme, suggesting his solidarity with the other villagers. When the billeting of the troops is discussed by the officers and the constable, the rustic theme is interrupted by snatches of the march theme played in the strings. This appropriation of the 'military' music by the instruments hitherto associated with the rustic setting vividly suggests the infiltration of the enemy into the life of the village.

Walton breaks all the Hollywood rules of dialogue scoring in a later scene from the film, where genuine British troops plan a counter-attack on the invaders. The Hollywood code of practice for dialogue scoring did not allow for the various contingencies which are likely to arise in secondary dialogue. The matter-of-fact communication of strategy by the commanding officer to his subordinates in an exterior setting does not require delicate orchestration to enhance the nuances of his vocal timbres. Walton creates a mosaic, passing a rapidly repeated single chord between trumpets, horns and woodwind. This perfectly suggests the urgency of the communication, and demonstrates how much more flexible the approach to the scoring of secondary dialogue can be.

Walton's most widely acclaimed film score is undoubtedly the one written for *Henry V*, released early in 1945, and intended as a morale-raiser for the weary British public. The lavishness of this production, which was shot in Technicolor and used over a thousand extras, contrasted strikingly with the production values of the average British wartime picture. The film did much to raise the profile of British cinema internationally, but the very features which led to its acclaim dissociated it from the body of films which had come to characterize the British and their way of life. Olivier, as director, had intelligently approached the problems of translating a Shakespeare play into the medium of film. He used a framing device which sets the opening and closing scenes as a contemporary performance at the Globe theatre in London. Siegfried Kracauer was unusually complimentary about this technique:

> The whole arrangement does credit to Olivier's film sense. It is an attempt to put the theatrical spectacle in brackets and offset the effect of its stylizations with a touch of camera-reality.[43]

However, Kracauer's observation reveals the reasons why the film stood out from the 'new type of national cinema' admired by John Huntley. Theatrical spectacle is not a good basis for realistic cinema, nor is any form of stylization. Much as literary scholars may wish to see Shakespeare's language as perennial, it sounds hopelessly archaic to those who are not educated to appreciate it, especially in the 'stylized' delivery encouraged by Olivier. For these reasons, the scoring of the film was exceptional to the general techniques of scoring in contemporary films. Much of the music functions as if for a theatrical production, with diegetic fanfares and drumming. Despite the inclusion of

---

[43] Kracauer (1961), 260.

numerous music cues, there is comparatively little nondiegetic scoring of dialogue. As the American commentator Stanlie McConnell observes,

> The background music never clouds the rendition of important Shakespearean lines. It is used infrequently to stir up imaginative power, but for the most part the music of this film is used as a distinct factor in the dramatic action.[44]

Because of the subject-matter and construction of the play, there is very little opportunity for the scoring of primary dialogue. The early scenes, including the prologue, are deliberately acted as a theatrical performance, with exaggerated vocal inflection and projection. One of the most interesting examples of 'dialogue' scoring occurs in the scene depicting the death of Falstaff. Because of the unusual nature of the exchange, with Falstaff crying out to the absent king, and the king's echo-enhanced voice-over reply, Walton was able to score freely, and he chose to use an expressive passacaglia for the whole scene.

Most scored dialogue scenes in the film involve more than two people, and contain varying degrees of physical action. The scene with Pistol and his cronies before the battle is essentially an exterior comic action scene, one requiring very little consideration from the composer for the interpretation of the dialogue. Equally, in the scene where the leaders of the English army discuss the superior position of the French, the whole emphasis is on the pictorial image presented by the figures in full armour standing among the tents and brightly coloured banners. Much of the film is simply a 'decorative pageant',[45] and the scoring enhances the image rather than the spoken word.

The film's message to its audience, that the English are invincible even against extreme odds, seems to have elicited an echo from Walton. The composer Hubert Clifford felt that Walton's score revealed a new facet of his work:

> I had never previously been aware of the essential Englishness of Walton, but in *Henry V* there was an authentic English musical voice, just as English in its own way as that of Elgar or Vaughan Williams.[46]

Walton, like many other British composers in the war, had responded not so much to the direct appeal to patriotism, by producing deliberately aimed 'nationalist' music, but to the threat to the nation's cultural heritage. Just as *Bredon Hill* had become a symbol for the enduring spirit of England, so had music for film during the war years acknowledged its legacy from those masters who had sought to eternalize that spirit.

War had focused British people's attention on what they stood to lose by the destruction of their culture, and had thereby created conditions conducive to the development of a genuinely national cinema. Every element of British film was required to validate the identity of this new national cinema, and not the least of these elements was the music.

[44] Stanlie McConnell, quoted in Huntley (1947), 172.
[45] Kracauer (1961), 227.
[46] Hubert Clifford, quoted in Manvell and Huntley (2/1975), 95.

While few British films produced during the war missed the opportunity, however discreetly, to serve the cause of patriotism, there were many different ways to serve that cause. *Henry V* had done much to boost the flagging morale of the British people, and to enhance their reputation in the eyes of their allies:

> *Henry V* rouses again our appreciation of the indomitable spirit of our English ally, whose artists made this rare thing of beauty, while the sound of war still resounded in their land.[47]

It was, however, an exception in a world where all the resources needed for film production were in short supply. Ealing studios had continued to produce films on a very tight budget throughout the war. Two of their films released in 1944 demonstrate different techniques of introducing propaganda through subject-matter, and how they affected the scoring of the respective films. *For Those in Peril*, Gordon Jacob's first feature film, is essentially a documentary film about the rescuing of pilots from British coastal waters, with a veneer of narrative. The plot does not include women – apart from a brief appearance by a barmaid – and the entire dialogue is conducted on a hearty man-to-man basis. The bulk of the scored dialogue scenes take place within action sequences, and is nearly always directed to the matter in hand. There is no necessity and no attempt to interpret the dialogue musically, and the scoring is often developed from the fully orchestrated music for the main titles. Strangely, all but one of the cues contain dialogue – a curious proportion for what is essentially an action film.

In contrast, *The Halfway House* demonstrates how a film which has a multi-layered plot, of which propaganda is but one element, can result in extremely complex dialogue scoring. Berners's dramatically effective use of themes in his scoring of the film has already been discussed. It is worth noting that only in the scene between Terence and Rhys, the one most directly concerned with the subject of patriotism, does Berners score for solo violin. British composers, in direct contrast to the directives of the Hollywood code of practice, rarely scored dialogue scenes solely for strings, and hardly ever for solo violin. Berners's dialogue scoring, in company with that of many other British composers, used wind instruments for characterization and narrative interpretation. British composers in general have shown a predilection for woodwind and nowhere is this more apparent than in a comparison between a British film and its classical Hollywood counterpart.

As British cinema found its own voice during the Second World War, the native composers had refined and developed the techniques of dialogue scoring. They did so, however, in accordance with the principles of the newly emerging national cinema. The most popular film of 1945, the one which encapsulates both the British character and the British way of life in wartime, is *The Way to the Stars*. Dealing not only with the pressures of life endured by airmen and the torment suffered by those who love them, but also with the conflict of cultures

---

[47] Stanlie McConnell, quoted in Huntley (1947), 176.

occasioned by the arrival of American pilots, the film has a broad emotional canvas and contains many primary dialogue scenes. Much of the power of the film derives from the flawless acting of its leading players. Jeffrey Richards describes how British treatment of the subject of sudden loss compares with the treatment it would have received from Hollywood:

> These losses are invariably received with a pain that is doubly moving by its restraint. There is no flag waving, no soupy soundtrack music, no over-the-top emotionalism. As Campbell Dixon put it at the time, declaring that 'few films have been more essentially English', 'Just imagine how Hollywood would have treated it – the tears from the women, the maudlin sentiment from the dead men's friends and at least one big bout of hysteria from somebody.' The Englishness is thus seen to lie in emotional restraint.[48]

The credit for the lack of 'soupy soundtrack music' during these scenes can be given to the film's director Anthony Asquith, who preferred such moments of controlled emotion to be played without music. It is unfortunate that Asquith did not extend this policy to every scene of the film, as he was later to do in *The Browning Version* and *Carrington V.C.* He would have spared this excellent film the inappropriate treatment it suffered at the hands of its composer. The whole integrity of *The Way to the Stars* is compromised by its score, which is totally out of sympathy with the film's portrayal of the British character in wartime. There is one simple explanation for this – the music was not written by a British composer. Jacques Feyder should have added one further requirement for the creation of a national cinema in Britain – 'no more foreign composers'. It is necessary to examine the contribution to British film made by foreign composers in order to establish the nature of its impact on the evolution of a British national cinema.

[48] Aldgate and Richards (1986), 283.

9.   A look at some British films scored by foreign composers

Although Korda was an ardent anglophile, his intention had always been to create international pictures that would appeal to as wide an audience as possible. He had little interest in establishing a national cinema in Britain, and he saw no need to adopt a policy of employing British artists and craftsmen for the various departments involved in film production, preferring to give key positions to his compatriots. In his autobiography Miklós Rózsa describes how this preference affected the working environment at Denham when he arrived there in 1935:

> It was the easiest thing in the world to be a Hungarian at the Denham studios. The three Korda brothers were Hungarian; so were Lajos Biro, the head of the script department, and Stephen Phallos, the head of the sales department. Alexander Korda was, I know, inundated with letters from Hungarians demanding work. It was said that he had a sign on his desk saying, 'It is not enough to be Hungarian. You have to be talented as well.' I used to think he had got it the wrong way round, and that it was not enough to be talented, you had to be Hungarian as well! There was an underlying resentful feeling against this Hungarian invasion of the British film industry, and a popular joke was that the three Union Jacks flying over the Denham Studios were one for each of the Englishmen working there.[1]

From this description it can be seen how remarkable was the appointment of the young Muir Mathieson as musical director, particularly in view of his stipulations regarding the employment of composers. As Leslie Mitchell points out,

> At this time these were rather startling demands. To begin with it was not at all an accepted or acceptable fact that British composers could offer anything like the same quality of work as those from other countries. In fact, British artists in the musical world had for long been changing their names to acquire a Russian, French or Italian ring which would automatically increase their chances of a worldwide reputation.[2]

Although we now appreciate that British music was enjoying a long-awaited resurgence, this was by no means the general perception at the time. It was not

---

[1] Rózsa (1984), 70.
[2] Towers and Mitchell (1947), 55.

easy to shake off the reputation engendered by long years in the wilderness. As late as 1947 Mathieson, in response to the question whether British composers' film work would be in demand from outside Britain, was to say

> Not until we can break down the idea that we have no composers in England. Hollywood, for instance, seems to be sold on the idea that only middle-Europeans are musicians, and it'll take a lot of argument and propaganda to persuade them that they are wrong.[3]

It was not only those from outside this country who refused to recognize the importance of British music. Mathieson's unshakeable faith in, and enthusiasm for, contemporary British music was not shared by all its exponents. Writing a year earlier, in 1946, the composer Christian Darnton had revealed how little it was appreciated that English music was experiencing a genuine revival:

> We can glance at contemporary activity in the country, and pass on. It does not appear that there is to-day in England any music of significance as far as the big issues and long historical view of the art as a whole are concerned.[4]

Few music historians today would share Darnton's opinion, but at the time there was a general bias against British composers, and a belief that in order to be taken seriously as a composer, it was necessary to be a foreigner.

From the earliest days of the British sound picture, when it was realized that an original score was a desirable adjunct to the soundtrack, foreign composers, most notably mid-Europeans – some looking to this country for a safe haven – were pressed into service. They were mostly well-trained musicians who had much previous experience of working for theatre and silent cinema. Hans May, born in Vienna in 1891, is representative. He studied piano and composition at the Viennese Academy of Music, and after working as a conductor for a touring opera company, he arranged and composed music for hundreds of silent films. His first score for a sound film in Britain was for *Flame of Love* in 1930. He continued to score dozens of British films until the late 1950s. How can the film scores of a composer from a different cultural background be distinguished from those of our indigenous composers? What, if any, were the consequences for the integrity of the films for which they were composed?

Probably the most important British film that Hans May scored was *Thunder Rock*, a discreet piece of propaganda released in 1942. Several factors separate this film from the standard British war picture. It is an adaptation of a play written by an American, and is set in a lighthouse on the shores of Nantucket. The play is 'given over almost exclusively, and unusually, to a discussion of ideas and competing philosophies of life'.[5] Although the action is set in 1939, and centres on the deliberate isolation of the main protagonist from the outside world, the film is also a ghost story and a period piece, as well as a psychological drama.

---

[3] Muir Mathieson, quoted in Towers and Mitchell (1947), 62.
[4] Darnton (1945), 123.
[5] Aldgate and Richards (1986), 174.

Despite all these factors, and despite its American financing, the film is unmistakably British. Michael Redgrave leads a predominantly British cast in uniformly restrained, understated performances. The appearances of the ghosts – immigrants shipwrecked in 1849, who exist only in the mind of the tormented lighthouse-keeper Charleston – are treated simply by a subtle use of distorting camera techniques. The first ghost to appear is the captain of the wrecked steam-packet. He is in the confidence of Charleston and, to reflect their affinity, he is filmed without distortion. It is entirely justifiable that the music should be relied on to indicate that there is something supernatural about this character despite his solid appearance. Hans May makes use of an eerie thematic fragment played on the musical saw. The unusual tone colour makes this seem more like a special effect than part of an integrated music cue, and it predates Miklós Rózsa's use of the theremin in *Spellbound* by three years.

The use of an unusual musical effect to indicate psychological disturbance is not, in itself, particularly alien to British scoring, as Brian Easdale was also to use the musical saw for that purpose in the 1949 Archers film *The Small Back Room*. The score of this tense, tightly controlled drama is remarkable for its almost complete absence. Apart from one orchestral cue used to illustrate a rather startling expressionist sequence involving a giant whiskey bottle, the score has only two short cues, played on the musical saw, to suggest the central character's problem with alcohol.

May's use of this special musical device is not the only feature of the score to suggest the unusual nature of *Thunder Rock*. He also uses vibraphone chords, in the main titles music and elsewhere to hint at the supernatural element of the drama. The destabilizing impression of the vibraphone's timbre was to be exploited by British composers for similar purposes. Richard Addinsell used it in the ghostly comedy *Blithe Spirit* in 1945, and, as previously mentioned, Malcolm Arnold used it to good effect in *Home at Seven* to indicate temporary amnesia.

It is the use of a far more familiar instrument, the solo violin, used for the theme for the main titles, which distinguishes May's score from British film scores of the period. It would be absurd to assert that the use of the solo violin could always be equated with sentimentality or with a cynical intention to manipulate the feelings of an audience. However, an unfortunate legacy of Hollywood scoring is the Pavlovian emotional response, almost impossible to avoid experiencing, when hearing the sound of a solo violin in the cinematic context. The melodic line would have to be very astringent indeed for the listener to be diverted from a response pattern acquired through association. For that reason British composers were wary of the solo violin, and tended to use it sparingly, and only when making strong dramatic points. As we have already seen, Berners uses the solo violin only once in *The Halfway House*, in the scene where Rhys cleverly manages to unlock Terence's closed attitude to the unconstructive nature of his patriotism (see Chapter 6, example 20). By restricting its use, Berners avoided the trap of sentimentality, and skilfully conveyed to the audience that Rhys's words had struck home to Terence on the emotional level.

Alan Rawsthorne's film music has been described by Ernest Irving as 'acidulated',[6] and his music could certainly never be considered sentimental. In his best-known film score – for *The Cruel Sea* (1953) – he too uses the solo violin on only one occasion. This is all the more memorable in a score which makes no other use of any solo instrument, relying instead on an almost uniform orchestral texture. The cue is heard at the moment when the captain and his first mate are reunited after a long, bitter night in open boats on the Atlantic, when many of their comrades have perished. As the two men exchange the laconic greetings 'Hello, Number One', 'Hello, sir', the solo violin plays a fragment of the main theme. The film itself has only one basic subject – the implacable and impersonal cruelty of the sea – and there is consequently little opportunity to develop the associated musical theme for dramatic purposes. Only here, the sea being deprived of its prey, is the theme permitted to express emotion. The use of the solo violin serves another purpose. The acting of Jack Hawkins and Donald Sinden in this brief scene equals anything in the area of emotional restraint achieved by Michael Redgrave or John Mills. Unlike the painful scenes in *The Way to the Stars*, where the audience can only too easily identify with the emotions that are held in check, this scene needs music because the two men are incapable of revealing or even recognizing their emotions. For the heterosexual British male, love between two men – even love that is borne of shared tribulations – can rarely be acknowledged. Without the use of this music cue, the significance of the scene – particularly as it takes place on the vast expanse of the Atlantic – would be lost.

This example of emotional complexity, where the characters' unrecognized feelings are revealed to the audience by the music, provides validation for the use of the solo violin. However, its use in main titles music, where the intention is to provide an indication of the film's main narrative threads, is a little misleading. Hearing May's main titles music for *Thunder Rock*, one could be forgiven for supposing that the film was a romantic 'woman's' picture.

Example 1. Main theme from the main titles music for *Thunder Rock*

Hans May, *Thunder Rock*. Composed by Hans May. (© 1942 Cinephonic Music Company Limited, 8/9 Frith Street, London W1D 3JB. Used by permission of Music Sales Ltd. All rights reserved. International copyright secured.

---

[6] Ernest Irving, quoted in Huntley (1947), 83.

The theme is not really adequate to convey the torment of a man driven to isolate himself from all human contact, or the persecution suffered by the ghostly characters for the sake of their beliefs. The main narrative theme of the film is the need of each character to find the courage to live his life according to his beliefs, no matter what the consequences. It could be argued that Hans May is emphasizing this by repeatedly returning to the starting note. It could equally be argued that such a device is a time-honoured compositional contrivance for eliciting an emotional response.

May's score is also full of nineteenth-century clichés, both in its orchestration and in its grammar. In the sequence where the keeper goes about his duties in the lighthouse, May uses a formula which is more than a little reminiscent of Tchaikovsky. The strings repeatedly give out a statement of the motif associated with the lighthouse, pausing on the final note of each repetition. The sustained note is reinforced by a minor triad held by the woodwind, or woodwind and brass, while the harp executes a progressively rising arpeggio figure. Sequential, chromatically based string figures are also extensively used, encouraging the experienced opera-goer to anticipate the breathless arrival of the heroine's confidante. Such backward glances were not helpful to a medium which was still struggling to establish itself.

May's scoring of *Thunder Rock* demonstrates that specific experience is not invariably beneficial for a composer. In film work it can sometimes result in a stale, unquestioning approach. The extent of May's work in silent films is obvious in another sequence from *Thunder Rock*, and is not to the film's advantage. In a series of scenes which serve to indicate the political climate in various countries during the months before the outbreak of war, May uses the kind of musical illustration formerly employed by the silent film accompanist. In a dialogue scene involving a Japanese delegate, the main theme is played in parallel perfect fourths, exactly the type of encoding formula employed in the classical Hollywood score that is lambasted by Claudia Gorbman in *Unheard Melodies*.[7] Such formulaic writing is rare in film scores by British composers, and, indeed, the leading figures among them eschewed it rigorously.

Unlike May, who had long been familiar with English people and English films by the time he came to score *Thunder Rock*, arguably the most distinguished European composer to write for British films was new both to the art and to the country when he composed his score for *Knight without Armour* in 1937. Miklós Rózsa was not initially employed to work for Alexander Korda simply because he was Hungarian, but because the director of *Knight without Armour*, Jacques Feyder, had been impressed by Rózsa's music for the ballet *Hungaria*, and felt that his compositional style would be particularly well-suited to the subject-matter of the film. There is a certain irony in the fact that a Hungarian who was to become one of Hollywood's best-known composers should have been invited to cut his teeth on a British film because it was considered particularly suitable for his style.

---

[7] Gorbman (1987), 83. See above, p. 25.

As luck would have it, Rózsa was asked to score another British film at the same time as *Knight without Armour*. *Thunder in the City* was produced by two Hungarians, Akos Tolnay and Alexander Esway. Tolnay had for some time promised Rózsa the chance to score one of the films that he planned to make in Britain, but there was nothing very British about this picture, as Rachel Low indicates:

> With a Hollywood director, writer, cameraman, editor and star, and a story by the American playwright Robert Sherwood about an American businessman in England, it was clearly designed as Esway's ticket to Hollywood.[8]

Rózsa was no more prepared for the previously untried art of scoring for film than any of the British concert composers had been. In his autobiography he describes how he approached the task:

> So here I was, about to write the music for two different films, without any idea of how to set about it. How I envy the training available to young composers nowadays, with its wealth of technical advice! I became a regular visitor at the Gaumont Palace and the Chelsea Classic, where I saw some terrible films and heard some equally terrible scores. For me, film music meant Honegger's score for *Les Miserables*; that was what I wanted to hear and what I hoped to achieve myself.[9]

Honegger may not have been the most appropriate model for a composer who was preparing to score British films, and it is unfortunate that Rózsa never had the opportunity to score a good British film that was free of some form of internationalism. The Britishness, or otherwise, of Korda's films has already been discussed at length. *Thunder in the City* was the first of four films scored by Rózsa – all made at Denham between 1937 and 1940 – that were not Korda productions. None of these four films, from *On the Night of the Fire*, with its 'unlikely story and characterization',[10] to *The Green Cockatoo*, whose release was delayed for three years, and *Ten Days in Paris*, a contrived comedy thriller set in a foreign location, could be described as a typically British film. Rózsa was to leave England with the production team of *The Thief of Baghdad* in 1940, at the time when British films began to establish their own identity. With the exception of *The Thief of Baghdad* – without question the furthest removed of all Korda's productions from any suggestion of Britishness – Rózsa scored no British films in the decade that saw their greatest achievement. He scored five nominally British films in the 1950s, but these were the MGM pictures that happened to be made on British soil. Rózsa himself described *Ivanhoe* – one such film dating from 1952 – as 'A typical Hollywood historical travesty . . . cliché-ridden and conventional'.[11]

---

[8] Low (1985), 205.
[9] Rózsa (1984), 66.
[10] Low (1985), 214.
[11] Rózsa (1984), 155.

Rózsa's visits to the Gaumont Palace and the Chelsea Classic did not prevent him from making the kind of errors that must have been common to many composers fresh to the art of film scoring. His description of his early attempts at dialogue scoring gives an idea of how many masterpieces must have ended up on the cutting room floor:

> When I finally came to do the music for *Thunder in the City* I made any number of novice 'howlers'. In one scene an English family was taking tea outside on the lawn, all talking animatedly. This I underscored with an energetic scherzo for full orchestra. The director patiently explained to me that in order to allow the dialogue to be heard the music would need to be dubbed at such a low level that all we would hear would be a vague irritation of upper frequencies, principally in the piccolo. So far from enhancing the scene the music would merely distract the audience. A pastoral oboe over a few strings or something of the sort was all that was needed. Well, I soon learned.[12]

Rózsa was fortunate to gain this kind of experience on the relatively unimportant *Thunder in the City*, because *Knight without Armour* is one of Korda's most convincing films, and one which presents a challenge to the composer. Although he was chosen on the strength of his music for *Hungaria*, by a French director who presumably imagined that Hungarian music was sufficiently similar to Russian for the purposes of a film about the Russian Revolution, Rózsa went to great pains to study the folk melodies of Russia. His scrupulous research into the music of the period and cultural setting of a proposed film was to become a feature of his later scores. *Knight without Armour* is one of the rare Korda films where the emphasis on production values does not get in the way, or distract attention from the actors and the storyline. It can be argued that in no other Korda film are the characters allowed such genuine and convincing self-expression. For this reason, despite its attempts to emulate some of the great moments from Russian silent cinema, the film is almost more British in its ethos than Korda's Empire pictures.

In the final analysis, however, *Knight without Armour* is a dramatic adventure story set in Russia, dealing with the subject of conditions in the country before and during the Revolution. The score is unusually extensive for a British film of the late 1930s, and this can be attributed directly to the nature of the film's subject-matter. The film requires many diegetic cues, as well as nondiegetic marches, all of which call for traditional Russian music. But the entire score is redolent of Russian folk melody, and the love scenes are dominated by the sound of the solo violin. Only in the scene where the hero – an English journalist, overtaken by events and temporarily disguised as a revolutionary – recites from Browning's poem *Fear Death* does Rózsa change style. As Robert Donat delivers the lines (whether his spoken English is intended to be, like the rest of the film's dialogue, fluent Russian, or whether he is literally quoting in his native tongue, is unclear), Rózsa's scoring for strings and lower woodwind is

---

[12] Rózsa (1984), 66.

a pastiche of Vaughan Williams's style. That this use of an English composer's style was intentional on Rózsa's part, and was not meant to serve as a blanket effect for the slightly embarrassing business of reciting poetry in film, is borne out by the second half of the cue. As the heroine reciprocates by quoting from a Russian poem, the music immediately changes to a pastiche Russian folk-dance melody played on two clarinets in thirds. The first part of the cue is the only moment in the score which indicates that the film has any connection with England.

Rózsa's approach to the scoring of the film was heavily influenced by the director, who emphasized the importance of its intensity. Rózsa reveals that this input from the film's director was a welcome one to the comparative novice:

> Feyder helped me greatly with the music for *Knight Without Armour*. He kept impressing on me that he did not want 'polite' music, but something violent and strong. He said, 'This is a revolution. You can be as sweepingly dramatic as you like, as symphonically passionate and tempestuous as possible, and when it comes to the love scenes you can be really poetic and warm. ['] . . . What Feyder said was a marvellous guide, because I needed to be told how far I could go, what kind of orchestral colours I could employ.[13]

Feyder's reference to 'polite' music indicates that the composer Korda had had in mind for the film, but to whom Feyder had objected, may quite possibly have been English. Such categorizing of musical styles was responsible for the practice of casting composers for different genres of film. Rózsa had proved himself capable of producing a colourful score for a fairly large-scale dramatic picture. This may explain why he was chosen in preference to John Greenwood – composer of *Elephant Boy* and *The Drum* – to score Korda's final Empire picture, *The Four Feathers*. It was Zoltan Korda, not Muir Mathieson, who wanted Rózsa for the film. It would seem that the conditions agreed with Mathieson when he accepted the job as musical director at Denham were not always honoured. Rózsa's comments on his engagement to compose the score for *The Four Feathers* is most revealing:

> This was a big step forward for me because, knowing nothing of the Englishry of Parry or Elgar, here was I being given this most English of films, against the will of the very chauvinistic musical director.[14]

Rózsa had certainly known enough of the Englishry of Vaughan Williams to write a very convincing pastiche of his *Serenade to Music* in *Knight without Armour*. But it says everything about his imperfect perception of England and the English that Rózsa should consider *The Four Feathers* to be the 'most English of films'. The main body of the film is set in the Sudan, and the central character – the Englishman Harry Faversham – spends most of his time disguised as a native Arab. Even if the customs and demeanour of the English upper classes are

[13] Rózsa (1984), 68–9.
[14] Ibid., 70.

reasonably well conveyed in the scenes set in England, the film is still a foreign-location epic – a genre far removed from the more typical English film.

The main theme from the main titles music shows that Rózsa had decided to place the musical emphasis on the film's location.

Example 2. Main theme from *The Four Feathers*

Miklos Rósza, *The Four Feathers*. Music by Larry Sturm and Miklós Rózsa. © Chappell Music Ltd, London W6 8BS. Reproduced by permission of IMP Ltd. All rights reserved.

This theme is used not only for the scenes in the Sudan, but in the non-diegetically scored dialogue scenes that take place in England. Harry Faver-sham's dilemma, and the retrieval of his reputation from the slur of cowardice – the main narrative threads of the film – are the subjects of three of these important dialogue scenes. Their treatment with this theme implies that Harry cannot be separated from the context of the place where he will retrieve his honour. Thus his Englishness, as far as Rózsa's scoring is concerned, is an irrelevance. There is only one single scene in the film where the nondiegetic music indicates the significance of England to the storyline. In the scene where Harry's comrade, John Durrance, after his return to England from the Sudan where he has been blinded as a result of sunstroke, is seen riding with Ethne (Harry's former fiancée), her father and Dr Sutton, Rózsa uses an accompani-ment suggestive of an English pastoral scene. At this point in the film, Durrance is trying to put behind him his experiences in the Sudan, while Ethne is trying to forget Harry by devoting herself to Durrance. Rózsa could not use the main theme without misleading the audience as to the dramatic meaning of the scene.

The Four Feathers provides a rare opportunity to compare the scoring of a foreign and a British composer for the same subject-matter. The film was remade by Zoltan Korda in 1955, using very much the same screen play and a great deal of the original footage. The filming of *Storm over the Nile*, as it was re-titled, seems in retrospect a rather pointless exercise, and, in common with many remakes, it falls short of the quality of the original. It is fairly obvious from comparing these two that Zoltan Korda expected the composer of the later film, Benjamin Frankel, to follow the example set by Rózsa, and at least two of the music cues are taken from the original score. In the scene which establishes the Egyptian setting, the cue is directly lifted from Rózsa's scoring of the same scene, and is an extended version of the main theme from the earlier film. It would be difficult to imagine that Frankel was happy about this incorporation of Rózsa's music, but as it was Zoltan Korda who managed to get his way, against Mathieson's will, over the choice of composer for *The Four Feathers*, it can be presumed that Frankel had little say in the matter. Rózsa was particularly proud of the music he had written for the scene where the barges are pulled up the Nile by scores of slaves. He had used a Sudanese melody that he had discovered in the British Library to create an antiphonal work song. This, too, reappears in the music for *Storm over the Nile.*

All Frankel's scoring for the scenes set in the Sudan emphasizes the scale and the setting of the film. Even if Zoltan Korda had not wanted to retain the ethos of the original film in its music, a composer would be concerned to acknowledge the dominating influence of both these features. However, Frankel treats the dialogue scenes set in England quite differently from Rózsa, and, as a result, these scenes have more impact than in the original film. The first of these scenes is when Harry receives the three white feathers from Durrance, Willoughby and Burroughs, his former fellow-officers and close friends. Harry's fiancée (Ethne in the original, Mary in the remake) tells him that he was wrong to turn his back on the tradition into which they were both born. Harry demands that she give him a fourth feather, and then leaves. In the original version, Rózsa scores this scene with the material of the film's main theme. There is no attempt to register the impact of its events or to develop the characters' identities.

Frankel, by contrast, drops all reference to the connection between Harry's redemption and the Sudan, and focuses on the dramatic meaning of the scene. As Harry realizes who the feathers are from, his shocked distress is conveyed by the use of a repeated chord in upper woodwind and strings played with the back of the bow, juxtaposed with a military drum repeating the rhythm. As Mary says 'It was cruel to send those', a solo oboe reflects her sympathy for Harry in his distress. But as she goes on to reveal what she thinks of his conduct, by saying 'You've destroyed yourself, Harry – both of us', her anger and disapproval are evident from the angularity of the clarinet solo. As Harry insists 'Go on, give me this feather!', the music for the discovery of the three feathers returns, and thus Mary is identified with Durrance, Willoughby and Burroughs. Her personality and her feelings are brought into much sharper focus by Frankel's musical treatment. In this scene there is one curious difference between the two films, a difference which is emphasized by Frankel's treatment. Ethne is not seen to give Harry her feather, but Mary *is*, and the significance of the gesture is reinforced by a subdued stinger in the horns.

In a later scene, the heroine's feelings are again given more attention by Frankel. Dr Sutton tells her that Harry left England a year before and, as no word has been received from him, the inference must be that he is dead. Rózsa again treats this dialogue scene with material from the main theme. Even as Ethne utters the words 'So that's the end', there is no corresponding gesture in the music. Only at the end of the scene does Rózsa indicate Ethne's emotion by the use of a solo violin. Frankel, on the other hand, heightens the intensity of this scene. As the Doctor tells Mary that Henry left England a year ago, her demeanour appears calm, but her inner reaction is conveyed by the use of solo timpani, followed by slow-moving minor chords in brass and lower woodwind. A dissonant chord is sustained under her delivery of 'So that's the end.' As she goes on to say 'I failed him when he needed help', the solo clarinet recalls her anger at her last meeting with Harry. In place of the solo violin of Rózsa's score, an expressive atonal melody is played by tutti violins – a much stronger effect.

In one of the most dramatic scenes in the original film, after Durrance has recounted at the dinner table his tale of how a mute Arab helped him to safety and then tried to rob him, the feather that Durrance sent to Faversham falls from Ethne's letter to Durrance which had been kept in his uniform in the Sudan. Ethne immediately realizes that the mute Arab must have been Harry, and that he may still be alive. The scene is all the more powerful because Durrance cannot see the feather or the reactions of Ethne, her father and Dr Sutton, but senses the tension in the atmosphere. Rózsa again elects to score the scene predominantly with the main theme, and again pays no attention to the nuances of the drama. In the remake Frankel once more highlights Mary's emotional response to the unfolding of events. Dissonant horns indicate her initial shock at recognizing the feather. An eerie timpani solo conveys the apprehension of the other two men as they realize that Durrance may now face another personal tragedy. The solo clarinet recalls Mary's part in the reappearance of the feather, and her anguish at Durrance's words, 'I was never able to trace him', is portrayed by a clashing major seventh played by two horns. Frankel's treatment of these three dialogue scenes involving Mary gives her far more individuality than Ethne enjoys at the hands of Rózsa, whose blanket scoring of these scenes with the main theme implies that Ethne has no identity save as an adjunct to Harry's efforts to retrieve his honour.

Rózsa's score for *The Four Feathers*, and for the fantastical fairytale *The Thief of Baghdad*, which gained him his first Oscar nomination, were to establish him as a composer of full-scale exotic productions in Hollywood. He was never to be brought into contact with the true national British cinema that was emerging as he left these shores. It is fascinating to speculate on the nature of the scores he might have produced for *In Which We Serve* or *The Way to the Stars* – two films that are widely considered as the acme of national British cinema. If Rózsa had scored the latter film he would surely have done it a greater service than did the Russian composer Nicholas Brodszky.

Brodszky was another example of a foreign composer who had written for film extensively in Europe before coming to England. His first score here was for *French without Tears* in 1939. John Huntley, in his biographical notes on Brodszky in *British Film Music*, politely obscures the fact that in reality he was little more that a tunesmith:

> Brodszky is one of the most prominent of our film musicians who employ the Hollywood system of having a large number of collaborators and orchestrators engaged on each score, whereby the composer may concentrate on the production

of the straightforward melodies, which are then passed on for orchestration and working-out. The excellence of this system may be judged by the fine *Way to the Stars* music.[15]

It is hard to understand why Brodszky should have been chosen to provide the themes for this film when so many admirable scores had been written by British composers. Was there something of particular value in the melodies Brodszky produced? Roy Douglas gives a very amusing account of how he and James Turner were expected to construct an entire score on one love song that Brodszky had composed several years previously; he seems to have few doubts regarding the Russian composer's melodic writing.[16] The reader may judge for himself the quality of the main titles melody for *The Way to the Stars*.

Example 3. Main theme from the main titles music for *The Way to the Stars*

Nicholas Brodszky, *The Way to the Stars*. Music by Nicholas Brodszky. © 1945 Chappell Music Ltd, London W6 8BS. Reproduced by permission of IMP Ltd. All rights reserved,

The influence of a much-loved fellow Russian is unmistakable in the theme, but how appropriate is such self-indulgent emotionalism for a film which was praised for 'its admirable emotional restraint [which] is far more moving than any picture deliberately designed as a tearjerker'?[17] The orchestrators of *The Way to the Stars* either did not have the presence of mind or the same degree of autonomy as Roy Douglas and James Turner, who had dropped Brodszky's theme for *Tomorrow We Live* as often as possible. Although the most moving scenes In *The Way to the Stars* – in which the characters are told of the deaths of their loved ones – are screened without music, the integrity of many other primary dialogue scenes is compromised by the inappropriate nature of this theme.

The curious parallel between one such scene and one from another classic British film made in the same year is described by Jeffrey Richards:

---

[15] Huntley (1947), 197.
[16] See Appendix A, p. 200.
[17] *Daily Sketch*, 8.6.1945, quoted in Aldgate and Richards (1986), 279.

The last parting of David and 'Toddy', interrupted by the eternally complaining Miss Winterton, was made without fuss. He just squeezes her shoulder and departs, using the same gesture that Trevor Howard uses in that other tribute to emotional restraint *Brief Encounter*, when parting forever from Celia Johnson, trapped by a gossiping neighbour in the refreshment room at Milford Junction.[18]

Whatever criticism may be levelled against David Lean for using Rachmaninoff's music, at Noel Coward's suggestion, for the tortured romance of Laura Jesson and Alec Harvey, he had the good sense in this scene to stop the music abruptly at the words 'Laura, what a lovely surprise!' – the moment when the couple's intimacy is shattered by the intrusion of the outside world. Unfortunately, in *The Way to the Stars* the dramatic impact of the parallel is lost, as the main theme pointlessly continues through the trivial complaints of the hotel guest.

Brodszky, however, was at least resident in this country when he was asked to score *The Way to the Stars*. Inviting a foreign composer to score a British film while still domiciled in his native land would seem to be another step away from an integrated approach to film making, and yet this is exactly what the musical director of Ealing Studios – the supposed bastion of Britishness – did in 1945. It is ironic that while Mathieson fought to have British instead of foreign composers at Denham, Ernest Irving should, of his own free will, ask Georges Auric to compose the score for *Dead of Night*. This film has parallels with *The Halfway House* in that it deals with the supernatural, and with a group of people who assemble under one roof. What contribution could a member of Les Six be expected to make to such a production that would in any way enhance its peculiarly British idiosyncrasies? Auric, who spoke no English, seems to have had very little contact with the film. John Huntley describes how this naturally led to problems for the musical director:

> The music was written in Paris and sent over to Irving who conducted and supervised the recording at the H.M.V. Recording Theatre in St. John's Wood. The problem of synchronising music and picture presented some headaches, working with a score written in Paris, recorded in London, and filmed at Ealing, especially on sequences like the golfing scenes, featuring Basil Radford and Naughnton Wayne, in which the music has to fit closely shots of a wavering golf ball in a ghost-hindered drive off the first tee.[19]

Irving had never previously employed a foreign composer (apart from using the music of Handel, Skryabin and Mendelssohn) for any of the Ealing films and he clearly intended to find the best composers for them:

> One of the tasks I set myself in Ealing was to see that this Tom Tiddler's ground was populated by the right people.[20]

---

[18] Aldgate and Richards (1986), 284.
[19] Huntley (1947), 71.
[20] Irving (1959), 162.

Ernest Irving was far more cosmopolitan in attitude and experience than the considerably younger Muir Mathieson. For Irving there was no incongruity in including Auric in his 'catches':

> It was a grand thing to get a composer of Walton's calibre associated with Ealing films. Afterwards we had Rawsthorne, John Ireland, Georges Auric and Ralph Vaughan Williams[21]

If, by using Auric, the intention was to introduce an element of freshness and excitement to Ealing films, it may not ultimately have been in the best interests of a national cinema. It is revealing that Auric himself appeared to be unaware of the implications of using foreign composers, even for French cinema, which has always been fiercely nationalist. This is clear from Muir Mathieson's description of Auric's ideas for a cultural exchange of composers:

> Before [Auric] left he said that we certainly had no need to be ashamed of the quality of our native music and that he would like to see the return visit of an English composer to France in connection with a French picture . . . from the point of view of having an English composer to write the film score for a French film which could make the best use of contemporary British music.[22]

Auric appears to have seen no irony in the notion of contemporary British music being put to its 'best use' in a French picture, and this disregard for the significance of national cinema is evident in his scoring of British films.

Although as a group Les Six had been banded together somewhat arbitrarily and temporarily, some of their ideals for 'an aesthetic of flippancy and determined anti-Romanticism',[23] and for music to be 'straightforward, drily witty and up to date',[24] were preserved by Auric. His music – whether for the refined horror of *Dead of Night*, or for the gentle comedy of *Passport to Pimlico* and *Titfield Thunderbolt* – is too densely scored, too relentless in its rhythmic patterning, and too dependent on the patchwork juxtapositioning of repeated two-bar phrases in place of any formal development. Although much has been said about the fragmented nature of film music, there are many instances in cinema where an extended music cue is required to reach a climax or a resolution. If the function of a music cue is gradually to increase the level of tension and dread, this cannot be accomplished by music that is consistent throughout in texture, dynamics and phrase structure. Even in the more boisterous comedy of *Hue and Cry*, the frenetic busyness of Auric's music, does nothing to enhance the humour of the film; its fussy complexity merely distracts the listener. The reason that Auric continued to be employed as a composer for British films, both by Ealing and by other studios may simply have been a matter of convenience, because Auric had one quality that endeared him

---

[21] Irving (1959), 145–6.
[22] Muir Mathieson, quoted in Towers and Mitchell (1947), 61.
[23] Griffiths (1986), 71.
[24] Ibid.

to producers and musical directors alike – 'they found that he turned out the stuff that they wanted quickly and without any trouble'.[25]

It is not without significance that the most memorable and popular score ever created by a foreign musician for a British film was one that deliberately evoked the ethos of the time and place in which the film was set. *The Third Man* – a 'stud[y] in disillusionment and the melancholy of innocence brought face to face with corruption'[26] – was one of the most successful British films that was at the same time genuinely international. Any portrayal of Britishness in the film forms a very minor part of the narrative, which takes place in post-war Vienna, and which centres on American, Russian and Viennese characters. Roger Manvell and John Huntley describe how the score for the film came into existence:

> From the first moment when Sir Carol Reed heard Anton Karas playing his zither in a Viennese café, the Harry Lime theme was born in his mind.[27]

With the exception of two diegetic cues featuring solo violin and solo guitar, all the music in the film is provided by the zither. It creates an atmospheric background to the film generally, but it also reflects the contours of the narrative – intimate primary dialogue scenes and dramatic chases through the dingy streets being contrasted with more tender or more agitated cues respectively. Manvell and Huntley describe the effectiveness of a solo instrument in the context:

> The zither music in *The Third Man* is a famous example of the use of a local instrument to establish the atmosphere of the place where the action of a film is set. The few melancholy, haunting notes from the zither were enough to create a romantic nostalgia for the legendary Vienna vainly trying to recapture after the war the remnants of gaiety in the face of the new social evils represented by Harry Lime's criminal activities.[28]

It was an impressive achievement that a dramatic film was musically upheld in this way by the use of a single instrument. The only other example of a British feature film of the period similarly accompanied was *Genevieve*, and that was a comedy with a very light touch for which Larry Adler's deft harmonica playing was delightfully appropriate. The extraordinary popularity of the music for *The Third Man* (the Decca recording of the Harry Lime theme sold 4 million copies) drew attention away from its success as an atmospheric film score. The fact that Karas's music achieved more recognition than any score by a foreign composer written for a British film suggests something of the inherently unsatisfactory nature of the association.

---

[25] Roy Douglas, in Appendix A, p. 204.
[26] McFarlane, 'Literary', in Barr (ed.) (1986), 133.
[27] Manvell and Huntley (2/1975), 110.
[28] Ibid., 109.

10. The decline of British cinema in the 1950s, and the consequences for British film scores

If the music for *Things to Come* had marked the birth of the British film score, it was the music for *Henry V* which brought it recognition outside this country. The film had received wide, though not universal, acclaim. Olivier's deliberate and somewhat idiosyncratic stylization had not been to everyone's taste, but the nature of the film, and the director's intelligent interest in its music, had offered Walton a rare opportunity to write a score which 'shone forth in a manner rarely witnessed before'.[1] The impact of Walton's score on American audiences may be judged by this extract from John Huntley's article in *Sight and Sound* written nearly two years later:

> From the files of 'Film Music Notes', journal of the National Film Music Council of America, comes a special issue of this magazine devoted entirely to the music William Walton wrote for this screen interpretation of a classic of English literature. 'Like all works that can truly be described as art', they wrote, '*Henry V* will enrich its beholders in proportion to their ability to absorb all aspects of its beauty, not only the beauty of the Shakespearean language, the quality of Mr. Olivier's and his supporting cast's performance, the magnificence of its color, costumes and settings, but also the masterful achievement of William Walton's musical score.' Full data on the picture was circulated to every music school and university in the country, while special concerts and lectures on *Henry V* are still in progress throughout the States at present.[2]

Such unprecedented interest in a British score led to the recognition of other British composers' contributions to film. In the same article, John Huntley lists the items of a concert conducted by Mathieson at the conclusion of the 1946 Prague Film Festival:

'Spitfire Prelude and Fugue' (William Walton)
From the film *First of the Few*
Suite from the film *49th Parallel* (Ralph Vaughan Williams)
'Calypso Music' (William Alwyn)
From the film *The Rake's Progress*
Suite from the film *Henry V* (William Walton)

[1] Huntley (1947), 74.
[2] Huntley (1946–7), 135.

'Variations and Fugue on a Theme by Purcell' (Benjamin Britten)
From the film *Instruments of the Orchestra*
'Seascape' (Clifton Parker)
From the film *Western Approaches*
Suite from the film *Things to Come* (Arthur Bliss)
'Waltz into Jig' (John Greenwood)
From the film *Hungry Hill*
Suite from the film *Malta G.C.* (Arnold Bax)[3]

This positive feast demonstrates the range and depth of British film music at the time. John Huntley optimistically concludes

> Today the once obscure 'background' music to British films is making a valuable appeal to the new world markets now opening up to our productions as it continues to advance, under the sure guidance of such men as Muir Mathieson, to maintain Britain's sound tracks 'second to none'.[4]

In fact, so much attention was paid to the British film score in the years immediately following the war that Anthony Thomas felt compelled to write in defence of Hollywood composers:

> A great deal of praise and many emoluments have been bestowed upon the musicians of the British film industry in the last few years, and although it has been justified and deserving, the attention paid to British film music has, rather unequivocably [sic], overshadowed the same field in Hollywood pictures.[5]

The 'marked renascence of British films during the war years'[6] was to continue its momentum through the first four years of peace. These years represented 'a period of immense vitality, invention and drive'[7] in British cinema. Conditions in post-war Britain were severe:

> Food was strictly rationed and so was almost everything else – clothes, fabrics, furniture, domestic fuel and petrol; many other things, from bananas and pepper to motor-cars and children's toys, were practically unobtainable. No houses had been built for six years and five million had been destroyed or damaged. Factories had to be brought back to peace-time production at a time when raw materials were scarce and world trade was dislocated. Yet millions of men and women were about to leave the Forces and war-factories wanting jobs and homes.[8]

It was hardship of this kind that had brought the best out of the British people in wartime. Michael Balcon could equally have been referring to the immediate post-war years when he wrote concerning the conflict itself:

[3] Huntley (1946–7), 135.
[4] Ibid.
[5] Thomas (1947), 97.
[6] Balcon (1946), 66.
[7] Marius Goring, quoted in McFarlane (ed.) (1992), 101.
[8] Unstead (1966), 221.

> One of the sweet uses of adversity is its stimulus, not only to physical courage and endurance, but to the creative mind, and this is the first and most important explanation of the better British film.[9]

There was also a general optimism that social conditions would improve:

> As peace broke out, I think we held, with many others, a belief that, after all people had endured, it must result in a more just and equitable society. That this sentiment was felt by the overwhelming majority had already been reflected in the landslide Labour vote at the first post-war elections.[10]

In these challenging post-war years, the British film industry produced many of its finest examples of national cinema, in most cases enhanced by an outstanding British score. Ealing's *The Loves of Joanna Godden*, although not representative of British cinema's best, provided Vaughan Williams with the nearest example of a straightforward romantic drama that he was to score. In it he demonstrated not only an ability to use themes to good dramatic effect, but also to score primary dialogue – even going so far as to employ a stinger at one point. His powers of atmospheric writing came into their own in a most unusual way:

> It called upon him to describe, for the first time in his life, foot-and-mouth disease, which he did with such fidelity that one could almost smell the burning carcasses.[11]

Vaughan Williams's best-known film score from this period – *Scott of the Antarctic* – has attracted much comment, not all of it favourable. Hans Keller, in particular, criticized the composer for the 'over-economy and . . . "repetition-compulsion" of the thematic material'[12] which he felt tended to 'interpret monotony by monotony'.[13] It is difficult to imagine what else Hans Keller expected Vaughan Williams to do with a film when its 'emotional range is narrow'.[14] A composer would be failing in his duty to the film if he did not reflect its almost suffocating monothematicism, and Keller is clearly not thinking of the music's *dramatic* responsibility when he complains that the main titles music's 'reappearance (in its original keys, too) during the last stage of the journey up the glacier weakens its own effect as well as that of its musical surroundings'.[15] Keller was not to know that Ernest Irving had had a hand in the reappearance of this music for a specific reason. Writing of the score, Irving reveals that:

[9] Balcon (1946), 66.
[10] Roy Boulting, quoted in McFarlane (ed.) (1992), 34.
[11] Irving (1959), 175.
[12] Hans Keller, in Blom (ed.) (1954), iii, 99, s.v. 'Film Music: British'.
[13] Ibid.
[14] Ibid.
[15] Ibid.

it was all so akin to the thoughts and emotions that stirred that devoted little party of explorers that I was often able to move it about inside the film, applying some of it to incidents for which it was not designed. For instance, the music composed for the main titles – or overture – to the film, exactly fitted the climbing of the Glacier and stopped with a shuddering roll on the bass drum as the party reached the very edge of the fathomless crevasse – one more crotchet would have swallowed up the whole expedition![16]

Music could occasionally be used to dictate the pacing of action in a British film, and the best example of this occurs in *Odd Man Out* (1947). This film was the first of three directed by Carol Reed in the late 1940s which constituted 'his main contribution to Britain's "literary" cinema'.[17] These three films – *Odd Man Out, The Fallen Idol* and *The Third Man* – are an important constituent of the body of classic British films that emerged in the fertile period after the war. William Alwyn wrote two of his finest scores for the first two films. He was assisted in this by the close collaboration not only with Reed, but with the effects department. Alwyn complained that he could not always 'allow for the sound effects which are pre-conceived but dubbed on after the music has been recorded'.[18] *Odd Man Out* and *The Fallen Idol* represented the ideal that Alwyn was seeking when he wrote

> I should welcome a much closer co-ordination with the effects department, as my most satisfactory scores have nearly always matured when this close and intelligent co-operation has existed.[19]

The musical conception of 'Johnny's walk' has been much discussed. Alwyn wrote the music for the dying IRA gunman's wanderings before the scenes were shot. James Mason, who took the part of the character, and who had shown himself to be 'keenly interested and involved in the music'[20] during the making of *The Upturned Glass*, has described how this unorthodox technique influenced his performance:

> There was a relentless underscoring of Johnny McQueen's dying march through the streets of Belfast in the last part which it was necessary to pre-record so that I would never escape from the beat as I played these scenes.[21]

Because of the close collaboration with the director and effects department he enjoyed during the making of *Odd Man Out* and *The Fallen Idol*, Alwyn had been able to produce scores that demonstrated his keen dramatic sense. John Huntley goes some way to explaining how the record companies' need for catchy themes to sell their records had done a disservice to Alwyn's reputation:

[16] Irving (1959), 176.
[17] William McFarlane, 'Literary', in Barr (ed.) (1986), 133.
[18] William Alwyn, quoted in Manvell and Huntley (2/1975), 229.
[19] Ibid.
[20] Stevens (ed.) (1989), 143.
[21] Mason (1982), 215.

William Alwyn's music is so familiar to cinemagoers that it seems a pity to represent him on record by a rather ordinary march (*Desert Victory*), an amusing and pleasant piece of nonsense (Calypso Music from *The Rake's Progress*) and now a delightful but unpretentious waltz theme from *The Cure for Love*. What is needed is an extract from the last reel of *Odd Man Out*, the little boy's flight through the streets in *The Fallen Idol* or the vocal effects of the 'More Money' theme from *The Rocking Horse Winner*. Alwyn's great contribution to the cinema has been in the field of drama; so far the record companies have only shown him as a martial expert, a rhumba writer and a composer of 'boy-meets-girl' motifs.[22]

In this respect the record companies, while undeniably promoting some fine music from Britain's top composers, misled the public as to the proper function of music in film, and as to where the real skill in film composing lay. The increasing and undiscriminating promotion of film music by record companies reached its first peak with the music for Reed's third film in this trilogy, *The Third Man*. Antony Hopkins was prepared to defend Reed's choice of the zither:

> Had it been orchestrated, however consummately, even the average cinema-goer would have felt it to be inadequate. But the true genius of Carol Reed showed itself when he realised that the zither, as sheer sound, was something fresh enough and new enough to excite the listener's interest and attention whatever the quality of the music it played. This subtlety of taste is something that few directors have.[23]

Whether Reed's choice of music on this occasion could be regarded as subtlety of taste is debatable, but it must be admitted that Reed showed great originality in dispensing with orchestral forces. It is difficult from today's perspective to appreciate the impact this had on contemporary audiences accustomed to orchestral sonorities with their films.

Oliver Twist had been preceded by Lean's adaptation of *Great Expectations* (1946), which critics almost universally acclaim as the superior film. It was with *Great Expectations* that the 'post-war literary cinema boom really got under way'.[24] Much of the superiority of *Great Expectations* may be attributed to the novel itself. It was written twenty-three years after the early *Oliver Twist*, and its characters display a much wider emotional range. All the more to be regretted, therefore, is the rather inferior score by Walter Goehr. Coming from the tradition of Schoenberg and Eisler, Goehr compromises both his own integrity and that of the film by adopting a harmonic language akin to Max Steiner's. Only at certain moments of dramatic action – the pursuit of the convicts across the marsh, Pip's first arrival at Miss Havisham's, and his attempt to save Miss Havisham from the fire – does Goehr write in a style closer to his own. If he had been as convinced as Hans Keller that 'twelve-note technique is congenial to cinematic treatment',[25] he need not have produced such an inconsistent score.

---

[22] Huntley (1950), 223.
[23] Hopkins (1950), 23.
[24] William McFarlane, 'Literary', in Barr (ed.) (1986), 132.
[25] Hans Keller, in Blom (ed.) (1954), iii, 102, s.v. 'Film Music: British'.

Plate 6. Muir Mathieson, with his arm in a sling following an accident, William Walton, Laurence Olivier and John Hollingsworth, who took over the conducting during the recording of *Hamlet.*

Following the huge popular success of *Henry V*, Olivier turned his hand to an adaptation of a very different Shakespeare play. His approach to *Hamlet* – intense, low-key and claustrophobic – was in direct contrast to the glamour of *Henry V*. Possibly for this reason, the film has never been popular, and Olivier's attempt to breathe cinematic life into this particularly stagey play has been the target of much criticism. As Siegfried Kracauer observed,

> On the one hand, Olivier emphasizes the dialogue, inviting us to revel in its suggestive poetry; on the other, he incorporates the dialogue into a texture of meaningful shots whose impact prevents us from taking in the spoken lines.[26]

Olivier's interpretation of *Hamlet*, whatever its shortcomings, provided Walton with an opportunity to exercise his musico-dramatic skills in a way which the more visually stimulating *Henry V* had not done. Even Keller, who despised leitmotivic use in films, described Walton's music for *Hamlet* as a score 'wherein the *Leitmotiv* technique is handled with unfailing and original

[26] Kracauer (1961), 106.

mastery'.[27] Walton's dramatic interpretative skill in his juxtaposing of diegetic and nondiegetic music in the 'play within the play', where Hamlet attempts to expose his uncle's guilt, is unsurpassed in film scoring. Walton, in the queen's monologue recounting the death of Ophelia, rivals Britten's achievement in *Night Mail* (see p. 135, above). As Ophelia, strewn with flowers, drifts slowly downstream, the unseen queen recites the speech beginning 'There is a willow grows aslant a brook.' This fusion of music, image and word produces a rare and poignant moment of cinematic perfection.

It was for another extended moment of cinematic perfection that, for the first time, a British composer won the Academy Award for best original film score. *The Red Shoes* ballet, described by Raymond Durgnat as '*the* peak of cinema',[28] is the centrepiece of the film *The Red Shoes* based on a fairytale by Hans Christian Anderson. Just as Carol Reed and David Lean had produced some of their best work in the years immediately following the war, Powell and Pressburger, in three consecutive years starting in 1946, delivered the three films that are now considered their greatest: *A Matter of Life and Death*, *Black Narcissus* and *The Red Shoes*. The score for *A Matter of Life and Death* was composed by the Polish-born Allan Gray, who had scored most of Powell and Pressburger's films up to that time. His scores were generally competent and unmemorable. It was not until *Black Narcissus*, the first feature film to be scored by Brian Easdale, that the music in the Archers productions attained the level of the other elements of their films.

Easdale's scoring of *Black Narcissus* is a unique achievement. Watching this film, it is difficult to believe that this rich, exotic, yet finely judged and dramatically intelligent score is the work of a novice at feature-film composition. The extraordinary sensuousness and beauty of this film – it still has the power to make audiences gasp in astonished delight – isolates it from the often drab black-and-white British films of the period. Yet the film is a study of the British character challenged to confront the lure of the senses, the film's title being the name of a heady perfume symbolizing this challenge. The score for *Black Narcissus* is exceptional for another reason. The music credit reads 'Music and Sound Score Composed and Conducted by Brian Easdale.' Easdale had been privileged with an exceptional degree of authority in the handling of the soundtrack.

In some respects it may be regretted that Easdale won his Oscar for the score of *The Red Shoes* rather than *Black Narcissus*. The music for *The Red Shoes* is, in effect, a ballet score, not a film score. From a dramatic point of view, it serves essentially the same function as for a musical where the central characters are stage artists. There are very few nondiegetic cues in the film, and they seldom serve to interpret the drama. *The Red Shoes* achieved great success in America, whereas the taut psychology and unusual storyline of *Black Narcissus* had less universal appeal.

---

[27] Hans Keller, in Blom (ed.) (1954), iii, 100, s.v. 'Film Music: British'.
[28] Raymond Durgnat, quoted in 'Top 10 Films', *Sight and Sound* (December 1992), 20.

Plate 7. William Walton, standing centre, and John Hollingsworth conducting at a recording session of *Hamlet.*

The post-war boom in film making in this country ended abruptly at the turn of the decade. Referring mainly to the year 1949, Rank freely admitted that 'many of the films we produced were not of a quality to ensure even reasonable returns'.[29] Film companies throughout Europe were suffering from inflationary rises in production costs. So serious was the situation in Britain that Roger Manvell wrote

> Only the sheer love of film making, and the fact that the British, as we are told, do not know when they are beaten and so work on through defeat until they emerge to victory, are keeping us in production today.[30]

In 1950, the effect of Rank's words were felt by the industry:

> The year following Mr. Rank's admission was one of gloom for the people who work (or who used to work and hope to do so again) in British studios. Some of them lost their jobs, for at least an alarmingly indefinite period, when it became clear that the post-war expansion in production, with all its untidiness, careless-

---

[29] J. Arthur Rank, quoted in Manvell (ed.) (1950), 18.
[30] Manvell (ed.) (1950), 8.

ness and lack of planning, had been achieved only at a financially prohibitive loss of quality.[31]

One of the most serious consequences of this financial difficulty to British films was the involvement in their production by Americans, deliberately encouraged by the Government in an attempt to keep British film companies afloat. James Monahan describes how this insidious infiltration came about:

> It is no new thing for American directors, actors and even companies to make films in Britain, but one of the measures introduced by the British Government, partly to keep dollars in this country but also in order to help our film studios in their time of dejection, increased this 'Americanization' in 1949, and, still more emphatically, in 1950. Because the dollar assets of American film companies in Britain were frozen, these companies were persuaded if not obliged to make films in our studios – films which might qualify as 'British' in the quota, though, in respect of filmcraft, they might be as American as could be.[32]

This American invasion was to prove disastrous to the British film industry:

> British feature production has consistently suffered . . . from the American power and influence, and, perhaps most perniciously, from the recurrent dream of breaking into the American market. This dream is an enticement to 'Americanize' British films (by making use of American stars and directors), an enticement also to make films of such costliness that they must succeed in the United States as well as in the British home market if they are to pay their way.[33]

It was an enticement that Rank was unable to resist. Apart from the financial consequences of Rank's determination to compete in the American market, the consequences to the individuality of British films was equally problematic, as James Monahan foresaw:

> The danger is that the separate personality of British feature films may dwindle in this familiar, often repeated process.[34]

The potential danger to British film in abandoning its greatest strengths was also perceived beyond Britain's shores:

> It would be fatal to over-estimate at present the commercial possibilities of British pictures in this country. Going by the remarkable successes scored in Paris, it would be more fatal still, however, to imagine that the trick can be done by challenging the Americans on American lines. It is now commonplace and markedly out of date to say that *Brief Encounter* has done immeasurably more good to the English cinema than *Caesar and Cleopatra*. But it is a remark which is still worth bearing in mind. The documentary school has taught the French to

---

[31] James Monahan, 'Feature Film', in Manvell (ed.) (1950), 18.
[32] Ibid., 19.
[33] Ibid., 20.
[34] Ibid.

Plate 8. Brian Easdale, the leader of the London Symphony Orchestra and Michael Powell during the recording of *Black Narcissus*.

> appreciate England's self-portrayal. As a French critic, I can see no good in renouncing this valuable formula.[35]

Rank would have been well advised to have considered Thorold Dickinson's words in praise of Michael Balcon's achievements at Ealing:

> His successes aim to have their roots in contemporary British life, whether developed through comedy, fantasy or straight drama. Moreover, in twelve years he has cultivated an organization which is respected in every country where Ealing films are shown, and is the only one in Britain which has weathered the post-war financial slump under its own power.[36]

Not even the memory of the disastrous financial and artistic failure of *Caesar and Cleopatra*, however, could prevent Rank from pursuing the dream of competing with the Americans on their own terms.

The injurious effect of American involvement with film production in this country was quickly perceived by commentators. Indeed, one of the striking

---

[35] Quéval (1950), 200.
[36] Thorold Dickinson, 'Balcon', in Manvell (ed.) (1950), 9.

things about the decline of the British film in the 1950s was the extent of awareness of the problems and their causes. It seemed that everyone except Rank knew that the Americanization of British films could only destroy the qualities that had led to the greatest achievements in British cinema:

> The high-pressure showmanship of Hollywood has been uneasily and ineffectively assimilated by the British production machines. It is very rare [sic] that a British studio turns out a successful spectacle film . . . On the other hand, the modest, essentially unshowman-like British semi-documentary has always proved reasonably successful. It is no accident that the war, which provided a wealth of material that lent itself admirably to realistic treatment, provided the source of some of Britain's most successful films.[37]

By laying itself open to American influences, and loosening its connection with the documentary tradition, British feature film was to suffer the negative effects of the one while denying itself the advantages of the other. With this worst of two worlds, British films drifted back to the stagnation of the 1930s:

> We cannot console ourselves with the thought that we are nevertheless getting the best in motion-picture art and technique, and that our industries are subject to fine imaginative influences. For American producers are on the whole the least experimental and the most rigidly conservative, with unrelenting views concerning the forms of satisfactory and profitable film entertainment, and – for the present anyway – a strong tendency towards intransigent rejection of anything progressive.[38]

The American influence should not bear the entire blame for the stultification of the film industry in this country at the turn of the decade. A general malaise seems to have gripped the British people. The sense of purpose and achievement inspired by the war had evaporated in the face of continuing dreariness:

> People were bored with 'austerity' and with Labour's apparent fondness for all kinds of controls; the war had been over for five years and they felt that life should be less grim and restricted.[39]

Much of the early post-war optimism had vanished with the realities of peace, as Peter Ustinov observed:

> Not only is there precious little magic left in a life of increasing averageness, but the dull and the drab have crossed the frontier into the unconscious, and are already colonizing our most secret privacies.[40]

Without the pressure and stimulus of war, and yet still living with its consequences, the British people found themselves unmotivated and direction-

---

[37] Reisz (1951), 166.
[38] Roger Manvell, introduction to *The Cinema 1951* (1951), 8.
[39] Unstead (1966), 236.
[40] Ustinov (1950), 125.

less. The nation's impetus had gone. In an informal conference on the state of British cinema in 1950, Henry Cornelius observed

> To me, it seems that the post-war mood in this country is merely symptomatic of the general apathy and staleness. Compared to Italy, for instance, I do not think the shock of war has been nearly as acute here, and so the response is not as acute either.[41]

The French commentator Jean Quéval went a stage further when he wrote in the same year

> As a Frenchman whose anglophilia is undoubted, may I be permitted to say without the slightest intention of offence, that one sometimes has the impression that, as far as British present-day films are concerned, there has been no war.[42]

This only goes to prove the point that 'the great test of a national film industry is when it is making films in time of peace'.[43] British national cinema was under threat because the British people had grown weary of being informed and educated by their entertainment. Increasingly they wanted the kind of experiences that American audiences had traditionally enjoyed. In America there had long been 'a widespread tendency not only to equate screen entertainment and relaxation, but to consider anything informative an undesirable admixture',[44] and British audiences increasingly expected that films should 'be about exceptional situations or people, made to "take you out of yourself" rather than to reflect on common situations and ordinary people'.[45] British audiences, by their attendance, or, rather, by their absence, were in a position to influence the nature of the product they were patronizing.

The conditions of the early 1950s, both in society and in the film industry, inexorably forced a return to the entertainment formulae of the 1930s. One noticeable departure was the extraordinarily high proportion of crime films. Whilst the genre had been fairly popular in the 1930s, its appeal had faded during the war. In 1942, during the height of the conflict, crime films accounted for less than 10 percent of feature output, but by 1952 the figure had risen to over 40 percent. The genre was to flourish throughout the 1950s. This can in part be attributed to financial considerations. Crime films made up the bulk of second features because producers felt they could get away with a minimum of expenditure on production values if the story was sufficiently gripping. Unfortunately the screenplays were seldom of a high enough standard to distract attention from the typically dreary settings and poor lighting. The actor Harry Fowler described the differences between 'A' and 'B' pictures in the 1950s:

[41] Henry Cornelius, quoted in Wright (ed.) (1950), 115.
[42] Quéval (1950), 200.
[43] Thorold Dickinson, quoted in Wright (ed.) (1950), 116.
[44] Kracauer (1950), 145.
[45] Sue Aspinell, 'Women', in Curran and Porter (eds) (1983), 280.

> There was much more time taken over an 'A' film. To light a shot for an 'A' film could take two hours, whereas to light a 'B' film they'd give you the script and a candle![46]

The subject of crime occupied pride of place in 1950s British feature film. No other genre could boast such a high proportion of the output. There is, however, a curious general misapprehension that 'there were a great many British war films made in the 50s'.[47] In his interviews with actors and directors in *Sixty Voices*, Brian McFarlane repeatedly asked such questions as; 'What did you feel about the preponderance of war films still being made throughout the 50s?',[48] the responses unfailingly endorsing the apparent validity of the questions. The fact that war films accounted for only 5 percent of the output of British films made in the years 1950–55, rising to 7 percent in the years 1956–59, is a testament to the extraordinary impact that these films had. They stand out in the memory from the welter of dreary thrillers, trivial comedies and the newly emerging genres of horror and science fiction. McFarlane was correct in asking why 'British cinema of the 50s seems to have been dominated by war films'[49] when emphasis is added to the word 'seems'. Richard Todd's reply to the question gives a clue as to why these films were so memorable:

> The only action films that we made with any sort of reality were war films.[50]

Todd's words reveal something more about these retrospective war films. They were nearly all action films dominated by the mystique of male camaraderie. There was no looking back at the lives of ordinary people on the home front, coping with the everyday realities of war as exemplified by *The Way to the Stars* or *Millions Like Us*. Through different types of action – *The Cruel Sea*, *The Wooden Horse* and *The Dam Busters*, for instance, each deal with a distinct facet of co-operation within a male group – women were assigned insignificant or subservient roles.

Another damaging effect on British films in the 1950s was caused by this retreat of the industry from the advances it had made in the portrayal of women during the 1940s. The status and independence of women had been greatly increased by conditions arising directly from the war. These developments had often, though not invariably, been acknowledged and reflected by the industry. Women were increasingly depicted as individuals rather than as stereotypes. Apart from the more obvious, and perhaps misleading examples of Margaret Lockwood's roles in the Gainsborough melodramas, women were allowed to appear more as independent characters than as adjuncts. This development in the characterization of women was not destined to survive the next decade:

---

[46] Harry Fowler, quoted in McFarlane (ed.) (1992), 89.
[47] McFarlane (ed.) (1992), 130.
[48] Ibid., 84.
[49] Ibid., 219.
[50] Richard Todd, quoted in McFarlane (ed.) (1992), 219.

In the early 1950s, films continued their tradition of categorizing women in terms of their functions for men. These stereotypes were by no means new but this kind of reductive characterization became more common, even in serious films.[51]

As the majority of British films in the 1950s increasingly relied on action rather than on interaction to direct the course of the narrative, it might be supposed that they became more inherently cinematic. However, for the British, this was merely a question of substituting the weak hand for the strong. Without the psychological drama characteristic of its best films, British cinema could only limp pathetically after its American rivals. Such rare performances as Michael Hordern's masterly portrayal of emotional repression in *The Spanish Gardener* (1956) must be treasured, particularly coming from a year which produced such dross as *X the Unknown* and the risibly awful *Fire Maidens from Outer Space*, notorious for being a 'strong candidate for the title of worst movie ever made'.[52]

Of course, there were good films made in the 1950s in this country, but they were in a small minority. Serious composers began to shun the medium. Vaughan Williams wrote his last feature film score for Ealing's 1950 production *Bitter Springs*. Under growing pressure from more important work, he was content to let Irving take over the job for him. Walton wrote only one film score in the decade, for Olivier's final adaptation of a Shakespeare play, *Richard III* (1955). This film, although equally conscientiously crafted by Olivier, lacks the charm and spectacle of *Henry V* and the inventiveness of *Hamlet*. The subject-matter, and the film's duration, held little appeal for audiences acclimatized to an increasingly unliterary cinema. Walton was not to score another film until *The Battle of Britain* – a project which ended in débâcle.

Alan Rawsthorne continued to write scores for feature films in the 1950s, but he was not by temperament a musico-dramatist. His score for *The Cruel Sea* is the most successful, partly because the film itself is the most impressive and memorable, and partly because his rather arid atonal language fortuitously coincides with the bleakness of its subject-matter. Since the main titles music of all his feature films sounds remarkably similar, they did not all benefit from such a happy coincidence. Rawsthorne displays little interest in the possibilities of dramatic interpretation by way of variety in his orchestration. His use of the solo violin in *The Cruel Sea* (described on p. 161 above) is a rare exception to almost uniform orchestral textures. His score for his first feature, *The Captive Heart*, contains a cue which must stand as one of the worst examples of dialogue scoring by a British composer. In the film's dénouement, where the central character reveals his true identity to the object of his affection – a scene which the audience has eagerly anticipated for a good portion of the film – the dramatic impact, and the timing of the actors' delivery, are all but obliterated by a barrage of frenetic repetitions of the associated theme from the full orchestra. The acting of Michael Redgrave and Rachel Kempson could have carried this scene without

[51] Sue Aspinall, 'Women', in Curran and Porter (ed.) (1983), 289.
[52] Walker (ed.) (8/1991), 381.

assistance. Irving should have let his judgment overcome any nicety of feeling, and left the music where it deserved to be – on the cutting-room floor.

If Rawsthorne had not espoused the cause of film music, there were three composers who combined extensive work in films with serious composition. The reputations of Alwyn, Arnold and Frankel have all suffered from their involvement with film. To be dubbed a 'film composer' was to be viewed by critics and the musical establishment in a dubious light. While many comment-ators have praised Walton for his film scores, especially those written for the three Shakespeare adaptations, it would never occur to any of them to categorize him as a film composer. Although John Huntley, even before the success of *Henry V*, had described him as 'perhaps our most consistent and brilliant film composer',[53] Walton was generally regarded as our most successful *contributor* to the medium, not as a film composer by definition. As far as the establishment was concerned, film scoring could never be regarded as an art. Those composers who had whole-heartedly embraced the medium certainly regarded it thus, and Vaughan Williams saw the potential in film for achieving Wagner's dream of the total art-work. But for all that, Vaughan Williams would never have let work on a film score come before his 'real' work, as witness the scoring of *Bitter Springs*.

Much of the blame for film composing's lack of prestige may be laid at the door of critics. Mathieson was all too aware of the problem. His efforts to encourage the country's top composers to raise the profile of film music by taking up its cause would all be wasted if critics and the establishment insisted on viewing such involvements as amusing but temporary aberrations. When Mathieson bemoaned the fact that 'to date, film music has been nobody's baby',[54] it was essentially to film-music criticism that he referred. Without 'experienced or constructive criticism'[55] film music could not hope to reach the status of concert music. This lack of interest in, and understanding of film music on the part or critics is responsible for a general misapprehension of its value. As Alwyn himself observed,

> One cannot label this music as mere 'background' music in a derogatory sense merely because film music in the minds of uninformed music critics has always tended to be associated with the lush outpourings of third-rate hacks.[56]

Alwyn has suffered possibly more than any composer from this association because it was recognized that he 'perhaps to a greater extent than any other composer in this country, has embraced the art of film background music'.[57] The very qualities that film required from a composer could damage him in the eyes of the critics, so far as his credentials as a serious composer were concerned:

---

[53] Huntley (1944), 91.
[54] Muir Mathieson, quoted in Huntley (1947), 7.
[55] Ibid.
[56] Alwyn (1967), 40.
[57] Huntley (undated), 7.

Versatility is sometimes regarded as a debatable asset in a composer – contemporary criticism is inclined to question the ability of the creative artist to be versatile: the composer must be channelled and clocheted [sic].[58]

Alwyn, Arnold and Frankel all demonstrated great versatility in their scoring of films during the 1950s. All three covered a wide range of subjects in their outputs, requiring distinct and individual treatment for each film. Whether composing for comedy – both contemporary and period – or for war films, thrillers or serious dramas, all three proved Alwyn's point that 'versatility does not mean an abandonment of individuality'.[59] Each composer's individual style was preserved no matter what techniques were employed to meet dramatic requirements. The technical prowess of these three composers could have been injurious to their concert music only if they had failed to make a distinction between the two media. But it would be impossible for any intelligent composer to mistake the differentiation in function between the two:

The conscientious composer brings to 'absolute music', or 'serious music' if you like, an utterly different approach from that which he adopts towards film. In 'absolute music' he in concerned with the technical problems of formal design and construction – even an essentially atmospheric work such as Debussy's *La Mer* is more dependant on its exquisite sense of line, phrase and climax rather than on 'the sea' which is its inspiration: and with evocation rather than description.[60]

Alwyn, Arnold and Frankel were all symphonists who happened to be highly successful composers for film. If their film work did not encroach on their serious output, neither did they bring symphonic expectations to their film scores. Dramatic requirements should dictate the musical forces:

I would often far rather use a small group of players than a full symphony orchestra – primarily because I like to choose my palette to suit my canvas.[61]

This was not only true of Alwyn, who, alone of the three, had been reared in the documentary tradition. Arnold, too, had occasion to leave the symphony orchestra behind:

Arnold has found that a small orchestra is best suited to this type of work [comedy]. Even in his dramatic work, he is a believer in the smaller ensemble for the microphone. For *Hobson's Choice* he used an orchestra of twenty-five, for *I Am a Camera* an orchestra of fourteen, and for *The Belles of St. Trinian's* he had only twelve instrumentalists.[62]

---

[58] William Alwyn, 'Film Music – Sound or Silence?', lecture delivered for the British Film Association at Edinburgh Film Festival, 31.8.1958.

[59] Ibid.

[60] Ibid.

[61] Ibid.

[62] Manvell and Huntley (2/1975), 154.

Curiously enough, film producers in the 1950s were generally reluctant to let composers have their own way in this matter, hence Alwyn's complaint that 'it is rarely now that one is allowed to use economic means to secure one's intentions in the feature film'.[63] It seems extraordinary that a composer should find it difficult to be 'allowed to use economic means', but Alwyn can offer an explanation:

> Unhappily the symphony orchestra is like the all-star cast, it provides a sort of Hollywood gloss and a pseudo-prestige value to the films. To put it at its worst – important sounding music makes the picture sound important.[64]

The most surprising thing about British film scores in the 1950s was the continued use of the symphony orchestra as the standard musical medium. The introduction of the country's symphonists to film scoring in the 1930s and 1940s had reinforced the relationship between the feature film and the orchestra, but the experimental work in documentary film carried out by these same composers indicates that they did not necessarily approach the task with a fixed idea about the supremacy of the orchestra. Cinema audiences in the 1940s had become conditioned to accept the sound of a symphony orchestra as a natural part of their entertainment, and it was rarely that they were offered an alternative. *Waterloo Road* (1945) is highly unusual, being a wartime film with a non-symphonic score. The music, by Bob Busby, is played by a salon orchestra, or more accurately, the kind of pit orchestra associated with stage musicals of the day. The film deals with an issue that concerned many men serving in the armed forces – what their wives were doing when they were away. As such, it falls into the category of 'social problem' film, and, especially in view of its cockney setting, the non-symphonic treatment seems more appropriate.

The social problem film was to gain in popularity through the 1950s. As the balance of the social structure continued to shift, film makers turned to three sectors of society that were beginning to claim attention: the working class, the teenager and regional Britain – subjects that had hardly existed in British films of the 1930s. There were difficulties with these subjects, however, because of 'the unwillingness of realistic ideas of society to come together filmically whilst conforming to the narrow censorship of the 1940s and 1950s'.[65] Hampered by censorship laws, these films nevertheless attempted to portray convincingly the lives of those other than the affluent middle classes of the Home Counties. And yet, throughout this, the symphony orchestra clung on tenaciously. It can be understood that the orchestra might continue to be considered suitable for certain types of film, particularly those that represented a continuation of traditions established in the 1940s. If it had been accepted as appropriate that an action war film made in the 1940s should be scored for orchestra, there was little justification for treating the subject differently a decade later. But, with

---

[63] Alwyn, 'Film Music – Sound or Silence?'
[64] Ibid.
[65] Sellar (1987), 118.

hindsight, it seems extraordinary that the more contemporary genres – thrillers, science fiction and the social-problem film – should so frequently have been scored for orchestra.

It was not until the latter years of the 1950s that examples can be found of scores written for other instrumental forces. Comedy films were the exception. Alwyn had been allowed his 'economic means' for *The Card* (1955), and the films sparsely scored by Arnold, *Hobson's Choice* (1954), *I Am a Camera* (1955) and *The Belles of St. Trinian's* (1954), were all comedies. Comedy films by definition have no need to sound important. Comic effects can be achieved much more easily by reduced forces, as Larry Adler's solo harmonica in *Genevieve* proves. It is surprising to discover that the score for the crime thriller *Nowhere to Go* (1958) is very much the exception. This score features the Dizzy Reece jazz quartet, and the limited resources inspire some innovative scoring, with certain extended action sequences played only on the hi-hat cymbal – a very economical means of building up tension. The electronic score for *Escapement* (1958), a science-fiction thriller, is another rare fugitive from the orchestral score.

British film music in the 1950s thus maintained the domination of the orchestral score even in areas that would have been better characterized by smaller, more 'popular' forces. There were other, less well-known serious composers working in the field. John Veale, Buxton Orr and Bruce Montgomery all continued to write concert music while working for film. This new generation of composers were no more inclined to subvert their individual style than their predecessors had been. As Hans Keller pointed out,

> While it is also true that there is hardly any British film music which could be regarded as advanced in style, neither have all leading British composers become reactionaries as soon as they started to work for the commercial cinema.[66]

This is borne out by such uncompromising offerings as Orr's title music for *The Fiend without a Face* (1958) and Montgomery's titles and opening sequence to *Checkpoint* (1956). Serious composers were still discovering that film provided them with an outlet and a captive audience for their music. But cinema audiences had dwindled alarmingly in the second half of the decade. Patricia Perilli's statistical survey shows that cinema admissions in Britain fell from 1,396 million in 1950 to 1,182 million in 1953, and to 501 million in 1960. In the same years, the number of television licences increased from 343,882 to 4,503,766, and finally to 10,469,753.[67] Quite apart from injury to the film industry, there was a less obvious consequence of this rapid growth of television viewing, as the term 'background music' took on a whole new meaning. At the same time, the British public were increasingly subjected to the involuntary consumption of background music in shops, pubs and restaurants. Alwyn was all too aware of the impact this had on film music:

[66] Hans Keller, in Blom (ed.) (1954), iii, 102, s.v. 'Film Music; British'.
[67] Patricia Perilli, 'Survey', in Curran and Porter (eds) (1983), 372.

A public who has become conditioned to a continual background of musical sound in every-day life, will still expect it as a background to its entertainment. It is with regret and foreboding that one sees this encroaching on the film score. Looking back over my own career as a film composer, I find that 10 years ago an average film score for a feature film was about 20 minutes – today it is normally 40 minutes to an hour. This cuts at the very roots of film music as an *art* – without silence the composer loses his most effective weapon.[68]

So destructive did Alwyn consider this tendency to be that he decided, some five years later, to part company from an art to which he had contributed so much. His relationship with film had been one of enduring commitment; it was not the brief encounter of Bliss, Ireland or Bax. They could never have said, as he did in 1958,

I am an unrepentant idealist and believe that only by giving of my best, and being given the opportunity of giving of my best, shall I work out my salvation whether in the concert hall, the theatre pit, or the cinema auditorium.[69]

But by then the days were over when Alwyn, or any other concert composer, was given the opportunity of giving of his best to film. With the beginning of the 'new wave' of British cinema the old guard of composers gave way to a coming generation who were happy to be known as film composers – Stanley Black, Ron Goodwin, John Barry. British film music, while it continued to offer occasional opportunities to more 'serious' composers, took a step closer to its Hollywood counterpart as it passed into the hands of specialists.

[68] Alwyn, 'Film Music – Sound or Silence?'
[69] Ibid.

Appendix A
The author in conversation with Roy Douglas,
4 August 1993

JS: I've got this book, you must have seen it at the time.

RD: I don't think I've ever seen it; what does that say? Louis Levy?

JS: This is the John Huntley. You're in there, there's a biography of you in there.

RD: Oh, yes, I have an idea they got it wrong. I'd forgotten that. Somebody did tell me. Contributions by Louis Levy! I was always given the impression that Louis Levy wasn't capable of putting any notes on paper at all. It was all composed by either Charles Williams, or Hubert Bath, who, I think, did a few scores on his own.

JS: Louis Levy's name is attached to many films, but hardly in the capacity of composer, though he is credited with that sometimes. Didn't he come from the dance-band world?

RD: I reckon he was a dance-band leader, yes, but Hubert Bath wrote symphonic works and choral works.

JS: How common was it for concert composers to orchestrate their own films?

RD: I should say that most of them, apart from people like Addinsell, did their scores *entirely* themselves – certainly Vaughan Williams did. I shall have to go back a bit now. There was always such a terrible hurry to get things done – they never gave you enough time to write the music – and people who wrote slowly like Walton and John Ireland, got into a terrible panic and realized they couldn't finish the composing and the scoring in time, so they would get somebody like me to orchestrate some of the less important sections, lasting about 16 or 32 bars, or something like that.

JS: So was there no concession made to the fact that they were coming from a different angle? Obviously composers who were used to doing film scores were used to doing it in a very short space of time, but if they'd employed someone like Walton or Vaughan Williams to do that score –

RD: [In the case of] VW, I think he sometimes used to give them about 45 minutes of music to pick out what they wanted.

JS: It's well known that he wrote from the script, and the inspiration came from that.

RD: I dare say he saw the rough-cut of the film.

JS: There are certain instances where he just said, as you very much imply: 'Here's 40 minutes of my music, and use it as you wish.' There's a letter from Irving to him which says: 'I've tried not to disrupt the structure of the music for you.'

RD: I dare say perhaps *Scott of the Antarctic* was more carefully planned as regards timing.

JS: How much did Irving engineer the thing? *Scott* is an interesting score because it's quite open-ended, isn't it? and therefore he was able to manipulate it without losing the structure.

RD: I always admired Irving, I think he was a very good musician, and he admired VW tremendously, and he could be entrusted not to falsify the composer's intentions.

JS: There can't have been that many people who were concerned with the composer's intentions.

RD: Film producers hadn't the least idea what a composer was, they just told you that they wanted music. The fact that you had to wait for inspiration, well, there wasn't time for inspiration. The only film I did for Ealing was for the film *The Bells Go Down,* about the fire service. I was given three weeks. A band of 44 – absolute riches: 8 first fiddles and 6 seconds! 4 horns, 3 trumpets, 3 trombones and tuba. 22 minutes music, 566 bars had to be composed in a fortnight. It's all very well, but I saw the film through once, then they sent me the list of timings. Have you seen a list of timings? Do they have them nowadays? Then you are at the mercy of the conductor. If he doesn't conduct it at the right speed the music doesn't fit, that was another snag.

JS: Did you work fairly closely with Irving on that score?

RD: Not really, I just sent in the scores and they were copied, and, as far as I remember we met at the recording sessions.

JS: But that would have been rather different in your case because you were experienced in film work.

RD: Not a great deal by then. I'd done three dreadful films in the 30s for little firms which went bust before they'd paid me.

JS: Why do you think it is that there's so little interest in British film music compared to the great tomes they're writing now about Hollywood?

RD: Did you listen two or three years ago, there was a series of five or six programmes on film music on Radio 4, because they came and recorded about 14 minutes of me and they didn't use a single word of what I said. They wanted to know all about British film music and British film composers. One entire broadcast was about Hollywood, another one was about cinema organists, and every one of them wasn't about British film music at all, they just weren't interested.

JS: It seems to me that there's this massive interest in what Steiner and Korngold were doing, and it just doesn't compare to what was happening here in terms of the quality of the music.

RD: I suppose during the war there weren't the American composers over here in film music, so it gave us all a chance. They got Walton, Anthony Collins, Arthur Benjamin and the smaller people. The other people who were very experienced, and didn't, I felt, ever have much trouble in writing for film, were William Alwyn and Hely-Hutchinson.

JS: Alwyn, though, is generally regarded as a film composer although he wrote superb symphonies.

RD: Oh, yes. You see, I was really a pianist in the London Symphony Orchestra, and so I took part in the recordings and played the piano in every session of *Things to Come*.

JS: Were you the regular pianist with the LSO or were you first-call extra?

RD: I was the pianist, organist and harpsichord player, celesta player, and I was fourth percussion and librarian.

JS: Were you fourth percussion? One of those jobs!

RD: Pianist and organist in the last sessions of the Proms at Queen's Hall, before it was bombed, and the first session at the Albert Hall. I did play in all the sessions and harpsichord in *The Ghost Goes West*, mostly on two Sundays in the Cambridge Theatre, and on the second Sunday we'd got there about nine o'clock, and we'd recorded on and off until about six, and all the orchestra left except for me on the harpsichord and Leon Goosens the oboe to do a solo bit and the actual sound was difficult, so they put the microphone inside the harpsichord, so every note you played – at the end of a nine-hour session!

JS: As if the harpsichord wasn't bad enough to start with!

RD: Yes, I know, terrifying! I also played the harpsichord in all the sessions of *Henry V* – you can hear it, I think, once or twice. There's a bit clanging about when they're getting their armour ready for Agincourt, and I played for the gramophone records of it. You very often had a piano to accentuate the bass because the bass didn't come through, you used to spend half your time playing octaves in the left hand.

JS: So did that happen more than one is aware of when listening to these scores? The bass is always a problem, isn't it, when writing for orchestra?

RD: I played in a lot of the William Alwyn scores, and Hely-Hutchinson's, and other people's whose names I can't remember. They weren't so bothered about it because I think they did all their own scores, they were more used to it than people like Walton and Ireland.

JS: People like Walton and Ireland you say, essentially because they ran out of time, they weren't used to producing work so fast, but they would have wanted to do their own orchestration had they had the opportunity?

RD: Yes. I think I told you on the phone, I did the Stampede and the fugue in *The Overlanders*.

JS: Is that your writing in the original score?

RD: I don't know, because I was told afterwards when they made a suite of it, when it was recorded, he scored them himself, which is understandable. I went to see him – was it Edith Grove he lived? and he gave me these [sketches], as usual, written on two staves, or perhaps three staves, and a couple of days later I delivered the scores to him, and 'How on earth did you put all these notes on paper?' he said in his funny little high-pitched, rather London voice.

JS: Yes, I've seen the sketches.

RD: He couldn't believe that anyone could put notes on paper so quickly.

JS: Only those who know how.

RD: Walton – I used to have to stay at Ashby St. Legers where he was living with Lady Wimborne, and he would disappear and strum about on the piano – he did most of his film composing on the piano – and then at the end of the day he would just say: 'Would you score these three bits for me?', and I used to get down to it the next day while he was writing some more bits.

JS: Would he indicate general ideas as they do in America, it wasn't a complete free hand?

RD: Yes. 'Strings with a clarinet solo' and that sort of thing. That's very different from putting all the notes on paper for a full score, isn't it?

JS: Incredibly different. When working with composers did you ever find it necessary to change radically any orchestrations because of misjudgment or inexperience?

RD: Well, I never saw their scores.

JS: You would only be given their sketches?

RD: Just the piano sketches, yes.

JS: There was never an occasion when you had an aside from somebody to say: 'Look, this isn't going to work'?

RD: The only time was the first time I met Vaughan Williams. He wrote me a card, and all I could read was: 'The White Gates, Dorking', and the telephone number, so I rang up and asked him what the card was about. He wanted me to go over some advice on film writing, film scoring, because he knew I was experienced and he wasn't, and he showed me some of the things he'd done. I think it must have been for *Coastal Command*, and I explained to him that in those days you must never have oboe solos over dialogue, because it didn't mix on the sound track, and that sort of little thing. I was nervous of him, I was half his age, and he was the greatest composer, and he was nervous of me, Ursula told me, because he was shy of a professional musician.

JS: He would, perhaps, have felt some inhibitions with you, knowing that you were an absolute expert in your field.

RD: That's my favourite story. He said, 'Did you go to the College or to the Academy?' I was terrible embarrassed. I said: 'No, I'm one of those people, a self-taught musician.' He said: 'Thank God for that. I can't bear these young men who think they know everything from the College.'

JS: It's interesting that so many of these people went to the College. It's a bit like today, when everybody comes from Cambridge.

RD: Well, I think the answer is that Muir Mathieson went to the College, he was a protégé of Sargent.

JS: Yes, and of Arthur Benjamin.

RD: There was a short film called *Yesterday's Over Your Shoulder*, which was a ministry propaganda film, and the tune was a piece called 'Yesterday's Over Your Shoulder', composed by Robertson Hare, the man who lost his trousers every night in the Aldwych farces. He wrote this Lumty Dumty Da Da Da Dumta, Dumta Dumta Dum. I had to compose the entire music for that film, and turn that into a patriotic march, and a waltz – thematic metamorphosis I think you call it, the whole thing was based on that – and when it came to the recording sessions, it [the credits]said: 'Music by Muir Mathieson'.

JS: I think Muir Mathieson would be the last person to try and grab credit for composing, because he was really responsible, wasn't he, for getting these guys in.

RD: These 'wonderful' suites he did of Walton's music. He just took the original scores and did a modulation via a cymbal roll and a side drum roll.

JS: But Mathieson is generally given credit for bringing these chaps in.

RD: Oh, yes, he did.

JS: And what do you think would have been the situation if he hadn't been on the scene?

RD: I think the Germans were all in it. Dr. Ernst Toch I seem to connect with *Catherine the Great*. I had to play the piano, and I had to rehearse a chorus, up at Elstree I think it was, and I was introduced to a young man who was very interested in film music, about 18 at the time, named Muir Mathieson. I don't know if in 1933 that works out with the date.

JS: He would have been 22.

RD: He had been recommended by somebody, probably Sargent, I'm not sure, and that's how he first got in.

JS: I was wondering how he got in so smoothly, because he became assistant at about that time, didn't he, to Kurt Schroeder.

RD: Yes, that's right, and there were quite a few German and Austrian Jewish composers around at that time, but Muir obviously wanted to –

JS: Yes, we could have ended up, given that the British film industry was absolutely overrun with the Korda collection, with a situation like Hollywood, but we didn't.

RD: Yes, you see Brodszky got quite a few films because he was a pal of Joe Pasternak in Hollywood, he was always talking about his friend Joe Pasternak.

JS: What about Spoliansky?

RD: Yes, he was another. Now, he was a nice chap, I liked him, a very thoroughly competent musician, but some of them were very pushing.

JS: A lot of British films, which, I think, can be distinguished by being very British in their essence, used foreign composers. I'm thinking here, for example, of *Hue and Cry*, which I think is not served by using somebody like Auric. What was your opinion about that?

RD: We all resented it very much. Now, Pascal did ask Walton to do *Pygmalion*, didn't he?

JS: Yes, it was at the time of his violin concerto. He made the decision not to do it.

RD: So instead of getting another British composer they got –

JS: Honegger, wasn't it?

RD: Somebody like that. There was another film he [Walton]was asked to do, (I found out quite recently, and that was, I think, in Stuart Craggs's book), *The Bells Go Down*. He's been able to see a lot of letters from Walton and he found this business about *The Bells Go Down*.

JS: Which, of course, you didn't know at the time.

RD: I was told at the time – it may be true – that they also had asked Addinsell, and he was too busy, and it was that that started my divorce from the music of Richard Addinsell, because he had a film at the time, and I had to tell Muir Mathieson I was too busy writing my own music.

JS: With your three weeks to write it I'm not surprised you were too busy.

RD: And he didn't like that at all.

JS: Addinsell himself didn't like that, or Muir?

RD: I think, basically, Muir. He got his knife into me about that. What was the date of the last thing I did for Addinsell?

JS: *The Day Will Dawn* of 1942

RD: *The Bells Go Down* was early '43.

JS: So that was the final film that you did for him.

RD: I did do a short called *The New Lot* for him in the January, and I think that was the very last.

JS: Had you enjoyed a good personal relationship with Addinsell before?

RD: Oh, yes, yes, except that I was always kept well in the background. At the recording sessions I wasn't allowed to say anything about the balance. I was able to correct wrong notes.

JS: You were a backroom boy.

RD: I was very much a backroom boy, and any parties that took place I was never invited to. The great fun was the Walton violin concerto, the first performance with Henry Holst. I'd spent a week or so rehearsing it with him at the piano, so I was invited to the first performance and to the party at Grosvenor House. I managed to get Addinsell an invitation to the party, at his request, and there was Addinsell sitting in a corner at the party surrounded by some of his boyfriends, and Walton, who was a devil like that, came over and said: 'Will you be wanting Roy to write some of your music next month, because I want him to help with some of mine?' Addinsell went very red, and got very embarrassed! It made me chuckle.

JS: So, just to take a step back for a moment. If you were more or less self-taught, how did that come about?

RD: You don't want the life story of me!

JS: I'd like to know how you became such an expert orchestrator on your own.

RD: In my teens I was a shop assistant in a music shop, then I left that and became a member of the Folkestone Municipal Orchestra, which was a band of about 25, reduced to 18.

JS: You were playing the piano?

RD: I was playing the Mustel organ. You know the Mustel organ? It was made so that various stops imitated orchestral instruments, particularly the bassoon as there was no bassoon in the orchestra. Thursday afternoons we had a symphony concert, with a band of 18 or 25. We used to play things like Glazunov's and Brahms's symphonies – so I was filling in from the piano part – then I managed to fill in from a Haydn score, a Mozart score, a Beethoven score. From miniature scores, playing with one hand and turning over! and then on Saturday mornings we had a children's concert, and we had community singing, we had all these popular songs, old folk songs and whatnot that had to be orchestrated for this band of 18. Sometimes the conductor did it himself, and sometimes he was too lazy, and got me to do half a dozen of them. You got used to sitting next to a horn player who was rather inefficient, and a trombone player who got nervous, and I used to be able to pick out the instrument and try and play some of them, and that's how it started. Eventually they reduced the salary from six pounds a week to five pounds a week for about 14 performances. Then they decided to reduce it by another pound, so I went to London to seek my fortune – which I didn't find – but after I'd been there a while I had a telephone call from Rae Jenkins. He was a fiddle player, a viola player, and finally became the conductor of the Welsh orchestra, and he said he knew of somebody who wanted someone to write film music for an Indian film, based on Indian tunes. I knew nothing about Indian music, or about writing film music – it was one of these small firms in Wardour Street – and I spent two days listening to recordings of Indian native music and I never want to hear another note of it! I produced this horrible score, and the orchestra that played it happened to include four members of the London Symphony Orchestra, and they realized I had talent. Eventually I was engaged to play and write music for another film which they played in, and eventually they said: would I like to be the librarian of the LSO, did I play the piano and organ, and that was that. That's all the experience I had.

JS: Yes, but that's a lot.

RD: *Practical* experience.

JS: So when it came to films themselves and writing for film, did you find a great personal interest in that, or was it just part of the orchestrator's job for you?

RD: It was awfully interesting to see how other composers handled it, and to try and score in their manner. To try and make Walton's piece sound as if Walton had scored it himself. I thought you might ask how one felt about composing music for films. First of all, one was flattered, and I think most people were flattered to be asked, whoever it was. I think even VW and

Walton were pleased that they were asked to do it. If you were asked a
second time that was even better. And then there was the money, because
during the war there wasn't a lot of work for composers to earn money
straight away.

JS: There isn't at any time, is there?

RD: You had to write something, get a publisher, who then published it after a
long time, then you had to wait for the royalties, whereas with a film you
perhaps didn't have to wait more than a couple of months. All of us did a
lot of Ministry of Information films. They paid badly, and the other,
smaller firms you were lucky if you got it at all within a couple of years.
For *The Bells Go Down* we were just watching it and I was sitting next to
Irving. He said: 'We haven't talked about terms, have we? I think we'll be
needing about 30 minutes of film music, would 300 pounds do?' I'd never
had more than about 25, 30 at the most. I said: 'Yes, that sounds
reasonable', after a gulp, and that was the biggest sum I ever got. The
film that James Turner and I did for Brodszky –

JS: *Candlelight in Algeria* was it?

RD: Yes. The first was *Freedom Radio*. For *Tomorrow We Live*, he [Brodszky]
produced 'My Love Song', which was something he'd composed when he
was in Austria or somewhere, he played it on the piano, and said: 'Do
somezings viz zat – develop it', and that is all the instruction we got. We
composed the whole ruddy film, transforming his tune, and dropping it
whenever we could. At the end the producer said: 'Look, it's quite obvious
to us that Mr. Brodszky hasn't composed a note of this music. Are we
right in thinking you composed the lot, as well as orchestrating it?', and
we said: 'Well, I'm sorry, but I've got to say yes.' 'Well, will you do our
next film *Candlelight in Algeria*?' He got 400 pounds, I think, and we got
100 pounds to share between us for *Tomorrow We Live*.

JS: Is *Candlelight* credited to you, then, on the main titles?

RD: The composition – all of it – is to me and James Turner. There was the
money, as I say, which was very useful. How else would a composer earn
money? Oh – the BBC. That's what happened to me eventually, by the
time I'd finished writing music for films. I was doing a great lot – once a
month, pretty well – of short propaganda broadcasts of various topics to
do with the war.

JS: Nearly everybody who became involved in feature films started with the
documentary as a sort of run-up. How important do you think that was,
as a comparison again with Hollywood composers, do you think it was a
very valuable practice run?

RD: Useful, I wouldn't say valuable! The Hollywood film scores, so few of
them live apart from the films, do they?

JS: That's a dangerous area, though, isn't it? Don't you feel it's detrimental if
a composer writes a film score with one eye on the concert platform? Isn't
it detrimental to what the purpose of a *film* score is?

RD: As far as I can see, the composers I worked with, for, and played the piano for, they were solely concerned with the film, to do a good job. That was the other thing I was going to say: flattery, as well as being flattered to do it, being paid, and having the incentive to compose – a definite incentive. You hadn't got to think: 'Now, shall I write a concerto for so-and-so?' Here was somebody who wanted you to write music, and you did it to the best of your ability to suit the film, what you thought was going to help the film, and was not going to injure your reputation as a composer. I think everybody probably felt like that.

JS: And yet many of them did adapt them for concert, and they do stand up as concert pieces.

RD: I think probably they were invited or encouraged to by their publishers.

JS: So you think it was less a cynical attitude on their part, it was more coming from outside.

RD: I think Walton was always wanting to earn money, however it was done. He was quite pleased, I think, when Muir Mathieson did suites. Then he did the ballet *The Quest*, and he didn't like the music for *The Quest*, he wasn't at all happy about it because he did it in a great hurry. There again, I did some scores, Irving did some scores, and then Vilem Tausky said he'd like to do a suite, so Walton said: 'Yes, do a suite – more money', same as [inaudible] does now with Christopher Palmer and his hashings up!

JS: Do you feel, then, that they've been a little bit maligned? This is a comment that's quite often made, that they were too concerned with writing music that would stand up. Bliss felt that it wasn't valid if it couldn't stand on its own as a concert piece, and there's the other side which says that is detrimental to film music whose function is to serve the film.

RD: I'm sure Bliss was only concerned with writing music for the film. The fact that it became popular as a suite – as I say, possibly the publisher thought: 'Can't we make a suite?'

JS: It was only something that happened afterwards, it wasn't something that was considered at the time?

RD: I'm sure Walton never thought of *The Battle of Agincourt* being made into a piece in the middle of a suite.

JS: In the early stages, were people like Walton and Vaughan Williams, certainly Vaughan Williams, capable of writing a score [for film] and going through the whole process of it unaided, or were they always supported and advised by the musical directors?

RD: I imagine that they just did what I did, they just saw the film, got the list of timings, went home and composed.

JS: And what happened to it afterwards, was it out of their control – in the sense of the cutting room floor?

RD: Oh, yes.

JS: They had no say in that?

RD: I don't think so. I don't know about the more practical ones like Hely-Hutchinson and Hubert Clifford – they may have.

JS: But they don't really belong, in the same sense, to what I would call the concert composers, do they?

RD: The top composers were just completely at the mercy of those people.

JS: Because Walton's first film, *Escape Me Never,* got completely butchered, didn't it?

RD: Yes. I was just trying to remember, things like *Candlelight in Algeria* and *Tomorrow We Live.* I think we were invited to the rush theatre to see the sections with the music, to see if it fitted alright. One or two of the Ministry propaganda things, I was let loose in the cutting room to cut the film. I was terrified!

JS: But that's what some composers would consider to be ideal.

RD: Yes, as long as you know what you're doing!

JS: Brian Easdale, in his score for *Black Narcissus*: on the main titles it says he was in charge of the soundtrack. He was allowed to use, in the ideal way, the effects. He was in control, and, surely, that's almost unique, isn't it?

RD: I think the last film I ever wrote music for was called, to start with, *Victory in Burma.* It was for a little firm to do with the Ministry at Merton Park. I saw the film, with the commentary. I was given the timings, and I wrote all the music, and after I'd composed it they rang up and said: 'We've submitted the commentary to the Ministry of Defence' – the War Office – and the victory in Burma wasn't being a victory, it was becoming a defeat, so: 'we've had to rewrite the commentary and all the timings are different.' All the score then had to be changed. Then we were allowed to record it, and after we'd recorded it and it was on the soundtrack, we lost, pretty well, the war in Burma. It [the film] was then called *War in Burma*, and the stuff was on the soundtrack with a different commentary again, and then I was given this wretched little machine that made horrible noises in your ears, and I had to cut my own soundtrack bar by bar to fit. Terrifying, because nobody was there to help me, they just left me to it. I don't think the film was ever made, but I was paid for it. [It was released as *Central Front, Burma.*]

JS: So that's a very unusual circumstance. When you say that composers were given the timings, that implies that it was very unusual for them to be able to decide with the producer where the music would go.

RD: Oh, the producer told you. Sometimes it would be when you saw a rough cut of the film, you'd say: 'I think we ought to have music there, I'd like to have music there, it could start there.' Then you'd get a list of the sections.

JS: You had very little control over that?

RD: Nothing at all.

JS: There was never any flexibility on that?

RD: Well, no. I think it was in *Tomorrow We Live* there was a session with dear Yvonne Arnaud, who[in the film]had lost her son in the war, and she was looking at his photograph, and she was a beautiful actress and excellent pianist. She did that scene so beautifully – restrained, without being sob stuff – and they wanted music under it. I said: 'No, you must not have music under it!' 'Well, we would like to have music, we'll record it, and perhaps you'll write something for it.' I wouldn't write anything for it, I gave that to James Turner, and when the film came out, it didn't have music.

JS: They had taken your judgment.

RD: Eventually, they decided. Years later I was turning pages for Yvonne Arnaud who was broadcasting a Fauré piece – *Ballade for Piano and Orchestra* – and I told her about this, and she was very amused.

JS: That impulse that made you feel very strongly that there shouldn't have been music under that, is again very different to American scores, where they wouldn't hesitate to write music under a scene like that. What do you think it is about British films and British composers that have that strong feeling that there shouldn't be music there at that point?

RD: I don't know. More restrained?

JS: Emotionally restrained?

RD: Yes. Certainly in that case.

JS: I've noticed with British films – especially in *Scott*, [at] two of the most emotional moments in that film – there is no music.

RD: I would say in that case, Irving, who was the musical director, would have had strong feelings.

JS: So you knew Irving quite well, presumably.

RD: Not really, I only met him a few times.

JS: He seems by his writings to have been a very cultured man.

RD: Very cultured, yes. He had a terrible temper, I'm told.

JS: As far as his job was concerned, I notice that in many of the early Ealing films, there is just a credit to him – whether as composer or just musical director. It was at a later stage that he began to use Walton in *The Foreman Went to France*, and so forth. But at the stage when Muir was eager to introduce the top composers, Irving was more or less on his own. What was the difference do you think?

RD: I don't like to think that he was using other composers and not putting their names up.

JS: Do you think that might have been the case?

RD: No, I think if there wasn't a lot of music he probably could turn it out.

JS: Yes, I'm talking about the films in the '30s, things hadn't become set by then. I mean the pattern of using more famous composers.

RD: I don't really know what he was like at all as a composer. He could probably knock things out.

JS: If you think of things like *Whiskey Galore!*, where he just takes Scottish traditional music and does a marvellous orchestration of it, perhaps that was the kind of thing he did. I just wondered if there was something different about his approach to the job from Muir's, where Muir was so concerned to get the best composers.

RD: I suppose it was just that he felt that it was the right thing to do, but it may also have been that he'd get a bit of credit reflected on himself for doing so.

JS: It might have been a tighter budget, that's another factor, because he [Irving] worked for Ealing all the time, they must have been on a tighter budget, certainly than Korda. But then, Ealing got into the habit of using Auric.

RD: I suppose they found that he turned out the stuff that they wanted quickly and without any trouble.

JS: He was fairly prolific, was he? What do you feel about Spoliansky and May and people like that?

RD: Oh, Hans May, yes. And, during the war, Francis Chagrin. Well, he was on the Arrangers, Composers and Copyists Section [of the Musicians' Union]. I was on it with Chagrin and Seiber when he proposed the formation of the CPNM, and Chagrin, Seiber and I were the three original members of that committee. Nowadays you only hear about Chagrin as the founder. The ACCS decided they should do something about composers for the Ministry of Information, that they should get proper composers and proper rates as the Ministry were paying just what they felt like – ten quid or something. So a little committee was formed to negotiate with the Ministry of Information as regards terms, and from that moment all, practically all the Ministry of Information films were composed by Francis Chagrin! Yes, you're hearing all the low-down now.

I must tell you about *All For Norway*. I won't say it was typical, but it was, I think, the worst thing. 1942, in July, I think – it's difficult to remember after fifty years – but the king of Norway had been smuggled over to this country, it was when Norway was invaded, or was going to be. They decided to make a film as a tribute to him, so on Friday, July 24th, I think it was, they rang me up, would I compose the music for the film which was going to be recorded on Tuesday? There wasn't time to go and see the film at all. They sent me a list of timings and a book of Norwegian national tunes. Would I compose continuous music for the 16-minute film? So you then had to take these tunes, harmonize them, spread them out and write sort of paraphrases on them to last 16 minutes, for a band of eighteen. There were 482 bars. Friday, Saturday and Sunday. I seem to remember on the Saturday I sent parcels up from the station which were collected by the copyists at Charing Cross. I finished composing those 482 bars, 16 minutes, on the Monday, and they were recorded on the Tuesday. I'll never forget that! And, of course, the producers liked the titles to be nice and full of brass – fanfares, rushes up and down in semiquavers on the strings, harp glissandos and such – which was rather difficult when you had a band of eighteen! Flute, oboe doubling cor, clarinet, one bassoon, one horn, two trumpets, one trombone, drums, and strings 3.2.2.1.1. Not even a harp for that – unusual.

JS: Difficult for the glissandos!

RD: Yes! That, I think, was my most rushed, though *The Bells Go Down* was pretty good – 21½ minutes, 566 bars, and that was done in a fortnight. That was not adapting existing tunes.

JS: Quite, you had a much bigger orchestration as well.

RD: Yes, more notes to put in the score!

JS: You must have been working night and day on that, or do you just work extremely fast?

RD: Yes. Another score I did, apart from film. Somebody told me the other day that Nicholas Cleobury had recorded Lord Berners's ballet *Les Sirènes*. You know *The Triumph of Neptune*? He did the ballet called *Sirens and Seagulls*, and it was later changed to *Les Sirènes*, and it has been recorded by Nicholas Cleobury or Barry Wordsworth, and they mentioned about the typical Berners orchestration. Well, I don't know about *The Triumph of Neptune* – I suspect Lambert and, possibly, Walton and a chap named Hyam Greenbaum. But in *Les Sirènes*, every note of that score was in my handwriting from beginning to end.

JS: Did you work on his films?

RD: No. Was there a film?

JS: There was *The Halfway House* and one of the Dickens – *Nicholas Nickleby*.

RD: I wonder who did that. I have an idea, by the little bits that he did scratch out on paper, that he *could* orchestrate. He did quite a lot of things for orchestra, didn't he, in his early days, but he certainly didn't do a note of that ballet.

JS: So it's quite likely he didn't do it for the films, then?

RD: I don't know how one could find out. Only by examining handwritings, but these scores are not available, are they, so frequently.

JS: There are very few scores extant, aren't there, very few.

RD: I was never allowed to keep my scores.

JS: What happened to your scores? Presumably they are the property of the film company.

RD: Yes.

JS: What did they do with them?

RD: Dumped, I suppose.

JS: A tragedy.

RD: I think the things that were done for Denham were probably put in Muir's library.

JS: What happened to that when he died?

RD: One or two people have been on at me about it. Stuart Craggs, in his tome on Walton, asks was it possible to find the scores of the films, but, no, I think they're all gone.

JS: Walton was very skilled at writing for dialogue, wasn't he? There's mention in Susana's book about how he would try to match Olivier's voice. He'd pitch it, and then he'd start there.

RD: There's a great deal in *Hamlet*. There's music under dialogue, and in *Henry V* – that long speech at the end, the French bloke about the countryside. It comes in the suite – fiddle solo. I only wish they would do less of it [background music] on the [television], isn't it awful?

JS: Unbearable.

RD: You can get teletext, and I rely on it a lot now, I think: 'I'm fed up with this bloody noise going on.' It's background music in the worst sense, not even incidental. It's not even in the background.

JS: It's not in the background, it's not incidental, it's absolutely meaningless. At least on the occasions in British films when it was used to underscore dialogue, it was used incredibly skilfully. It was meant to interpret the narrative for you, you were told what to feel. With this you get a meaningless stretch of jargon which just goes over a wide spectrum of things. Did you by any chance see the Russell *Lady Chatterley*?

RD: Yes, well, at least it was nice music! It was very nice music, I liked it.

JS: Well, I think that was the tragedy of it that such nice music was being squandered on that.

RD: If you listen to it, it takes your mind off what's being said.

JS: So all those skills that were built up in that period seem to have been completely lost. The leitmotif was so popular in Hollywood, and it doesn't seem to have been used anything like as much in the British film.

RD: I suppose not. Was it used a lot in Hollywood?

JS: Oh, yes. Particularly by Steiner, for each person and situation.

RD: I hadn't thought of that, actually, but I think you're right.

JS: This is part of the tradition of the mid-Europeans who went over to Hollywood and took with them this obsession with the leitmotif, for example *Gone With the Wind*.

RD: I've never seen *Gone With the Wind*.

JS: 3 hours and 20 minutes of music.

RD: 3 hours and 20 minutes of music? Good God! Somebody got a nice lot of money. Whether they still get royalties I don't know.

JS: So what do you think it was. Was it because composers here were allowed to write more in their own style?

RD: I think we weren't allowed to live with the film long enough: you just turned out each section to fit what was on the screen. Just a theory.

JS: They didn't have long to look at the film, very, very rushed. And yet they still seemed to be insistent on this motivic idea.

RD: I think most of it, you saw the rough cut, then a week, 10 days, a fortnight later you got the timings and the sections you'd got to compose, and at the same time, or a telephone call a day or two later, you'd be told the recording session was 3 weeks or a month ahead if you were lucky. Having seen the rough cut, I did start thinking about the titles and possible ideas. I don't know, but I fancy that with people like Walton, they didn't get much more than a month. That's why he got in such a panic.

JS: Do you think our composers did use their own style, or was there a certain amount of compromise in what they were doing?

RD: I think they unavoidably preserved their own style, if they had a style. Most of Walton's music is recognizable. I wouldn't say that Anthony Collins or Arthur Benjamin or anybody like that would be immediately recognizable. You wouldn't say: 'Ah, that's Anthony Collins' if you heard the music.

JS: You knew Anthony Collins – you worked with him, didn't you?

RD: Yes.

JS: So what makes you say that he didn't use the same style?

RD: I think Tony Collins was a practical man. He took it as a job to make some money and turned it out, conducted. He eventually went to Hollywood, didn't he, and stayed there. Always an eye to the main chance, all very practical. There was an occasion in the LSO when the conductor fell ill. They wanted some foreign conductor, and Tony Collins said: 'Well, I'd like to conduct the concert.' He had done a bit of conducting elsewhere, I suppose, and as he was one of the directors, and one of the people who took part in all the film sessions – the main directors and the main people who engaged the orchestras for Denham – Tony Collins was allowed to conduct. They said: 'Well, you'll have to conduct his programme.' 'Oh, no, I'm not conducting his programme, I want to do Dvořák Seven – and they let him. I always think of that when I hear Dvořák Seven now. That's how he got on, really – forceful and efficient. Everything he did was efficient and good.

JS: So his film music was very much in demand.

RD: Yes. The only two films I remember were the ones about Victoria, which were a sort of pastiche; *Victoria the Great* and *Sixty Glorious Years.*

JS: What kind of compositions did he write apart from his films?

RD: He wrote a few shorts pieces as suites, I think. He conducted an unknown Boccherini symphony at the BBC years ago, and he never got another engagement to conduct [at] the BBC when he admitted that he'd composed it, it wasn't Boccherini at all. They were so annoyed at having been taken in, they dumped him!

JS: I'm not surprised. How foolish to admit to such a thing!

RD: I suppose he wanted the royalties!

JS: You can't take the BBC by the ears like that and get away with it, can you?

RD: No.

JS: Who do you think of the top composers has been outstandingly successful in film music? – in the sense not so much of writing good music, but of writing successful film music, which I feel sometimes can be separate.

RD: I suppose it has to be Walton as far as I know, as far as I can think.

JS: Yes. He does seem to have been peculiarly well-adapted to it. He seems to have understood the process really well.

RD: It always seems to be right when you see the film, and listen to it again, and it's in his own style, he's not attempting something else.

JS: How do you feel about Vaughan Williams's scores? I mean, *Scott* is one of my favourite scores, but then, of course, it was a gift, wasn't it really, as a score, because of the nature of the film?

RD: It's really a one-off of itself, isn't it? It's not like anything else. I don't like the symphony. I was so much mixed up with it that I could see that it was bits of film music put together, not always joined very successfully.

JS: You worked on the symphony itself, not on the film? You didn't actually work with Vaughan Williams on his film scores?

RD: Not at all. You've seen his scores, have you?

JS: In the British Library, yes. I've seen examples of his handwriting and his scores there – just unbelievable. It must have been really informed knowledge on your part that you knew whether he was writing a G or an A at any given point, or was it second sight?

RD: Ursula once wrote: 'It's a good job you took your examination in second sight at the University of Salamanca!'

JS: Extraordinary, isn't it? Extraordinarily unclear.

RD: Have you come across Su Walton?

JS: No.

RD: She wrote to me and asked me if I had any letters from Walton that they could put in the museum in Ischia. And then I thought: 'I've got a lot of letters from Vaughan Williams.' I'd got 74 letters from VW, I could get a lot of money from these – five figures – and I thought: 'I cannot bear the thought of those going to America', so I asked the British Library if they would like to have them. Of course, they jumped at it. I thought: 'I don't need the money, I don't need five figures.' I'm not wealthy, but I'm well-off enough to be able to say I don't need it. I'd rather feel that they are in the British Library for posterity, all those original letters. After 40 years, then, I had to redecipher all those letters which wasn't easy, and I wrote about 10,000 words [of] commentary explaining what the letters were about. Then it dawned on Arthur Searle – he's the keeper of manuscripts, I think – it dawned on him that a lot of people can't go to the British Library to see those letters, so it might be a good idea to put them in print, so there's the text of all the letters, and about 30 thousand words to go with it. I think they've produced it beautifully, it's a lovely copy. [*Working with Vaughan Williams*] There's precious little about his film music, of course. I'm going to find a certain section. Are you a fast reader?

JS: Reasonably.

RD: 'On 2 November . . .'

[The extract from *Working with Vaughan Williams*: On 2 November I played the complete Ninth Symphony – twice through, as usual – to the 'inner circle' of expert friends. Malcolm Sargent was to conduct the first performance, so he had been invited, but made the excuse that he would be busy rehearsing on that day.

It was arranged that I should play it to him on the following Tuesday. To my disgust, and to Ursula's intense displeasure, we were all three obliged to go to Sargent's flat near the Albert Hall. R.V.W. himself did not, apparently, see anything unacceptable about this arrangement, but Ursula and I deemed it contemptible and typically self-regarding that

Sargent should expect a man of R.V.W.'s renown – and advanced age – to go to Albert Hall Mansions, when Sargent could (and should) have easily taken a taxi to Hanover Terrace.

An amusing sidelight on this visit was that before leaving the house to go to Sargent's flat, Ursula reminded RVW to inscribe the manuscript score with the words: 'Dedicated to the Royal Philharmonic Society'; this was to guard against the unwelcome probability that Sargent would ask – if not insist – that the Symphony should be dedicated to *him*.

On entering Sargent's office (vestibule? foyer? entrance hall?) I was confronted by a signed photograph of Vaughan Williams, a few inches in front of a signed photograph of Sibelius. Present in this impressive audience chamber were Sargent and two secretaries or amanuenses. I was airily greeted by the great man with: 'Ah, good morning Mr Douglas. You won't mind if I go on dictating letters, will you.' (A statement, not an enquiry.) I was then left to sit in isolation, totally ignored and inwardly fuming, until RVW and Ursula arrived; then, of course, dictating ceased, and we were ushered into the luxurious music room. Here was a large grand piano; on the closed lid was a signed photograph of the Queen, a few decorous inches behind was a signed photograph of the Duke of Edinburgh, and a signed photograph of the Queen Mother was on a side table.

I played the first movement, and Sargent immediately fired off a number of queries about speeds, balance, and expression marks; after the second movement he burst forth again, criticizing the metronome marking as being too little of a contrast to the speed of the first movement, and suggesting various accelerandos and rallentandos. The third movement set him off on a condescending lecture, explaining (as if he were instructing a first-year student) that there was no need to keep changing the time signature from three-four to six-eight: 'All you have to do is to write it all in three-four, and put in the necessary accents, and the orchestra will have no problems.' At that point he was called from the room to answer the telephone – it must surely have been a call from royalty. In his absence, R.V.W. looked over his spectacles at Ursula and me and said with a wry smile: 'Giving me a good lesson on how to write my music, isn't he?']¹

JS: This incident is in her [Ursula's] biography, isn't it?
RD: But much more restrained.
JS: 'It must surely have been a call from Royalty'!
RD: Well, I mean, to leave Vaughan Williams – unspeakable man! [Sargent] I've been wanting to get that off my chest ever since. You see, many years ago, I think soon after Vaughan Williams's death, the OUP published a little paperback called *Working With RVW*, which had only just tiny

---

¹ Douglas (1988), 91–2.

quotations from the letters, and just a few of the anecdotes, and they wouldn't let me put that in. Sargent was dead, but they said any adverse remarks might have an adverse effect on the Malcolm Sargent cancer fund.

JS: Yes, of course, that was going on at the time.

RD: Anyway, I asked the British Library, and they said: 'Put it all in.' What happened at the end I didn't put in. There was Sargent and the two secretaries he was dictating to, VW, Ursula and myself – six. When the session was over, we went back into the vestibule, or whatever it was, and the secretaries produced the Queen Anne silver coffee pot and the Dresden china cups and all that, for five people, and he turned round and he said: 'Would *you* like a cup of coffee, Mr Douglas?', just to point out that I *had been* left out deliberately. Of course, those secretaries must have been instructed to provide five cups.

JS: It's baffling, isn't it?

RD: Whereas dear old Boult, I remember one of the first times I met him, we'd listened to the [Vaughan Williams's] sixth symphony played over at the College of Music, and that was the first job I had to do, to write out a readable score of number six. I'd only been a member of the LSO under him conducting, we'd never spoken before. We came out of the College of Music together, and he said: 'I'm walking to the bus. Can I walk with you?' And we walked up the steps and got to the bus and chatted away, and he was waiting for a bus. None of the limousine waiting for him, and he said: 'Oh, you'd better take this bus, you've got a train to catch' – that's typical.

JS: These are the things you don't get to hear about.

RD: No. I'm full of anecdotes.

JS: I know that Sargent didn't have a very good reputation, but I had no idea he was quite so –

RD: Anything to get me down. I don't know why, just that sort of attitude. Unless, of course, I was sitting with VW and Ursula in the rehearsal room: 'Oh, yes, Mr Douglas, if you have any suggestions, do come . . .' – smarming all over me.

JS: I take it Ursula was a different kettle of fish to Susana Walton?

RD: She's a dish, Ursula.

JS: She's very much around, isn't she?

RD: Oh, yes. She's just come back from America on a poetry-reading tour. She's kept her age very quiet until recently. Now, as one is, she's very proud of the fact that she's just over 80. Oh, she's full of life.

JS: Who else did you rate from the established composers, as film writers apart from Walton? You seem to think that Vaughan Williams wasn't as successful, in a way, as Walton was.

RD: Apart from, possibly, *Scott*, he didn't get so much connected with interpreting the film in musical terms.

JS: You say you worked with Rawsthorne, what did you think of his work?

RD: I don't think I even saw his film – I just did it.

JS: You just did some orchestration?

RD: Yes. Taking part as a pianist in [recording] sessions, my chief recollections are from William Alwyn. Good serviceable music, musicianly and well scored. For a much lesser composer – Hely-Hutchinson. I don't know how many scores he did.

JS: Ireland only did the one score. There must have been a reason for that.

RD: I think he was so horrified at the conditions, he didn't take [any more] on. Oh, another little story. We've talked about how everything had to be done in a rush, and then, when you got to the sessions, Muir wasn't always right in getting the tempo right. I learnt that you had to prepare for the fact that a bar could be repeated or cut if he didn't – to get to the moment when somebody slams the door or falls downstairs. There was all that, and then sometimes the stuff was cut, and when you saw the film in the theatre, all the bits you liked best and were most proud of, were shoved behind dialogue or behind fires burning, or people clattering about and crowd noises. The bits you just wrote in a hurry came out full blast! There wasn't really much satisfaction, and quite often you had to wait and wait for the money. About 20 years ago I had a telephone call from somebody who's name I've now forgotten – would I like to write the music for a film? I immediately went tight up the back of the neck, I thought, 'I cannot take this on.' All very smarmy – 'Look, Roy old boy, I'll come down to Tunbridge Wells to talk about it' – somebody I'd never spoken to in my life before. I thought: 'This smarming business!' He talked about how they wanted to use Vaughan Williams's *Antarctic* Symphony and somebody had told them it had been used for a film before, so they wanted somebody to write imitation Vaughan Williams music. That, of course, settled it. The idea of me settling down to try and write Vaughan Williams's music – it would be difficult, it would be immoral and distasteful. I still go tense all over the shoulders. This was about 20 years ago: 'We're going to offer you two thousand quid.' I said: 'No, thank you.' Eventually they rang off, and I thought: 'I've refused two thousand pounds!' I rang Doris up who was in Devon then, my sister, and she said: 'You didn't accept, did you?' You know what the film was? *2001, a Space Odyssey.* I refused it. I think Rodney Newton will tell you that half a dozen people were asked to do that and they all refused it. I could have earned several hundred thousand pounds in royalties on soundtracks. I've never regretted it. I should be in the loony bin! I thought of all the terrors and horrors I've been through – I was in my 60s then – so they engaged a couple of Strausses, Richard and Johann.

JS: There's actually a thesis on the use of music in that film, an American one. All pre-existent music.

RD: So they didn't have to pay a composer.

JS: Just a few royalties.

RD: But I've never for one moment regretted it. I think they asked one or two pupils of VW. Elizabeth Maconchy was one, I think.

JS: Of course, Lutyens has written a lot of stuff, hasn't she? Did you ever come across her?

RD: I met her once or twice.

JS: What sort of a woman was she? I have an impression of her.

RD: Spiky.

JS: Yes, that's the impression, and the music, of course.

RD: She said unforgivable things about VW's music, anyway.

JS: Yes, that figures too, I suppose.

RD: She, of course, changed her style completely. She was writing atonal, 12-tone music, but not for films. Alan Bush, did he write for films?

JS: I don't think so, he certainly didn't do feature, you'd think he would have done some of those GPO things.

RD: I never came across Benjy Britten who, I think, did some good film music.

JS: One feature. Mostly documentary, wasn't it?

RD: *Night Mail.* He also did some other small feature for which I played in the orchestra he conducted. I think he was only concerned with making new noises on instruments; harmonics on the double bass on the other side of the bridge, that sort of thing. Being clever. As you've gathered, I've never been in that gang.

JS: How common was it for a composer to be credited exclusively with a score that other composers had contributed to?

RD: Well, Louis Levy. I can't think of any others at the moment.

JS: There's no famous miscarriage of justice that you can think of?

RD: I don't think so.

JS: You just mentioned this thing with Brodszky and Levy, and that's about it? I mean, unlike America where we know that up to 8 composers sometimes worked on one score because they were in such a rush, and they had this conglomerate type of thing. When it says that Rawsthorne wrote a score, he will have written that score?

RD: Oh, yes, definitely. Are you in contact with Christopher Palmer at all?

JS: No.

RD: Well he came to see me about two years ago. We talked for about six hours. We had a lot of things, of course, in common to talk about. He picked my brains and left his denim jacket behind. I was a bit doubtful, I said: 'I don't know how you get time, do you write all these books? Books on this, and books on that, and all these scores. How did you get all this music from *Henry V*?' It turns out he has a little team who take it down. I get these things about Walton concerts of new music arranged by Christopher Palmer.

JS: But does he actually do the arranging?

RD: I don't know. It's amusing that, although I worked with Walton for 30 years, from 1942 to 1972, and I got fed up for various reasons, he wasn't such a nice man as Vaughan Williams, let's put it that way. When I reached the age of 65 in 1972, I told the OUP: 'I am retiring from doing any work on Walton, but I will continue to do all the work you want on

Vaughan Williams.' All those 30 years, and since then, *The Quest* ballet was done by Vilem Tausky and when the string quartet was to be turned into a piece for string orchestra, during Walton's lifetime, Malcolm Arnold did it. I was never asked to do any of those things. Since then I heard on the radio Walton's violin sonata arranged for orchestra by Christopher Palmer. That's the latest. It's been recorded! Chandos will do anything if Christopher Palmer does it – I think he's a director by the sound of it! He gave me a copy of his book on George Dyson. It has a preface or foreword of about 20 pages, and the rest is nothing but Dyson's letters and facsimile reproductions of his talks on music. He didn't write another word.

JS: He did a book on Howells, didn't he?

RD: Yes. I've got that too, a small one.

JS: He makes a lot of money, I suppose.

RD: The whole of Walton's output Chandos are recording, and even the things which Walton didn't write.

JS: So in other words, for example *The Battle of Britain* score which was lost as well, has that been reconstructed for that recording of two years ago? These are all reconstructions? I mean, Stuart Craggs in his book says they're lost. As you know, it's possible to reconstruct, if you've got the patience to do it.

RD: But can they really reconstruct every line of Walton's orchestral score by listening to it?

JS: I suppose they can reconstruct it as well as you can hear it on a recording, and that's it, because it will be different.

RD: What I'm afraid is that eventually when I'm gone, perhaps, he will start on Vaughan Williams, digging out scores, because there's quite a few things.

JS: Scores that aren't known, do you mean?

RD: Years ago Chandos, before Christopher Palmer got mixed up, asked me to see if there could be a suite made from VW's music. Oh, God, which was that?

JS: That wasn't *Joanna Godden*?

RD: Was it *Joanna Godden*? or was it *Coastal Command*?

JS: *Coastal Command* was already a concert item, wasn't it, so I don't think it could have been that.

RD: Yes. You see, they could easily do that with *The Loves of Joanna Godden*.

JS: There are some lovely things in that, but that's one of the scores that was recorded at the time – there was a disc made of that in '47 or '48.

RD: I'm in my 86th year, and I've given up any composing, I never get any ideas or anything like that, I'm too exhausted to do much except read the papers and watch television – VW in his 86th year had finished the complete vocal score of a 3-act opera, with a libretto by Ursula, and a piano draft, on two or three staves, of a cello concerto, complete but no orchestration at all. Now, I've always said it must be left like that. Much as Ursula would like the opera, she hasn't had the courage to say: 'Let somebody have a go at it.' But when we're gone, I expect Mr Palmer will jump on them and score both, or get somebody to score them. Nothing you can do about it.

JS: No.

RD: Very plausible, very charming bloke, but entirely superficial.

JS: The people that were really a part of the business, how did they view people like Vaughan Williams coming in and doing this?

RD: I think most of them were rather proud of the fact, because it made it more respectable – that's what I would have said offhand. If Walton and Vaughan Williams can write film music, it makes it less a case of 'I write film music' and people turn up their nose, as it was at one time.

JS: It certainly did make it very respectable at that period.

RD: I suppose Bliss was one of the first, was he?

JS: Yes, Bliss was the start of it. Can you think of anybody who failed dismally, [composing for film] as far as you were concerned, who could be considered to be one of the good concert composers?

RD: No, I can't think of any offhand.

JS: There's mention in this book [Huntley] about people only getting asked once – that's why I asked you about Ireland, the fact that he only did one score. I can see that people would be scared off from doing the job.

RD: He would probably take about two years to compose something serious.

JS: But they all seem to have done a pretty good job.

RD: I should say so.

Appendix B
'The true story of *The Warsaw Concerto*'[1]

Roy Douglas

From December 1936 to January 1943 I orchestrated every bar of all Richard Addinsell's music for films and broadcasts. I must state very firmly that I did not compose any of it. We developed a method whereby he would play his music on the piano (he could stretch a twelfth with either hand), and I would rapidly take it down on paper as he played. His contribution to the orchestration was to say 'this is strings only, that is oboe, give that to the horns' and so forth, and I would eventually take my draft away and complete the scoring in all details.

During the winter of 1940/1 Addinsell was staying in Iffley with one of his boy friends, and I was in digs in Oxford, which meant that day after day I trudged a couple of miles into Iffley village and back, through rain, fog, wind, and sometimes inches of snow.

My diary for 29 November 1940 records: 'Started work on the Polish Concerto film', which was, of course, 'Dangerous Moonlight'. For the next few weeks we were very busy with his music for other films and broadcasts, until 31 January 1941 when I wrote: 'Started work on three minutes of the Polish Concerto film'. This was obviously the actual Warsaw Concerto section, because my diary entry for 5 February reads: 'Finished the score and piano parts of the Concerto'.

I'm not sure, but I think 31 January must have been the day when Addinsell was in a particularly happy mood because, after many depressing days of being unable to invent a satisfactory theme, he had at last succeeded. During a return journey to Iffley the previous night he had scribbled on an envelope the first bars of the famous theme for the Concerto; I remember clearly that he showed this to me, though, for some unexplained reason, he strongly denied the envelope story in later years. Incidentally, he secretly admitted to me that the middle section of the piece was roughly based on a rumba-like tune which he had written when he was an undergraduate.

Apparently the film director had originally wanted to use Rachmaninoff's 2nd, but this was either forbidden by the copyright owners, or was far too expensive, I have forgotten which. Knowing this, Addinsell understandably wanted the score to sound like an imitation of Rachmaninoff, and I unashamedly confess that,

---

[1] First published in *ICRC* Autumn edition 1999, no. 18. Reprinted by permission of Orpheus Publications Ltd.

while I was orchestrating the Warsaw Concerto, I had around me the miniature scores of Rach. 2nd, Rach. 3rd, and the Pag.–Rhap.

The final recording sessions for 'Dangerous Moonlight' were on 27 March, and during February and March I often had to sit up until 2 or 3 a.m., scoring Addinsell's music for this and other films and broadcasts.

For the earliest sessions of recording, the pianist was the young Noel Mewton-Wood, but for the final sound-track Louis Kentner agreed to perform the Warsaw Concerto, though only if his name was not publicised; presumably he thought his reputation might suffer if it were known that he had played for films. However, when he found that gramophone records of his performance on the sound-track were being sold in vast numbers, he decided to ask for some royalties, which he was given – at least, that is what I was told at the time.[2]

I was not so lucky.

It has been stated on the radio that I was given the choice of either accepting a lump sum or taking a royalty, and that I made the wrong decision. This is totally inaccurate – I was given no choice at all.

When I read in the newspapers that three million records had been sold, I meekly asked if I could be given a small royalty, on the grounds that my scoring had surely helped to make the work popular. This seemed to me a reasonable request, but it was greeted with horror and anger. I was summoned to a meeting with Addinsell and his agent, at which I was told very sternly that I had been commissioned to orchestrate the entire music for the film – all the 647 bars it – for £100 (yes, a paltry one hundred pounds), and as there had been no contract, I was not legally entitled to any royalties whatsoever. Furthermore, they threatened to take me to court if I dared to make any claim for royalties. I now suspect that this was a clever piece of bluff on their part, to prevent *me* from taking *them* to court, because they presumably knew at the time – but I unfortunately did not – that the law says: the first person who writes down the notes of a musical work on paper automatically becomes the owner of the copyright!

I went to the publishers, Keith Prowse, to consult them, and found that the only copy of the full score in their possession had been written by a professional copyist, and my original score had been destroyed; no doubt this had been done on the instructions of Addinsell's agent.

I had no proof that my score had been destroyed: it may well have been smuggled away by Addinsell or Muir Mathieson. But I could produce no evidence that I had orchestrated the Warsaw Concerto, and therefore I received not a penny in royalties. I worked out the simple sum that if I had been allowed just one penny on each of 3,000,000 records, it would have brought me in £12,500 – a colossal sum for me in the 1940s, when my annual income was around £700.

There is a rather more pleasant aspect of my connection with the Warsaw

---

[2] In a recent conversation with the author, Roy Douglas revealed that he has subsequently learned that Louis Kentner did not in the end receive any royalties.

Concerto. Someone at Keith Prowse must, I think, have felt sorry for me, because when they commissioned me to make an arrangement of the 'Theme from the Warsaw Concerto' for piano solo which was published by them at 2s 6d, they allowed me the munificent royalty of one farthing on each copy that was sold.

Much to my surprise, on 18 January 1944 I received a royalty cheque for £316-14-4. This I put into the bank towards paying off a loan in connection with buying my present home, though I resisted the temptation to rename it 'Warsaw Villa'.

Over the next few years, my farthings reached an impressive total of £913-16-9 which, to my reckoning, represents 877,284 copies bought by an admiring public. So, added to the £100 for the film scoring, my earnings from the Warsaw Concerto totalled just over £1000. It is worth comparing this with the sum which Richard Addinsell left when he died: well over £250,000.

Appendix C
Interview with Doreen Carwithen, 2 July 1997

JS: Let's return to the question of Alwyn's reputation being affected by working in film. I feel that the article here[1] tends to gloss over that, doesn't it? It sort of implies that it didn't affect his work or the reputation of his work. But you feel differently about that.

DC: I feel very differently about it. It still affects his music now. Imagine his name, 'Ah, film composer!' What else has he written? Five symphonies, concertos, songs, operas – are they played now?

JS: That's talking about reputation as people thinking of him. What about his reputation as far as bodies like the BBC and commissioning bodies were concerned?

DC: Yes, he did get commissions sometimes.

JS: But do you feel that his work there [in film] affected the way that that kind of establishment looked upon him?

DC: Yes I do, but other people were not affected like that. Take Malcolm Arnold. Not written as many films as my husband – written several successes, but none of them great films. But he's never affected, he's not dubbed a film composer. It's so unfair.

JS: I *do* think Arnold has been tarred with the brush a little bit, in the sense that I feel the establishment tended to ignore *him* a little bit.

DC: He hasn't had it all his own way. There are other composers, too, who have written a lot of films. They're not damned by it. That was one thing – the other was the concert music.

JS: Was there a particular identification, then, that Alwyn had with it?

DC: He was so successful – one of the greatest composers for the film.

JS: What you're saying, in effect, is that he subsumed, to a certain extent, his own interest for the interests of the film itself – the interests of the dramatic purposes of the film.

DC: He was fascinated with film, right from the beginning in '36. This was something new that had started, using music in a different way – not an opera, not a concert piece; something that goes with a visual.

JS: As a whole integration – more than opera in a sense.

DC: More than opera, even more, yes.

JS: As we've already noted, not many people think of it like that. I think musicologists still tend to think of film music as something that can be

---

[1] Lindgren (1951).

analysed as a piece of music that exists on its own.

DC: No, it's not, it's part of a film. That is what I was taught at Denham from the beginning. You've got dialogue, or you've got commentary. That is one thing you are writing *with*, not against – with. You always had to allow for that.

JS: Who did you most come into contact with then? Who was it that told you these things at Denham?

DC: I worked with Muir Mathieson and his assistant, John Hollingsworth. John Huntley was there, of course, every composer who was writing. Practically every week of the year I'd be attending recording sessions – to see, and to listen to how they coped with these things, how I could use it for myself, how I'd learn by it.

JS: And what sort of jobs were you put to do?

DC: Well, I'd start by copying parts, putting the parts on the music stands, and then, say they wanted a piece altered – they frequently had to be altered to fit the film – the composer would jot it down, and I would come along and put it into the score and parts.

JS: Were there occasions when you would, as it were, co-write for a film, where you weren't credited for it?

DC: I ghosted a lot – Jock Addison, I think I've written a lot of his films.

JS: I'm sorry! Could you say that a bit louder!

DC: No, it really did happen. People pressed for time would say 'Oh, come along, would you write my music, do this reel for me – this is the theme I'm using.' And I'd do it, they would pay me.

JS: Subcontract!

DC: Subcontract, ghosting. All sorts of jobs done there. Transpose, yes – 'I can't sing in this key, would you please transpose all this?'

JS: Instantly. What about Muir Mathieson? Because from my perspective he's quite a hard person to get an image of, apart from somebody who was very keen that British composers should be used for film

DC: Yes, he was. And people like Vaughan Williams, Bax, John Ireland dragged into it, and he didn't really like it.

JS: Although it was Irving, wasn't it, who dragged Ireland in.

DC: It's very hard to say anyone who was left out of that, musically who was left out in those years, the '40s and '50s.

JS: Only Rubbra, I suppose, and Tippett, of course, didn't write until he wrote one film score in the '70s, I think, funnily enough.

DC: Muir was encouraging everybody, said it was good for them. One thing he said: 'You will write a lot of good, considered music for the concert hall. There will be a lot of not so good music. OK, I don't like to think of it as not good enough for film, but we can use that music, it gives you experience. You're writing and you're hearing, you've got a first rate orchestra, and you learn by it.'

JS: Although some of them just didn't take to it, did they?

DC: Some of them, they just couldn't stand the pace, which was pretty killing, I must admit.

JS: Yes, it had to be produced, didn't it. Fineness of temperament couldn't be taken into account.

DC: No.

JS: How much orchestrating did you do?

DC: Mostly for my own scores.

JS: Did you think most of the composers that we know of as well-known composers now did their own full scores, because quite a few of them are lost, aren't they?

DC: Yes, unfortunately.

JS: I think it was only people like Addinsell who had a lot of their orchestrations done for them. Talking of concert composers, did they regard it as an opportunity for something new and creative for their writing, in a way that Mathieson obviously –

DC: As much as Muir thought, and my husband thought, and perhaps one or two other composers – but it was the money! You were paid well.

JS: And instantly, not like waiting for a long time. So how many of them do you think were really interested in the medium itself, rather than as an opportunity?

DC: Some of them were fascinated with documentary – what we always used to call down at the studio 'nut and bolt' composers, Lis [Lutyens] was a nut and bolt. Seiber, people like that, make lovely mechanical noises. And then there were the more romantic ones who liked to include a song in it, which they possibly can't.

JS: But again that comes away from the idea of being interested in the drama, interested in writing in that kind of way. Because writing for documentary in nuts and bolts – what we now call 'squeaky gate' music – again it's coming to the music as something that is experimental for itself rather than writing for drama, because writing for drama, especially dialogue writing is far more difficult, isn't it?

DC: I think writing under commentary is worse. I did a number [8] of *This Modern Age* films – you probably know them – which is non-stop commentary, and you had non-stop music. You mustn't blot out their commentary otherwise they just screw it down, screw the music down and let the commentary ride. But you had to have continuous music. I found the best thing under that was long lines of music, long tunes of music.

JS: Sustained but not complicated. One thing that interests me, how aware was Mathieson, and therefore, what he conveyed to you, about what was happening over in Hollywood? Were composers the least bit interested in that, as something maybe they should take as a guideline, or did they just get on with the job over here?

DC: I was always interested in every foreign film that came over and so was my husband. Some Japanese film of the early 60s; not only did we see it twice, we went and saw it three times because it had a fascinating score. Whether other people took the trouble I don't know.

JS: This country has always felt itself in competition with America, for obvious reasons.

DC: Well I know their composers were real professionals – people like Mickey Rózsa and so on.

JS: And the older lot, Steiner and Co. But they wrote to an extraordinary formulaic system of writing.

DC: Yes, it would be really.

JS: When you were starting the job, composing your first score or your second score, a feature film, how interested were you in the idea of thematic use, did it seem a natural thing to you to write thematically?

DC: Yes, it was something that was encouraged, something that linked it all together. It isn't just isolated pieces of music for this and that and so on, but it was a reference to what you wrote, the opening title even – incidentally, I always wrote the titles last.

JS: Was that general practice or was it something that you liked to do?

DC: They were never assembled as such, they hadn't got any reel lengths on them, you had to plunge straight into the film – then you come to the titles which were the most important music, the themes I've used I put those in the titles to prepare you for all the themes you'll hear.

JS: A little bit like the old-fashioned prelude to an opera or a ballet, so you get a preview musically. Yes, because that interests me, the way themes are used, it's almost an instinctive response to a dramatic situation, to write themes that relate to major issues in the drama.

DC: Yes, but Muir and John Hollingsworth, they'd discuss it with you in great detail always.

JS: Oh, they did?

DC: Yes. You see, you always saw a film in a little theatre and had a look at it. Would you like to do it? Sometimes you would, and sometimes you were told that you were going to do it! Then you'd have a much more lengthy session, reel by reel, discussing where we'd put music – where we'd start, where we'd stop, what the ideas should be, and that bit should tie up with later on when they climb a mountain or something.

JS: And where were those ideas coming from, from Muir Mathieson or from the film's director? Do you remember occasions when those ideas would clash?

DC: Generally it was the music director. Sometimes we had to have the director and the producer in. Sometimes we wanted their advice, wanted their permission to do something, or we were left to ourselves and hoped the director trusted you.

JS: Because the position of the musical director can vary depending on the musical strength of the film's director.

DC: Both Muir and John were extremely musical.

JS: And dramatically literate, if you like, as well, because that's the important thing.

DC: It's amazing how music can change the whole feeling of a sequence to a film. Something badly acted doesn't come across – you can change all that by music.

JS: And sometimes, as I've seen in some British films that are scored by foreigners, you can totally misrepresent that scene with music as well. It can be a negative thing as well, can't it?

DC: You can, you can make it absolutely laughable – it's just not true. Music can do so much, your audience shouldn't be so conscious of it as that.

JS: The power of it is sometimes because it's not conscious, isn't it? So that you're gently led without knowing it into an interpretation of a thing. What was the feeling in the studio about foreign composers writing for British film?

DC: They had a reputation. The director or producer thought: 'That name will add to this film's stature.'

JS: What sort of people are you thinking of there?

DC: People who came over from Hollywood, some people from Europe in the latter days – French composers.

JS: So it was generally the idea of the directors. I don't think Muir was particularly keen, was he?

DC: No, he was entirely for using British, English composers always.

JS: But he got overridden, didn't he? For instance, *The Four Feathers* – he didn't want Rózsa on that score, but he got overridden by Zoltan Korda. Do you think it's detrimental sometimes to what British film is trying to convey to use a foreign composer for the score?

DC: It depends how well they understand the English whom they're writing for. The world is getting wider now.

JS: *Now* it is, yes.

DC: That makes a difference.

JS: Yes it does. And to a certain extent the kind of encapsulation of British life which happened, I think, from, say, 1940 – in fact that decade of the '40s – I think it's in those films that using people like Auric and Spoliansky was detrimental to the film.

DC: Yes. They didn't really understand, do you think so?

JS: I think they didn't understand at all. I think particularly in the case of Auric, I'm still baffled as to why Irving –

DC: Did he do the Ealing films?

JS: Yes he did. It was Irving who –

DC: *He* wanted him, then? Did you know Christopher Palmer?

JS: Only by reputation.

DC: Alas, he died two years ago. I've got a book here somewhere.

JS: Yes, I've got that one, *The Composer in Hollywood*. He talks a lot about the factory way of life for the Hollywood composer.

DC: I worked with Christopher on *Odd Man Out*.

JS: On reconstructing that?

DC: Yes. I was lucky in finding sketches of *Odd Man Out*, no score, it was burnt, as you know.

JS: How many of Alwyn's scores have you got here?

DC: We've got a list of them and I can show you the cupboard. Occasionally an odd one turns up, and a few have flown off to America! We're pretty well off really. I did have a complete score of *Fallen Idol*, that was lucky. I wouldn't let Christopher *touch* that, apart from putting a cadence at the end of a section – the score had to remain exactly like that.

JS: That's one of Alwyn's most well-known scores, isn't it?

DC: It's a beautiful score, yes.

JS: The films that he scored – naturally because he did a wide spectrum of films – were of varying standards in the films themselves. To a certain extent, no matter how good a score is, it can't *rescue* a film can it?

DC: No, and some of them I really wonder why he did them – like *Lady Godiva Rides Again*, I thought was a shocker.

JS: Funnily enough, I saw that film only a couple of days ago and, yes, it's a shocker in one way, but it's quite a contemporary –

DC: Oh, yes.

JS: Which brings me to another subject which is how did Alwyn feel about that change, because there was a change in the way films – I don't know, the standard seemed to slip, if you like, from, say, about 1950, 1951 onwards. Did he ever talk about that? Did he ever feel that the films he was writing after 1950 –

DC: He continued writing – '62 was his last score, which was a Walt Disney, which he didn't score himself.

JS: Because he wrote quite a few films in the '50s.

DC: He wrote some very good ones in the '50s.

JS: I like *The Long Memory*, that's a score I like very much. But opportunities for that kind of score, which were harking back to the '40s became less, didn't they?

DC: Yes, they did.

JS: *The Card* is another film –

DC: That's a fine score. That is worth analysing, it's completely different.

JS: It's a very different technique he uses there to the films of the late '40s.

DC: Talking about Christopher Palmer and what he sent me – because he'd been over to Hollywood – and there came a very abbreviated score, just a few lines and odd sort of crosses and dashes and things like that.

JS: His own short-hand?

DC: He had a gang of rather lean and hungry young men who used to fill these in. I used to get a score back from him with various sorts of writing, this was a proper score.

JS: I think I was aware he had a team that did these things for him.

DC: I wouldn't let him change my husband's scores. *Odd Man Out* we had some of the piano score, not the full score. There was a *tiny* bit of the score, because William started writing before the film was shot. You know that, don't you? Johnny's scene for walking, he always walked at the same pace. I've just got that, which shows him [Palmer] the orchestra he wanted, and I insisted he kept to those instruments, and didn't use the tuba, because William didn't use the tuba. I cut that out. *Mr Polly* – again I've only got a piano score. By listening I knew what was wanted – what he used and what he didn't use, so again I cut that out. So they're pretty authentic. I sometimes did help him out – with the hallucination scene.

JS: That was one of the rare instances where the music was created first. Did you personally have instances where the composer had actually very little contact with the film.

DC: Did I?

JS: Yes, in your work in the studio, when all these composers were working there, did you notice a varied input into the film? You've said that a lot of composers were only interested in taking the money for the film.

DC: No, they had to work pretty hard. You know as a composer – you've written yourself – it's not like writing in English or French or anything else, it's got to come from *there*.

JS: But in the sense of how much involvement with the actual film did they have, because you said Muir was very helpful in encouraging you to use themes and to think of the drama in that way. But one does hear of instances where – I mean, for instance, Auric in his first film he did here, *Dead of Night*, he wrote it in Paris.

DC: Well, there are some people would do that – it's just a job.

JS: To some extent there was that here as well for some composers, whereas others would be very concerned to –

DC: Others have more conscience about it.

JS: And more interest.

DC: More interest. You do get wrapped up in a film you're writing for, you can't help it. I think Benny Frankel wrote some good scores – you know, Benny Honkle!

JS: Ben Frankel really sort of took up, in the '50s – he and Alwyn and Arnold were the three that were left, weren't they, when everybody –

DC: I started before Arnold.

JS: You started before Arnold, but in the '40s we had Walton and Vaughan Williams and –

DC: They had the finest films.

JS: Yes. The ones that were easier to score.

DC: A big one like *Scott of the Antarctic*. I did a little one with VW.

JS: He did some, like *The Loves of Joanna Godden*, that was a real drama, wasn't it? I mean *Scott* was something different which was mostly visual.

DC: Yes, he turned it into a symphony.

JS: That's getting onto dangerous ground again, isn't it, music that stands up?

DC: Yes, but he'd got the name and the reputation – that was alright. You write a symphony called *Odd Man Out* and I don't think it would have been.

JS: It's a good name! But VW did take writing for film seriously, do you think?

DC: Hmm. Yes, he was willing to have a go at it.

JS: Willing to have a go within his own parameters?

DC: Yes, yes.

JS: I mean, he admitted freely that he couldn't do the fine timing sort of writing, and that would never have suited his style anyway.

DC: No, using *Five Variants of 'Dives and Lazarus'*, the producer [Humphrey Jennings] was thinking that music all the way along [for *Dim Little Island*]. Would I go and see the old boy, and get his permission to do it, to use the music and what we'd do for it? So I went down to his home – took me up to his room, tiny little room, strewn with manuscript paper all over the floor, old upright piano – and I explained what we wanted to do, we wanted some title music as well. 'Oh', he said, 'you're a composer, you could write that.' He eventually wrote his own title music, he seemed keen to do it all. That was one of my meetings with VW. Then we went downstairs for tea. This was his first wife, crippled with arthritis, and I went to shake hands – she had hands like this. We had tea, he cut the cake – 'I always cut the first piece for my cat', he said. He was interested in [the film]: 'how are we going to use it?', 'what are we going to do with it?', 'what are the pictures here?' – it was good.

JS: He didn't alter his style, did he, for film? Do you think some composers did?

DC: Certainly Elisabeth Lutyens did, and some of the others, too.

JS: Who do you think, apart from her?

DC: I can't say, really . . . If you wanted completely different sounds in films, he [Alwyn] could do it. He had such a wonderful technique.

JS: For instance, like *Lady Godiva Rides Again*, the writing in that is idiomatic, isn't it, because again, it's a very contemporary film.

DC: He could change completely. In *The Card* – that's a very clever score – he uses clarinet for the 'card'. It was a very tiny orchestra.

JS: That interests me in the way he was prepared to adapt from the big symphonic style –

DC: He said of this film: 'I do something different in every film I do, and I learn something' – no two film scores alike. He found by the '50s, films were changing by the late '50s. Music scores were getting longer and longer. He said 'I'm not prepared to treat music like that.' The last one he wrote – *The Running Man*, '62 he wrote it. He wrote a very good short score, and he handed it over to Muir. After that he said 'I shall never write another film. The music has no meaning when it's got to this pitch.'

JS: It's the same with the television now, isn't it?

DC: It's just a wash.

JS: Exactly – wallpaper. Did Muir or any of the people you worked with when you were learning the trade ever discuss with you the use of orchestration in the sense of individual instruments for dramatic purposes?

DC: Up to a point, yes.

JS: Was that something you did quite naturally?

DC: You find out for yourself, I think.

JS: But it had meaning for you?

DC: It definitely had meaning for me, yes. I would work things out for myself.

JS: Because some British film scores in the '40s and '50s, too, you find they use a more or less full orchestral texture throughout. Actually, I'm thinking of Rawsthorne mainly there, who I don't think was as interested in the dramatic interpretation as some people were.

DC: In a way I preferred a more detailed score, rather than a full score.

JS: Because there's a sort of unwritten code – certain uses of instrumentation do represent dramatic meaning. Was that something you were interested in yourself?

DC: Yes.

JS: Or treatment of themes?

DC: Yes, I'm thinking of *The Men of Sherwood Forest*. I found the horns extremely important in that. It evolved somehow from the very first piece I wrote in that score – I found myself using it and using it.

JS: Yes, I like the score of that film, but the film is terrible, isn't it?

DC: The film is *ghastly*! I think it's one of the best scores I wrote. The hardest I ever wrote was the Wendy Toye.

JS: *The Three Cases of Murder*?

DC: No. I enjoyed writing hers [the story in *Three Cases of Murder* which Toye directed] not the other two. I meant *On the Twelfth Day of Christmas*.

JS: I haven't got that one. I quite like *Three Cases of Murder*.

DC: They played around with it and altered it. Eamonn Andrews announcing everything in between – that didn't happen in the beginning, it wasn't like that. It mucked it up, it really did!

JS: The middle one isn't a very good sequence, is it, but the two outer cases I think are good cinema.

DC: With Wendy Toye, we discussed the script, we discussed everything. I wrote the little tunes for her first, the little music box tune. So we knew exactly what we were doing, and I knew what she wanted.

JS: Because Wendy Toye latterly did opera productions, didn't she, so she was quite musically literate.

DC: She's trained as a ballet dancer. Everything's timed exactly with Wendy – the steps, the movements, you do this, you do that, and musically you have to follow that – very exacting to work for.

JS: But that's much more interesting, isn't it, to a certain extent.

DC: Yes, but it could be maddening at times – you weren't even working in seconds.

JS: Micro-seconds. That's a very '50s film, although the first sequence is almost timeless. But the concept of that film is '50s, with the three cameos, and that sort of thing. Did you find that less satisfactory than writing a score that was continuous?

DC: I was very happy to write for Wendy, I wasn't particularly interested in the other two – they had to come together.

JS: So you had much less involvement with the other two directors, they weren't bothered.

DC: No, they weren't bothered much. You don't know *On the Twelfth Day*?

JS: No.

DC: That was a marathon.

JS: What year is that from.

DC: Practically the last one I did.

JS: Did you stop writing for film for the same reason as Alwyn?

DC: Up to a point. I enjoyed my documentaries immensely because there were very nice people to work for – very intelligent, with great interest in the film, great interest in music. I found features weren't –

JS: The composer didn't have quite the same position? or didn't have as much freedom of –

DC: No, I found that documentary – working with Basil Wright, they were all delightful people to work for – though I love all the drama about feature films.

JS: With documentary it doesn't have the drama, does it?

DC: No – different.

JS: They serve a completely different purpose.

DC: The drama and excitement of the feature film, yes. But then, other people – not very kind to me.

JS: What sort of people?

DC: Well, somebody who puts a composer in touch with the film director, and says, 'here's a composer for you.' I worked for several with Wendy Toye – 'don't you think it would be a good idea if you had a change of composer, you must be getting a bit used to her?' – out!

JS: To what do you attribute that?

DC: Successful.

JS: What was it like being the first woman when you were working –

DC: That was very funny – I'd always shown an interest in films.

JS: Did you get treated there [Denham] as a second-class citizen?

DC: Up to a point, yes. *This Modern Age* of which I did a lot, they'd had a number of composers who 'Oh, no, they're no good.' I did one and that was lovely – would I do them all? I said, 'No, it's too much like hard work', which it was. It finishes a 20-minute film, for which you wrote 30 minutes of music, then you cut it. I said, 'Oh, I'll do every other one', and Malcolm Arnold did the alternate ones. I was at the studio one day when Malcolm was there – they were recording one of his. 'A lot of work for ninety pounds', he said. I said, 'do you get ninety pounds? I get seventy.' I was not going to sit down under this, so I went and I said, 'Are you pleased with my work?', 'Oh, delighted with it, yes.' 'I understand

Malcolm Arnold is paid ninety pounds, I get paid seventy.' 'Don't you think you're doing very well for a woman?' – my money didn't go up, but they didn't sack me.

JS: If they can get away with it, they will.

DC: I thought it was wicked.

JS: To a certain extent that still goes on, certainly the attitude it still there.

DC: With Pathé I always negotiated my own fees – I never had an agent, an agent wouldn't take me on. You know that, don't you?

JS: No, I didn't.

DC: Oh, all these people had agents.

JS: I knew that, but I didn't know one wouldn't take you on. Because you were a woman?

DC: No, I couldn't get an agent to fight my battles for me – I had to do it all myself.

JS: That's tough going, isn't it?

DC: Very tough going, you had to make sure your performing rights were covered. They tried to take them away from you – I had enormous battles. 'You'll never get another film if you don't sign this contract', which would give everything away. I said, 'I'm not signing it' – I won.

JS: You weren't going to be bullied.

DC: I was not going to be bullied, and my fee went up, more than they'd offered me. Instead of a hundred pounds, I got two hundred and fifty, and I kept my performing rights. But it was like that all the time.

JS: Yes, but it's people like you who have made it easier for us, for our generation of composers.

Sources of musical examples

Chapter 4

Example 1   William Alwyn, *The Winslow Boy*. Reproduced by kind permission of the William Alwyn Foundation

Examples 2–9   Bernard Stevens, *Once a Jolly Swagman*. Reproduced by the kind permission of the Bernard Stevens Trust.

Examples 10 & 11   Malcolm Arnold, *The Holly and the Ivy*. Reproduced by the kind permission of Sir Malcolm Arnold. CBE.

Example 12   Malcolm Arnold, *Home at Seven*. Reproduced by the kind permission of Sir Malcolm Arnold. CBE.

Example 13 & 14   Malcolm Arnold, *Sound Barrier Rhapsody*. Reproduced by permission of Patersons Publications Ltd, 8/9 Frith Street, London.

Chapter 5

Examples 1–23   Arnold Bax, *Oliver Twist*. Music by Arnold Bax. © 1947 Chappell Music Ltd, London W6 8BS. Reproduced by permission of IMP Ltd. All rights reserved.

Chapter 6

Example 1   Ralph Vaughan Williams, *Prelude 49th Parallel*. © Oxford University Press 1960. Extract reproduced by permission.

Examples 2–7   Ralph Vaughan Williams, *49th Parallel*. Reproduced by the kind permission of RVW Ltd.

Examples 8–23   Lord Berners, *The Halfway House*. © the Berners Trust. Reproduced by the kind permission of the Berners Trust.

Examples 24–39   Grace Williams, *Blue Scar*. Reproduced by the kind permission of Marian Glyn Evans.

Chapter 9

Example 1   Hans May, *Thunder Rock*. Composed by Hans May. © Copyright 1942 Cinephonic Music Company Limited, 8/9 Frith Street, London W1D

Example 2   Miklós Rózsa, *The Four Feathers*. Music by Larry Sturm and Miklós Rózsa. © Chappell Music Ltd, London W6 8BS. Reproduced by permission of IMP Ltd. All rights reserved.
Example 3   Nicholas Brodszky, *The Way to the Stars*. Music by Nicholas Brodszky. © 1945 Chappell Music Ltd, London W6 8BS. All rights reserved.

Appendix B

Filmography

Film title is followed by date of release, production company and then composer, in that order.

Action for Slander (1937). London Saville. No credit
All for Norway (doc.) (1942). Strand. Roy Douglas
Anthony Adverse (US) (1935). Warner. Erich Wolfgang Korngold
Battle of Britain, The (1969). Spitfire. Ron Goodwin. 'Battle of the Air' sequence composed by William Walton
Belles of St Trinian's, The (1954). British Lion. Malcolm Arnold
Bells, The (1931). Associated Sound Film Industries. Gustav Holst
Bells Go Down, The (1943). Ealing. Roy Douglas
Birth of a Nation, The (US) (1915). Epoch. Score composed and compiled by D. W. Griffiths and Carl Joseph Breil
Bitter Springs (1950). Ealing. Ralph Vaughan Williams
Black Narcissus (1947). IP-Archers. Brian Easdale
Blithe Spirit (1945). Two Cities-Cineguild. Richard Addinsell
Blue Scar (1949). Outlook. Grace Williams
Boys in Brown (1949). Gainsborough. Doreen Carwithen
Brief Encounter (1945). IP-Cineguild. Rachmaninoff Piano Concerto No. 2
Browning Version, The (1951). Javelin. No music credit, but the main titles music is the original soundtrack recording of cue 11m1. from Bax's *Oliver Twist*. The end titles music is an adaptation of the finale of Beethoven's Symphony No. 5
Caesar and Cleopatra (1946). IP-Pascal. Georges Auric
Candlelight in Algeria (1943). British Aviation. Roy Douglas and James Turner
Captain Blood (US) (1935). Warner. Erich Wolfgang Korngold
Captive Heart, The (1946). Ealing. Alan Rawsthorne
Card, The (1952). British Film Makers. William Alwyn
Carrington V.C. (1954). Romulus. No music
Catherine the Great (1934). London (UA). Ernst Toch
Central Front, Burma (doc.) (1945). Gryphon-Verity. Roy Douglas
Checkpoint (1956). Rank. Bruce Montgomery
Citizen Kane (US) (1941). RKO. Bernard Herrmann
Coastal Command (doc.) (1942). Crown Film Unit. Ralph Vaughan Williams
Cruel Sea, The (1953). Ealing. Alan Rawsthorne
Cure for Love, The (1950). London-Island. William Alwyn
Dam Busters, The (1955). ABPC. Leighton Lucas. March 'The Dam Busters' composed by Eric Coates
Dangerous Moonlight (1941). RKO. Richard Addinsell
Day will Dawn, The (1942). Niksos Films. Richard Addinsell
Dead of Night (1945). Ealing. Georges Auric. Song 'The Hullalooba' written and composed by Anna Marley

Desert Victory (doc.) (1943). MOI/British Army. Film Unit William Alwyn

Dim Little Island (doc.) (1949). GPO Film Unit. Ralph Vaughan Williams

Dr. Terror's House of Horrors (1964). Amicus. Elisabeth Lutyens

Drum, The (1938). London-Denham. John Greenwood

Elephant Boy (1937). London. John Greenwood

Elusive Pimpernel, The (1950). London-BLPA-Archers. Brian Easdale

Escape Me Never (1935). B & D (UA). William Walton

Escapement (1958). Anglo-Guild. Music devised by Soundrama, consultant John Simmons

Fallen Idol, The (1948). London-Reed. William Alwyn

Fiend without a Face (1958). MLC Producers. Buxton Orr Associates (Eros)

Fire Maidens from Outer Space (1956). Criterion (Eros). Music excerpts from Dances from 'Prince Igor' by Borodin. 'Oriental Suite' by Mona Liter. 'Challenge of Space' and 'Grand Vista' by Trevor Duncan

First of the Few, The (1942). Misbourne-British Aviation. William Walton

Flame of Love, The (1930). BIP. Hans May

Foreman Went to France, The (1942). Ealing. William Walton

For Those in Peril (1944). Ealing. Gordon Jacob

49th Parallel (1941). Ortus Films. Ralph Vaughan Williams

Four Feathers, The (1939). London. Miklós Rózsa

Freedom Radio (1941). Two Cities. Nicholas Brodszky, Roy Douglas and James Turner

French without Tears (1939). Two Cities Nicholas Brodszky and Clive Richardson

Genevieve (1953). Sirius. Larry Adler. Dance numbers by Eric Rogers

Ghost Goes West, The (1936). London. Mischa Spoliansky

Give Me the Stars (1944). British National (Anglo). No credit. Song 'Throughout the Years' by Mabel Buchanan

Gone with the Wind (US) (1936). MGM/Selznick International. Max Steiner

Great Expectations (1946). IP-Cineguild. Walter Goehr

Green Cockatoo, The (1937). New World. Miklós Rózsa

Gunfight at the O.K. Corral (US) (1957). Paramount/Hal Wallis. Dimitri Tiomkin

Halfway House, The (1944). Ealing. Lord Berners

Hamlet (1913). Hepworth (Gaumont). Silent

Hamlet (1948). Two Cities. William Walton

Henry V (1945). Two Cities. William Walton

High Noon (US) (1952). Stanley Kramer. Dimitri Tiomkin

History of Mr Polly, The (1949). Two Cities. William Alwyn

Hobson's Choice (1954). London-BLPA. Malcolm Arnold

Holly and The Ivy, The (1952). London-BLPA. Malcolm Arnold

Home at Seven (1952). London-BLPA. Malcolm Arnold

Hue and Cry (1947). Ealing. Georges Auric

Hungry Hill (1947). Two Cities. John Greenwood

I Am a Camera (1955). Remus. Malcolm Arnold

In Which We Serve (1942). Two Cities. Noel Coward

Informer, The (US) (1935). RKO. Max Steiner

Instruments of the Orchestra (doc.) (1946). Crown Film Unit. Benjamin Britten

Intolerance (US) (1916). D. W. Griffiths. Score composed and compiled by D. W. Griffiths and Carl Joseph Breil

Ivanhoe (US) (1952). MGM. Miklós Rózsa

Jigsaw (1962). Figaro. No music

Jungle Mariner (doc.) (1944). Crown Film Unit. Elisabeth Lutyens
Key to Scotland, The (doc.) (1935). Strand. Ursula Grenville
King Kong (US) (1933). RKO. Max Steiner
Knight without Armour (1937). London. Miklós Rózsa
Lady Godiva Rides Again (1951). London-BLPA. William Alwyn
Ladykillers, The (1955). Ealing. Tristram Cary
Lodger, The, (1932). Twickenham. Silent
Long Memory, The (1953). Europa. William Alwyn
Love from a Stranger (1937). Trafalgar. Benjamin Britten
Loves of Joanna Godden, The (1947). Ealing. Ralph Vaughan Williams
Love Story (1944). Gainsborough. Hubert Bath
Malta G.C. (doc.) (1942). Crown & RAF Film Units. Arnold Bax
Matter of Life and Death, A (1946). IP-Archers. Allan Gray
Men of Sherwood Forest, The (1954). Hammer. Doreen Carwithen
Midsummer Night's Dream, A (US) (1935). Warner. Mendelssohn arr. Korngold
Millions Like Us (1943). Gainsborough. Hubert Bath
Moulin Rouge (1928). BIP. Silent
Never Take Sweets from a Stranger (1960). Hammer. Elisabeth Lutyens
New Lot, The (doc.) (1942). Army Unit. Richard Addinsell
Nicholas Nickelby (1947). Ealing. Lord Berners
Night Mail (doc.) (1936). GPO Film Unit. Benjamin Britten
Night of the Party, The (1934). Gaumont. No credit
Nowhere to Go (1958). Ealing. Dizzy Reece
Now Voyager (US) (1942). Warner. Max Steiner
Odd Man Out (1947). Two Cities. William Alwyn
Oliver Twist (1948). IP-Cineguild. Arnold Bax
Once a Jolly Swagman (1948). Pinewood-Wessex. Bernard Stevens
On the Night of the Fire (1939). G & S Films. Miklós Rózsa
On the Twelfth Day (1955). Bahamian Productions. Doreen Carwithen
Out to Play (doc.) (1936). Short Film Productions. Molly Berkeley
Overlanders, The (1946). Ealing. John Ireland
Paranoic (1963). Hammer. Elisabeth Lutyens
Passport to Pimlico (1949). Ealing. Georges Auric
Passport to Shame (1959). United-Co-Productions. Ken Jones. Song 'Never, never more'
    by Jeff Davis
Pastor Hall (1940). Charter. Charles Brill
Peter Ibbetson (US) (1935). Paramount. Ernst Toch
Pimpernel Smith (1941). British National. John Greenwood
Place in the Sun, A (US) (1951). Paramount. Franz Waxman, Daniele Amfitheatrof and
    Victor Young
Private Life of Henry VIII, The (1933). London. Kurt Schroeder
Pygmalion (1938). Pascal. Arthur Honegger
Rake's Progress, The (1945). IP-Individual. William Alwyn
Red Shoes, The (1948). IP-Archers. Brian Easdale
Rembrandt (1936). London. Geoffrey Toye
Richard III (1955). London-Big Ben. William Walton
Rocking Horse Winner, The (1949). Two Cities. William Alwyn
Running Man, The (1963). Peet Productions. William Alwyn
Sapphire (1959). Artna. Philip Green

Scarlet Pimpernel, The (1935). London. Arthur Benjamin
Scott of the Antarctic (1948). Ealing. Ralph Vaughan Williams
Sixty Glorious Years (1938). Imperator. Anthony Collins
Skull, The (1965). Amicus. Elisabeth Lutyens
Small Back Room, The (1949). London-BLPA-Archers. Brian Easdale
Son of the Sheik, The (1926). UA. Silent
Sound Barrier, The (1952). London-BLPA. Malcolm Arnold
South Riding (1938). London. Richard Addinsell
Spanish Gardener, The (1956). Rank. John Veale
Spellbound (US) (1945). David O. Selznick. Miklós Rózsa
Storm in a Teacup (1937). London-Victor Saville. Frederic Lewis
Storm over the Nile (1955). London-Big Ben. Benjamin Frankel
Ten Days in Paris (1939). Irving Asher Productions. Miklós Rózsa
There Ain't No Justice (1939). Ealing-Capad. Ernest Irving
They Flew Alone (1942). Imperator. William Alwyn
Thief of Baghdad, The (1940). London-Korda. Miklós Rózsa
Things to Come (1936). London. Arthur Bliss
Third Man, The (1949). London-BLPA. Anton Karas
39 Steps. The (1935). Gaumont. Jack Beaver and Hubert Bath
39 Steps, The (1959). Rank (RFD). Clifton Parker
Three Cases of Murder (1955). Wessex. Doreen Carwithen
Thunder in the City (1937). Atlantic. Miklós Rózsa
Thunder Rock (1942). Charter. Hans May
Titfield Thunderbolt, The (1953). Ealing. Georges Auric
Tomorrow We Live (1942). British Aviation. Credited to Nicholas Brodszky [Roy Douglas and James Turner]
To the Public Danger (1948). Production Facilities. Doreen Carwithen
2001, a Space Odyssey (1968). Panavision. Johann Strauss, Richard Strauss, György Ligeti and Aram Katchaturian
Upturned Glass, The (1948). GFD-Triton. Bernard Stevens
Victoria the Great (1937). Imperator. Anthony Collins
Waterloo Road (1945). Gainsborough. Bob Busby
Way from Germany, The (doc.) (1946). Crown Film Unit. Elisabeth Lutyens
Way to the Stars The (1945). Two Cities. Nicholas Brodszky
Went the Day Well? (1942). Ealing. William Walton
Western Approaches (doc.) (1944). Crown Film Unit. Clifton Parker
Whiskey Galore! (1949). Ealing. Ernest Irving
Wind, The (US) (1927). MGM. Silent
Winslow Boy, The (1948). London-BLPA. William Alwyn
Wooden Horse, The (1950). BLPA-Wessex. Clifton Parker
X the Unknown (1956). Hammer. James Bernard
Yesterday is over your Shoulder (1940). Denham & Pinewood. Robertson Hare and Roy Douglas

Bibliography

Because the volume numbering and pagination of *Sight and Sound* are inconsistent, articles from it will be referred to by date only.

Adorno, Theodor, and Hanns Eisler, *Composing for the Films* (London, 1994; first edition New York, 1947)

Aldgate, Anthony, and Jeffrey Richards, *Britain can Take It* (Oxford and New York, 1986)

Aldgate, Tony, 'Comedy, Class and Containment: The British Domestic Cinema of the 1930s', in James Curran and Vincent Porter (eds), *British Cinema History* (London, 1983)

Alwyn, William, 'From Ariel to Miranda', *Adam International Review* (London, 1967)

Anon., 'Top 10 Films', *Sight and Sound* (December, 1992)

Aspinall, Sue, 'Women, Realism and Reality in British Films 1943–53', in James Curran and Vincent Porter (eds), *British Cinema History* (London, 1983)

Bacharach, A. L. (ed.), *British Music of our Time* (London, 1946)

Balcon, Michael, 'The British Film during the War', *Penguin Film Review No. 1* (1946)

Barr, Charles (ed.), *All our Yesterdays* (London, 1986)

Barr, Charles, 'Amnesia and Schizophrenia', in Charles Barr (ed.), *All our Yesterdays* (London, 1986)

Blom, Eric (ed.), *Grove's Dictionary of Music and Musicians*, 5th Edition (London and New York, 1954)

Brown, Geoff, 'Sister of the Stage: British Film and British Theatre', in Charles Barr (ed.), *All our Yesterdays* (London, 1986)

Carstairs, John Paddy, *Movie Merry-Go-Round* (London, 1937)

Cockshott, Gerald, *Incidental Music in the Sound Film* (London, 1947) (pamphlet)

Corrigan, Philip, 'Film Entertainment as Ideology and Pleasure: Towards a History of Audiences', in James Curran and Vincent Porter (eds), *British Cinema History* (London, 1983)

Curran, James, and Vincent Porter (eds), *British Cinema History* (London, 1983)

Darby, William, and Jack du Bois, *American Film Music* (Jefferson and London, 1990)

Darnton, Christian, *You and Music* (London, 1945)

Davy, Charles (ed.), *Footnotes to the Film* (London, 1938)

Dickinson, Thorold, 'The World of Sir Michael Balcon at Ealing Studios', in Roger Manvell (ed.), *The Year's Work in the Film: 1950* (Harmondsworth, 1950)

Douglas, Roy, *Working with Vaughan Williams* (London, 1988)

Foreman, Lewis, *From Parry to Britten: British Music in Letters, 1900–1945* (London, 1987)

Gianetti, Louis, and Scott Eyman, *Flashback: A Brief History of Film* (Englewood Cliffs, 1986)

Gorbman, Claudia, *Unheard Melodies: Narrative Film Music* (Bloomington and London, 1987)

Greene, David Mason, *Biographical Encyclopedia of Composers* (London and Glasgow, 1986)

Griffiths, Paul, *Modern Music: A Concise History from Debussy to Boulez* (London and New York, 1986)

Herbage, Julian, 'Sir Arnold Bax', in A. L. Bacharach (ed.), *British Music of our Time* (London, 1946)

Hopkins, Antony, 'Music', *Sight and Sound* (January 1950)

Hudson, Lynton, *The English Stage, 1850–1950* (Westport, 1972)

Huntley, John, 'Film Music', *Sight and Sound* (January 1944)

Huntley, John, 'British Film Music and World Markets', *Sight and Sound* (winter 1946/7)

Huntley, John, *British Film Music* (London, 1947)

Huntley, John, 'British Film Composers: William Alwyn', *Music Parade* i/7 (undated, acquired by the British Library 27.4.1948)

Huntley, John, 'The Music of *Hamlet* and *Oliver Twist*', *Penguin Film Review No. 8* (1949)

Huntley, John, 'The Sound Track', *Sight and Sound* (July 1950)

Irving, Ernest, *Cue for Music* (London, 1959)

Jaubert, Maurice, 'Music on the Screen', in Charles Davy (ed.), *Footnotes to the Film* (London, 1938)

Kalinak, Kathryn, *Settling the Score: Music and the Classical Hollywood Score* (Madison and London, 1992)

Karlin, Fred, *Listening to the Movies: The Film Lover's Guide to Film Music* (New York, 1994)

Keller, Hans, 'Hollywood Music – Another View', *Sight and Sound* (winter 1947/8)

Kracauer, Siegfried, 'National Types as Hollywood Presents Them', in Roger Manvell (ed.), *The Cinema 1950* (Harmondsworth, 1950)

Kracauer, Siegfried, *Nature of Film: The Redemption of Physical Reality* (London, 1961)

Kulik, Karol, *Alexander Korda: The Man who could Work Miracles* (London, 1990)

Lambert, Constant, *Music – Ho!* (London, 1948)

Landy, Marcia, *British Genres: Cinema and Society, 1930–1960* (Princeton, 1991)

Lindgren, Ernest, 'The Composer: William Alwyn', *Sight and Sound: Films in 1951, a special publication on British films and film-makers, for the Festival of Britain* (1951)

Low, Rachel, *Film Making in 1930s Britain* (London, 1985)

McFarlane, Brian, 'A Literary Cinema? British Films and British Novels', in Charles Barr (ed.), *All our Yesterdays* (London, 1986)

McFarlane, Brian (ed.), *Sixty Voices* (London, 1992)

Macnab, Geoffrey, *J. Arthur Rank and the British Film Industry* (London and New York, 1994)

Manvell, Roger (ed.), *The Year's Work in the Film: 1950* (London, 1950)

Manvell, Roger (ed.), *The Cinema 1950* (Harmondsworth, 1950)

Manvell, Roger, and R. K. Neilson Baxter (eds), *The Cinema 1951* (Harmondsworth, 1951)

Manvell, Roger, and John Huntley, *The Technique of Film Music* (London, 1957), revised and enlarged by Richard Arnell and Peter Day (London, 1975)

Mason, James, *Before I Forget* (London, 1982)

Mathieson, Muir, 'Music in British Film', *Film Review, 1948–9* (1948)

Monahan, James, 'The Year's Work in the Feature Film', in Roger Manvell (ed.), *The Year's Work in the Film: 1950* (London, 1950)

Murphy, Robert, *Realism and Tinsel: Cinema and Society in Britain, 1939–1949* (London and New York, 1992)

Nicoll, Allardyce, *Film and Theatre: The Literature of Cinema* (New York, 1972)

Palmer, Christopher, *The Composer in Hollywood* (London, 1990)

Parkinson, David (ed.), *The Graham Greene Film Reader: Mornings in the Dark* (Manchester, 1993)

Parlett, Graham, *A Catalogue of the Works of Sir Arnold Bax* (Oxford, 1999)

Perilli, Patricia, 'Statistical Survey of the British Film Industry', in James Curran and Vincent Porter (eds), *British Cinema History* (London, 1983)

Prendergast, Roy, *Film Music: A Neglected Art* (New York, 1992)

Quéval, Jean, 'France Looks at British Films', *Sight and Sound* (July 1950)

Reisz, Karel, 'The Showman Producer', in Roger Manvell and R. K. Neilson Baxter (eds), *The Cinema 1951* (Harmondsworth, 1951)

Rózsa, Miklós, *Double Life* (Tunbridge Wells, 1982)

Sabaneev, Leonid, *Music for the Films* (translated by S. W. Spring) (London, 1935)

Sadie, Stanley (ed.), *The New Grove Dictionary of Music and Musicians* (London and Washington, DC, 1980)

Sellar, Maurice, *Best of British* (London, 1987)

Stevens, Bertha (ed.), *Bernard Stevens and his Music: A Symposium* (London, 1989)

Thomas, Anthony, 'Hollywood Music', *Sight and Sound* (autumn 1947)

Tierney, Neil, *William Walton: His Life and Music* (London, 1984)

Towers, Harry Alan, and Leslie Mitchell, *The March of the Movies* (London, 1947)

Unstead, R. J., *Britain in the 20th Century* (London and Edinburgh, 1966)

Ustinov, Peter, 'The Modern Nightmare', in Roger Manvell (ed.), *The Cinema 1950* (Harmondsworth, 1950)

Walker, John (ed.), *Halliwell's Film Guide: 8th Edition* (London, 1991; first edition 1977)

Westrup, J. A., 'Lord Berners', in A. L. Bacharach (ed.), *British Music of our Time* (London, 1946)

Williams, Raymond, 'British Film History: New Perspectives', in James Curran and Vincent Porter (eds), *British Cinema History* (London, 1983)

Wilson, Garff B., *Three Hundred Years of American Drama and Theatre: From 'Ye Beare and Ye Cubbe' to 'Hair'* (Englewood Cliffs, 1973)

Wood, Alan, *Mr Rank: A Study of Arthur Rank and British Film* (London, 1952)

Wright, Basil (ed.), 'Round Table on British Films', *Sight and Sound* (May 1950)

Wythenshawe, Lord Simon of, *The BBC from Within* (London, 1953)

Index